Women on the Move
Globalization and Labour Migration

Women on the Move
Globalization and Labour Migration

M P Kumar

MD Publications Pvt Ltd
New Delhi
www.mdppl.com

Published by :

MD Publications Pvt Ltd
"MD House", 11, Darya Ganj,
New Delhi - 110 002
Phone : +91-11- 45355555
E-mail : contact@mdppl.com
Website: www.mdppl.com

ISBN : 978-81-7533-350-5

Published and Printed by Mr. Pranav Gupta on behalf of **MD Publications Pvt Ltd** at Repro India Limited.

Preface

Globalisation is a process of increasing interdependence, interconnectedness and integration of economies and societies to such an extent that an event in one part of the globe affects people in other parts of world. We have often heard of global culture and integration of the world economy. However, as this process is not consistent throughout the world, it leads to conflict and fragmentation. The world/global economy is one that both serves and promotes free and unregulated markets as primary arenas of exchange for goods, services and more recently, of money itself. This market is dominated by economic, financial and political institutions such as multi- and transnational corporations, financial speculators, investment firms, and governments.

The past two decades have witnessed the feminisation of the labour force both in the industrialised countries as well as in the colonial world. Women's employment has increased in most countries, whereas men's employment has either stagnated or has declined. Some academicians and activists have judged this as definite progress towards women's emancipation and empowerment. Others have pointed out that women workers cluster into low-skilled jobs, in specific branches, and that their working conditions are poor, while wages paid are much lower than the average wage of men workers. Naturally, a struggle for equal rights in the workplace should be the dominant agenda for women workers; but, to be successful, this struggle must proceed from an adequate theoretical understanding of the relationship of globalisation to the feminisation of labour.

There have been increased economic opportunities for women but also mounting threats. In the present global reshaping of labour, studies have shown that, as a company adopts labour casualisation, the higher is the number of women employed and the greater is their vulnerability to exploitative conditions. The impact of economic globalisation on women needs to be assessed in light of women's multiple roles as productive and reproductive labour in their families, as well as their contributions towards overall community cohesion and welfare, and maintaining the social fabric. Because of deep-rooted differences in gender roles and socio-cultural expectations, the impacts of economic globalisation are felt quite differently by women and men.

One of the biggest challenges of tracing and fully understanding the ways in which globalisation affects women is the absence of sex-disaggregated indicators and data in key sectors such as agricultural production and employment, services, and the informal sector. While independent researchers and institutions such as UNIFEM are gathering information and showing how women are affected by current economic trends, many of the indicators and methods used to monitor these trends are in and of themselves not gender sensitive.

I am very grateful to Mr. Pranav Gupta, Director of MD Publications Pvt Ltd, New Delhi, for his kind cooperation and support for this book.

M P Kumar

CONTENTS

1

New Migrations to Southern Europe

The title of this chapter refers to how the migration of women involves 'metaphors of home' that is movement of homes in terms of a movement physically in space, the movements and inter-relationships between these spaces and the impacts that the related symbolic and identity shifts have on women's lives in different ways. Migration, if nothing else, is both an escape (forced or otherwise) from the original homeland and a search for a better life and some kind of new home if not a new homeland.

In one sense it is not difficult to gender new transnational migrations to southern Europe because, unlike earlier migrations which were, paradigmatically, predominantly male (although women have always also migrated on their own), much migration today is female, particularly migration from the Philippines, Sri Lanka and Latin America. Gender is a relational concept as well as a central organizing principle of social relations. Within most approaches to women in migration, there has been a tendency to treat gender as additive and to reduce it to looking at women migrants.

However, gendering migration is not just a question of recognizing the proportions of women migrants or their economic and social roles. It is also important to consider the role of gender processes and discourses, as well as identities, in the migration and settlement process. This requires looking at the new processes that have given rise to the feminization of migration as well as the particular forms of insertion and mobilization that this involves. The extent to which this feminization may be part of the transformation of gender relations more broadly also needs addressing.

The family is a unit of reproduction and cultural transmission and women within the family play a central role in this. This involves what Walby (1997) amongst others now calls 'gender regimes' (as a substitute for the much-criticized notion of patriarchy), meaning broader sets of social relationships whose object of reference is the construction and reproduction of gendered social practices and using the term gendered social relations, treating gender as an ingredient that enters into different societal mechanisms rather than being constituted as a discrete system.

There are two sets of gender relations to consider with ethnic and migrant women: those within their own society/ group and those within the dominant group in the state. The focus on feminization not only needs to be done within this context (which includes the differential positioning of men), but must also pay attention to difference of social positioning in terms of migration, racialization and class subordination. In other words, the use of the gender category must avoid homogenizing women's experiences and practices and must be undertaken in relation to how gender intersects with other social divisions, such as ethnicity, 'race' and class. However, the discourse and practice of 'otherness'on the basis of racism and ethnicity defines the otherness of migrant women, where the European woman serves as the ideal woman.

Although some migrant women are pathologized as victims (for example domestic maids from Sri Lanka), others are desired for their supposed submissive nurturing natures (for example mail order brides from the Philippines) and others for their exotic beauty and as fitting better into Western lifestyles (for example Russian women). According to Helma Lutz (1997), Muslim women, on the other hand, are regarded as the 'other other' thus representing a dichotomy with the western European model of womanhood. Although discussion of gender issues certainly cannot be reduced to looking at the role of women, the latter has not been addressed adequately by most migration approaches.

As Buijs (1993: 1) states: 'Women were invisible in studies on migration and when they did emerge tended to do so within the category of dependants on men.'

This is echoed in the European Forum of Left Feminists statement (1993: 3), that 'black and migrant women's concerns are largely ignored in policy, in campaigns and in research'. So although it is important not to reduce gender to \romen'given the relative lack of focus on women, it is imperative to make them visible, paying attention to difference. There are at least 6.4 million women in Europe who are not full citizens of the countries where they live. It is estimated that there are more than one million domestic workers who are dependent on the good will of their employers. Indeed, more than 14 million non-nationals constitute second class citizens in 'Fortress Europe'.

THEORIES OF MIGRATION

Ethnic pluralism exists in all societies to a greater or lesser extent, but the phenomena of migration, as well as diasporization, produce ethnic diversity in new ways. Nation state formation usually involves the domination by one group, usually the larger or the most powerful economically, over other groups and the hegemony of its Vorld view'and its conception of boundaries of belonging. Migration can be seen as important in terms of testing the boundaries of \fho belongs to the community'or the nation. Moreover, migration from outside Europe tests the boundaries of inclusion and exclusion within Europe itself.

Although migration is a world phenomenon, it is also a diverse one. There have been and still are different stages and forms of migration although they are not necessarily either analytically or substantively distinct: the terms gastarbeiter, settler, refugee, exile, sojoumer, denizen all denote particular forms, as well as ways, in which the phenomena of migration have been distinguished. Much migration stems from economic imperatives linked to rural or urban poverty and tends to be from societies with a link to colonial powers, or involves people fleeing or forcibly expelled from political regimes. This has certainly been the case with regard to European migration in the post–war period.

For a long time, the push–pull model, dependent on neo-liberal economic theory, was used as the classic explanation for migration to Europe, starting from the observation that individuals migrated primarily for economic reasons and to better themselves and their families. Although at the descriptive level this approach seemed to capture the dual imperatives involved, it made a number of assumptions that are pertinent to issues of gender. In other words, gender was not absent in this approach, but deeply embedded in it. Firstly, men were the prototype migrant, being regarded as the decision makers and bread winners.

Women entered, therefore, as dependants. Secondly, migration was seen as a rational choice. Whilst giving a central role to human agency, that agency was treated in the light of the ideal typical rational economic action. Not only did this ignore the role of constraints around choice (for example why did some individuals migrate when others did not in similar circumstances) but it also ignored wider structural constraints imposed by a long history of colonialist or imperialist forms of domination. Moreover, it underplayed the role of the mythology of the West (not even adequately captured by the idea of adventure migration found in the work of writers like Bench 1975) and the continuing interaction between migrants and homelands (captured better by the notion of diaspora.

There is a case for looking at migration in terms of a threefold positioning of social actors: within the relations of the homeland, within the relations of the country of migration and within their own ethnic communities and networks. As an alternative, some of the important work by Marxists sought to emphasize the role of the mode of production – the macro or system level – as opposed to focusing on individual choices. The seminal text that gave an impetus in this direction was that of Castles and Kosack (1973). In this the focus was on migrants, not as discrete individuals who made choices but as particular categories of labour power, linked to the internationalization of the labour market.

Broadly speaking, Marxist political economy, particularly through the work of Castles and Kosack (1973) and Castells (1975) focused on migrants as a subproletariat forged out of the uneven development of capitalism. Such work has treated migrants as a reserve army of labour subjected to the power of capital, or as in Phizacklea and Miles's (1980) work, as a class fraction of the working class. The use of Marxist economic categories (like that of the reserve army of labour) for particular population categories, (like women or ethnic minorities) is itself problematic. This analysis was not only economistic but gender blind.

Moreover, although mainstream approaches to migration saw the actor as exercising free choice, the Marxist approaches erred in the opposite direction and deprived actors of any agency, thereby reducing the migrant to a category of labour power in the global labour market. Neither of these approaches consider how decision making takes place within family and broader social networks, both within the sending and receiving countries, nor the ways in which knowledge and communication channels and opportunities for work are mediated by social actors in specific social locations. The longing for return may also fundamentally influence settlement.

Class outcomes are also related to the ways in which migrants may be oriented in complex ways to a number of geographical locales including the homeland. Similarly imaginaries of the boundaries of the nation have been as important if often contradictory to class or economic relations in understanding migration and its reception. For example the imaginary of the colonial power as a potential home from home is found in much colonial migration. Most important, the ways in which migrants have been received by the countries of destination (involving, for example, practices of discrimination and racism) cannot be explained fully by economistic explanations, whether neo-liberal or Marxist.

The bulk of the literature produced in Europe has been on post-war migration to Western Europe. More recently, the focus has shifted to refugees and undocumented migrants. The most important tendency, however, is the shift away from a migration problematic altogether with the permanent settlements of population that Western Europe has experienced. This tendency is characterized by a focus on incorporation and exclusion in the receiving countries and has tended to take a problem-oriented approach.

In Britain in particular, the 'race relations' and ethnic studies problematic have dominated the field. Even more recently, a concern with identity, with new ethnicities, with difference and diversity has characterized debates in the area. Theories of diasporization and of new diaspora social forms, including consciousness, have emerged. The issue of gender has become an increasingly relevant issue as is the role that women play in the reproduction of the ethnic boundary.

NEW MIGRATIONS

New migration to Europe and particularly southern Europe in the 1990s has turned the attention of scholars once again to migration processes. The paradigms used to explain earlier forms of migration, with their focus on economic migrants from poorer sectors of their communities, primarily men or families led by men, can no longer yield a fruitful conceptual basis for understanding migration today. Such migration is more diverse and includes large numbers of educated people from the old Eastern bloc.

Some of these may experience downward economic mobility on migration rather than an improvement. It is diverse also because large numbers of the older type economic migrants have to come in as undocumented, as modern economies do not formally want them within their territories, despite needing them; this is particularly the case in Greece, for example, with its large informal and unregulated sector. In addition a large part of this migration is made up of women who migrate on their own, being involved in what can be termed a solo migration project. The diversity of these new forms of migration has therefore gone hand in hand with feminization.

Migrant women, however, have strong transnational family links and major responsibilities for providing for families left in the homelands. Migration is also diverse in terms of motivation: some migrate for family reunification, some migrate simply for work; others are asylum seekers and also what Mirjana Morokvasic (1994) has called commuter and brain drain migrants. The increasing diversity of the people on the move is linked to the disintegration of Eastern Europe and crisis in various world economies. This is particularly the case with regard to the more educated and 'brain drain' migrants. Return migration and family reunification processes have also been important in southern Europe, as in Europe as a whole, being one of the few ways in which women can migrate legally.

As Castles and Miller (1993) argue, in the wake of so many people on the move, the old distinction between refugees, economic migrants and exiles is diminishing. The notion of 'forced migration' has been advanced by others. Such a notion however, does not capture the multilayered processes for individuals and groups in the migration process. Examples from Spain, Italy, Greece and Cyprus show the extent to which movements are multiple and statuses, both legal and other, of individual migrants unstable and precarious. It is this tension between migrants as travellers and migrants as settlers in new territories that produces the new phenomena of migration.

New approaches to migration, therefore, require us to avoid the binary focus of traditional migration theory with its emphasis on the process of migration from and migration to particular nation states. Migration needs to be seen as part of the globalizing tendencies in the modern world and in terms of transnational processes. This involves a set of contradictions between the continuing imperatives of nationhood, on the one hand, and increasing economic and cultural globalism on the other. Moreover, all transnational population movements entail contradictory processes relating to particular forms of exclusion and inclusion.

These processes involve competing discourses: the idea of human rights and equality of treatment of all persons is accompanied by exclusion from full citizenship rights as well as the differential racisms experienced by different categories of migrants. In the case of southern Europe, as in much of the history of migration in the postwar period generally, there are contradictions that lie, on the one hand, in terms of the perceived needs of the economy (or at least action by employers to fill cheaply their needs) and the perceived needs of the 'integrity of the nation' and the borders of 'otherness' or alterity, that will construct migrants as a threat.

Different discourses and practices around ethnicity, or around civic rights, may be deployed in excluding and including differentially different groups of migrants in different countries and from different countries. This is particularly important where national identity is an important part of the agenda as it is within many societies; this is certainly the case in Cyprus, which will be drawn on substantively in this chapter. Transnational and global processes provide the context within which new forms of gendered migration to southern Europe need to be located.

TRANSNATIONALISM, GLOBALIZATION AND EXCLUSION

Transnational social spaces mean that the problematic of assimilation and ethnic pluralism may not be adequate. Whilst the assimilation problematic posits the potential disappearance of a migrant population, the newer ethnic pluralism problematic found in multiculturalist discourse posits the reproduction of ethnic culture. Both of these positions are no longer sustainable, given that transnational processes involve border crossings where migrants have complex relations to different locales and form new and different communities.

These include migrant networks involving social, symbolic and material ties between homelands, destinations and relations between destinations. Transnationalism is centred in two or more national spaces; this is found particularly in the case of Filipina maids. Transnational population movements may be seen as part of the globalizing tendencies in the modern world. Globalization involves a number of related processes: movement of capital in its various forms; the global penetration of new technologies, forms of communication and media; transnational political developments and alliances (such as the European Union (EU), the European Court of Human Rights and the Beijing Conference of Women); and the penetration of ideologies producing a 'world system' or Global Village.

Appadurai's (1990: 297) conception of the ethnoscape provides one way of understanding the movement of people: 'By ethnoscape, I mean the landscape of persons who constitute the shifting world in which we live; tourists, immigrants, refugees, exiles, guest-workers and other moving groups and persons 'Globalization challenges social scientific analysis with changing forms of governance and political participation, changing identities, values and, allegiances. These have a profound effect on social life and our understanding of it, with serious implications for the future of democracy, citizenship and nationalism.

Some categories have emerged excluded from society, through new technology and new flexible employment patterns. Many of those most affected by these processes are women. This is partly because the drive to attain greater flexibility in employment practices has encouraged casualized employment practices and especially the feminization of migration. Although globalized economic structures potentially break national borders, as well as established gender/patriarchal ones, they cannot ensure the equality and growth of status and respect to all groups equally and may reinforce borders in new ways.

The state/welfare system has become dominated by increasing privatization, dismantling the welfare states of liberal democratic societies and prohibiting the development of welfare regimes in southern Europe. Moreover, privatization and free markets are redefining the relationship between the state and their economies, families and public life and political and cultural life. Ihis is likely to reinforce divisions between rich and poor nations, on the one hand, and between different categories of people within them on the other.

Moreover, despite globalization, the reconfiguration of ethnic boundaries and exceptions such as the European court of human rights, nation states are still the determinants of juridical, social citizenship and cultural citizenship and the ethno-national project remains central. The borders of the nation state are still policed against undesirable others in formal and informal ways through migration controls, racism and the desire for the integration and management of minorities within (in the present phase of multiculturalism) while excluding others on the outside and the inside (such as Gypsies). Many nation states wish to retain the ethnic identity of their diaspora populations and encourage their reproduction as well as their return to the homeland (unrecognizable for those who were born outside it), a home no longer 'a home' or a place where they may feel 'at home'.

It may be the case that globalism as an ideology demands one culture which can be shared (what has been termed a global village), found in a more limited sense within the notion of Europe, but this involves a particular construction of 'Europe' as Christian and White, thus excluding Third World migrants and Muslims. Freedom of movement and trade has made boundaries between one European Union country and another less important, but in practice this is reserved for majority ethnic group members who have full citizenship. For many Third World and other migrants this process means that they need to carry additional identification, with passport controls at airports reinforced to exclude non-Europeans.

Being Black or obviously foreign is therefore an impediment to movement as racialized minorities within Europe may be targeted because of the growing ideology of Europeanism/whiteness. Moreover, there are different layers of citizenship and residence/ work permits for different groups and inequality both between the countries of the European Union and between Western Europe and southern Europe. Therefore, in practice, privatization and exclusionary nation state citizenships sit alongside differential border controls in the management of movements of population within Appadurai's ethnoscape.

Nation states have always had ethnic 'outsiders'or minorities within, who have demanded recognition of their practices. Within Eastern Europe, for example in Latvia, Rumanians are excluded from eligibility for citizenship. In ex-Yugoslavia this has been particularly horrendous. 'Ethnic cleansing' may be a relatively new term but it is an old experience. The European framework provides different instances of ethnic and racist practices: racism and hostility in Spain and Greece towards migrants from Tunisia and Albania; in Germany and the Netherlands the Turks have been targets of racist hostility but more recently Rumanians and Poles in Germany have been the subject of neo-Nazi attacks; in France, target populations are increasingly Muslims and Jews; in Britain there has been a growth of anti-Muslim racism. Such processes are essentially gendered.

GENDERING MIGRATION

The idea of migration as a male phenomenon has been seriously questioned since the mid-1980s by the focus on women migrants making independent choices or taking the initiative for their own families. The empirical picture of women that has emerged shows the diversity of social positioning entailed. There are class and ethnic differences amongst women migrants and the different countries of origin and destination provide heterogeneous contexts that need to be taken into account, but there are some broad areas that allow us to posit some general features of the new feminization of migration. It is not the case that women migrants migrate primarily as dependants or for family reunification. Instead, women migrants are more often than not a main source of family support and see their role in terms of a family strategy.

However, as noted previously, gendering migration is not simply attending to women migrants. For gender as a relational social category is implicated in a range of social relations linked to the process of migration. Therefore it is necessary to look beyond merely economic processes for understanding the position of migrant women and to attend to ethnic and national boundaries. Whilst nationalism, as Benedict Anderson (1983) notes, constructs imagined communities with a sense of belonging, it also requires an 'other' from which it can imagine itself as separate.

The migrant 'other 'is gendered as well as racialized and classed. Gender is a significant component of ethnic landscapes. Cultural groups, nations and ethnic groups are imagined as woman and women are particular objects of national and ethnic discourses and policies, in terms of the biological reproduction of the group/nation, its social and cultural reproduction and its symbolic figuration.

In addition women are active participants in economic processes and are particular political actors, often playing specific roles within the nation. It is necessary to incorporate women as active agents and to focus on the different ways in which they manage the migration process. Women as social actors are located at the intersection of their country of origin and country of destination, as they are economic and ethnic subjects within both locales. A contextual and situational analysis is therefore needed. Moreover, the importance of transnational connections requires us to look beyond the interaction between countries of origin and destination towards wider migratory networks.

The role of the state is central in understanding women's position. This entails more than looking at legal rules or social provision, although these are of fundamental importance. The public/private divide, reflected within state practices, with the relegation of women to the private space of the home and the family, has been extensively critiqued by feminists. In the receiving countries, the personal lives and experiences of women are socially constructed as private, so that for example, experiences of women migrants in rape and 'trafficking' is treated as private, although the women who are discovered to be illegally working in the sex trade, or who enter illegally as refugees, may be punished if this comes to the attention of the police. Rape and other forms of sexual abuse become explained as products of individual pathology rather than emanating from social processes of gender hierarchy and subordination.

WOMEN MIGRANTS AND GENDERED WORK

There is no doubt that economic incorporation into particular sectors of the economy provides an important context for understanding the position of migrant women, albeit in a heterogeneous manner. Women migrants provide the flexibility that global capital needs. Approximately two-thirds of all part-time and temporary workers are women. Women fill particular functions in the labour market, being cheap and flexible labour for the service sectors, and in some countries, small/light manufacturing industries.

They are located within a secondary, service-oriented or hidden labour market that is divided into male and female sectors and reproduces an ethnically and gendered divided labour market. Moreover, ethnic/migrant groups can use women as an economic resource. For example, family labour was one central pattern for many migrant groups in the post war period in Western Europe. In terms of the economic role of migrant women in southern Europe, there is a diversity in female participation, but there is a concentration in the service sector, particularly domestic service and within the sex or leisure industry.

Moreover, many migrant women are either illegal or do not have legal status as individuals, their legality being dependant on the permits held by employers. This places them under the control of their employer and potentially and actually leads to superexploitation and other forms of abuse. The undocumented nature of much migration is therefore important in structuring its relation to the market, in terms of the hidden or private economies within the service sector, the household (as in domestic service) and the sex industry. This raises the issue of the ways in which being deprived rights of entry and settlement, as well as broader rights of citizenship, are central reasons for the forms of domination faced by migrant men and women.

DOMESTIC MAIDS

The use of foreign domestic servants, many of whom live in, constitutes a significant growth industry in southern Europe. Sri Lanka, the Philippines, Albania and Latin America are favoured countries for this form of female labour migration. Southern Europe has increasing numbers of working women, many of whom are mothers. The inadequacy of state provision for the care of the very young and the elderly, or the inability of the state to actually provide those services has resulted in a massively increased demand for domestic workers. Local women with more disposable family incomes turn to poorer women, many of them migrant women, to take on the domestic role and responsibilities traditionally associated with women's role in the private sphere.

Few domestic maids have a migration status separate from their work entitlement on entry as domestic workers, and they are therefore vulnerable; if they leave their employer they could be deported. Some women are undocumented, which makes them particularly vulnerable and exploitable. Lack of formal regulation and person rights deprives them of any ways of countering potential forms of abuse and may trap them in unhappy and at times dangerous dependencies on the families that employ them. Often their employers complain loudly of the presence of too many foreigners in their country on the one hand and yet happily employ a foreigner in their own home because they are cheap.

The multiple domestic tasks such maids are given 'as part of the family' mean the extension of the subordinate role of women as unpaid family workers to paid family workers. The expectations that families have on the wife and mother now are placed onto the domestic maid but without the potential emotional and other rewards as well as the reciprocities involved in family structures. Women from poorer countries such as Eritrea, Sri Lanka, Albania and the Philippines are subjected to oppression by women from more affluent countries.

This problematizes the view that the source of women's oppression is men and shows how power relations not only exist between men and women but also amongst women. This supports the view that many of the gains that indigenous women have made have depended on the exploitation of other women from poorer countries in the international division of labour. It also shows the importance of state processes in the facilitation of subordination within the employer/ employee relationship.

This is an important instance of how differential labour market incorporation can be divisive for women. While women of the majority improve their position it is at the expense of migrant women. Moreover, this pattern reproduces traditional family arrangements where women remain responsible for the domestic sphere, even though they work. The employment of maids facilitates changes in the female participation of indigenous women whose reliance on the family (for example their mother and other unpaid female kin) can no longer be guaranteed.

Women migrants also often bear the responsibility for supporting their families back home and are an important familial resource. They thus carry the 'burden of reproduction' for their families and for its survival in the homeland or in the society of migration. Changing class relations and the importance of material display also mean maids are part of status symbolism in many societies such as Greece, Italy, Spain and Cyprus. Sex Related Migration There has also been a growth of the entertainment industry linked to sexual services such as in cabaret, dancing, and massages parlours etc.

The feminization of flows to southern Europe is linked to changes in women's employment, with the restructuring of labour markets towards the service sector, but the sex industry is also linked to continuing traditional maintenance of the family for local women. Prostitution, in fact, is hidden by some of these activities and has become very lucrative, sometimes for co-ethnic employers or pimps. Traditionally such women tended to come from south-east Asia and Africa, but today it is women from Eastern Europe and the former Soviet Union who are increasingly used in this way, being preferred as well as being more available with the collapse of Eastern Europe.

The traffic in women in the sex industry is largely illegal and undocumented. Where women are not illegal entrants they may be documented as cabaret artistes and musicians as in the case of Cyprus. Many of these women are promised jobs in clubs and other forms of leisure but find them forced into prostitution on arrival. If they are illegal entrants any attempt to avoid prostitution could lead to deportation. This shows how the illegality of women and the fact that the abuse they face may be defined as stemming from the private realm of relations with men, means that they cannot be protected by the state.

A related growth industry is that of mail order brides. In the past, women from south-east Asia were favoured for their submissiveness and as good housewives. Eastern European women are increasingly preferred, being promoted on grounds that they will fit in and they are not physically distinguishable. Some of these are educated women who may be escaping from countries that may be in political or economic disarray, searching for a dream in the West. The need to search for new homes involves recognizing individual and subjective components of choices being made by some of these women. If a mail-order bride wishes to leave the relationship that secured her entry to the migration setting, she too will be liable for deportation. Once women are shifted out of the private sphere, it is irtmigration law that determines their status, not family law or the laws against trafficking.

THE ECONOMY AND GENDERING MIGRATION IN CYPRUS

We can see some of these processes at work in the small country of Cyprus. It was traditionally a country of migration, but the tables have now turned. In the 1990s Cyprus has become a country that receives migrants from the Third World and from Eastern Europe. Like much of southern Europe it has experienced a feminization of migration, with a strong distinction between the calls upon men and women who migrate. More and more Cypriot women have been incorporated into the labour force, along with growing urbanization and the continuation of a gendered division of labour within the Cypriot economy and within the home.

Migrant women are therefore important in terms of the changing configuration of gender relations for Cypriot women. Cypriot women are more likely to be in full time employment, unlike many married women workers in Western Europe, whereas care and services for families are not provided through state agencies. This also relates to changing relationships with elderly parents who can no longer be looked after by their married daughters and who need a full time nurse at home. The demand for child care is high given the increase in the proportion of children under 5.5 years who are in child care: 60 per cent in 1996 compared to 27 per cent in 1987 according to published data (Dept of Statistics).

The expectations of women in the labour force are for greater parity, but there is continuing relative low pay for women compared with men. There is a shortage of local women going into nursing and care work but there are additional factors relating to the cost of labour (cheapness) and the greater comfort felt by many women in employing foreign maids compared with indigenous ones (also cited in Anderson and Phizacklea 1997). The use of Filipina and Sri Lankan maids and nannies can be understood in this context. Women became an important source of labour after the 1974 invasion, particularly after 1978.

The increasing participation of women in higher education (the latter had to be abroad by necessity, until the recent establishment of the University of Cyprus) provides opportunities for alternative lifestyles and concomitantly the development of less traditional conceptions of gender relations. However, there is a disparity between the attitudes and practices/experiences of women in Cyprus vis-a-vis an emancipatory and feminist consciousness.

Although, as more and more Greek-Cypriot women become active in the labour market some aspects of patriarchal control will be modified, there has not been any great transformation of gender relations to accompany economic participation. This issue has yet to be fully explored through extensive empirical research, but there is a continuation of women's responsibility for household and child care, particularly as the employment of maids has put on the back burner a transformation of social roles within the family.

The latest figures show 27,500 legal migrants and calculate an additional 10,000 illegal migrant's resident in Cyprus in 1997. The employment of artists, maids and foreigners working for offshore companies (calculated at 17,000) is regulated by the Irtmigration Office, whilst other categories are regulated by the Ministry of Labour. Over one-third of these are maids with about one-eighth as artists and musicians (all likely to be women); that is, women constitute approximately 50 per cent of migrants who come into Cyprus in this way. Major countries of migration to Cyprus are Greece, Bulgaria, The Philippines, Sri Lanka and Syria.

Of these the growth over the last few years has been primarily maids from the Philippines and Sri Lanka. There has been an increasing need for foreign workers over the last six years or so and this has extended to a need for domestic workers, governesses, gardeners, barmen and workers in offshore companies, which already employ a significant number of foreign personnel. Following the pattern found in the rest of southern Europe, women generally come in as maids for middle class professional families, or as artists and musicians, a euphemism for the sex industry, which in Cyprus caters largely for the indigenous population although it is also used by tourists. Sex-related migration has been very profitable and an integral part of tourism in many countries in southern Europe as noted earlier in this chapter.

Sex workers come particularly from Southeast Asia, Thailand, Eastern Europe and Russia. They come in as cabaret dancers but may be recruited as prostitutes. Because their activity is illegal they are heavily dependent on their employers. They are only allowed to come in for six months and then they must be away for six months before they are allowed to return. In the case of domestic workers, they come in on short-term contracts. Their employer has to apply for an employer permit for up to three years with the possibility of renewal for another year. At the end of the period, women may send a female relative in their place or change employer.

The likelihood is that a large number of women are also operating illegally. The issue of mailorder brides from south-east Asia and Eastern Europe has not arisen in Cyprus, although there is some evidence that domestic maids who are brought in by single men may be used as mistresses and there have been some publicized cases of marriages taking place with Filipina women.

There is little regulation of the terms of employment of many of these women. Regarding domestic maids who come largely from the Philippines and Sri Lanka, for example, there is some evidence of superexploitation. They are also a status symbol: in one middle class neighbourhood I visited in Nicosia out of 26 families living in a new prestigious development, 24 had a foreign maid. This is not only confined to women who work, but women who prefer leisure to doing their own child care and domestic work.

In addition, more and more women are taking maids as part of a materialist status symbol, even within the lower middle classes. Filipinas are regarded as top-class maids for status, being generally seen as cleaner, more deferential and more sensitive to privacy. Many are educated women, some of whom have degrees and were teachers or accountants in their own country. The issue of racialization is relevant here as they are regarded as less of an 'other'than Sri Lankans, largely because they are Christian.

Many of these women not only service the family that employs them but that of the employer's elderly parents, so they may be given tasks of cleaning parental homes and looking after sick relatives, as well as looking after the children of brothers and sisters. Bartering in maids is not unknown and a particularly pleasing maid may be passed on to other relatives or friends. The sisters and mothers of maids may also be brought in either concurrently or sequentially and there are cases where a mother may replace her daughter within a particular family. Most maids are not treated as part of the family and eat separately, often sharing a bedroom with the children, and they are not allowed boyfriends. They may be used for the dirtiest work and have little protection.

Like maids, particularly Filipinas, in other countries, remittances home form an important part of the transnational financial aspects of female migration. Women also save to buy consumer goods (particularly good electrical equipment) and fashionable clothes and jewellery to send back home. Networking gives maids strong systems of support. A usual practice is renting a flat where they meet and eat on their days off and they may be seen in the town squares on Sunday morning congregating and picnicking together. The different treatment of different groups of women from different origins suggests that economic incorporation cannot fully account for some of the ways in which migrant women have been received by the countries to which they migrate. Issues of nation and ethnicity are also important factors that structure women's lives.

MIGRANT WOMEN AND THE ETHNIC BOUNDARY

There is much evidence that women are central transmitters of ethnic culture: they reproduce the culture and tradition of the group and its religious and familial structures and ideologies. They reproduce the group biologically and are used as symbols of the nation or ethnic group. They are important as 'mothers' of patriots and represent the nation. For example in both Bosnia and in Cyprus, the rape of women involved the project of forcing them to bear the children of the enemy and being violated as mothers of the national enemy.

Migration can be seen in the context of the reproduction of national identity and the boundaries of belonging, both for the receiving countries (where it may lead to ethnic exclusion and racism) and the sending countries (where it may lead to a concern with retaining the ethnic bonds of migrants with their countries of origin). These processes are not given or static; they change around specific economic and political conditions. Gender processes may be regarded as important in understanding how nationhood and belongingness are retained and reconstituted, particularly through the role of women as ethnic actors. However, it could be argued, that women function as objects of discursive practices and social relations whereas men are its active agents. Wetherall and Potter (1992) argue that men are given the authentic voice to represent their communities.

It is not surprising that women as biological reproducers of the nation play a central role given the importance that ideas of 'blood' and 'common origin' have for constructing ethnic and national collectivities. The importance of this for the formation of nations, however, varies, from societies like Germany, which are based on ideas of essential Volknation' or true Germanness decided by blood and family, to ideas of common culture and civic virtues that best characterize the Swiss and Belgian context where several ethnic groups constitute a nation, as well as Italy.

Societies like the US, Canada, South Africa and Australia are largely what may be termed White settler societies and contain several ethnicities; nationhood is constructed out of the acceptance of the political reality of the nation and identification with its future. This could be seen in terms of the importance of 'collective destiny' rather than origin and common parameters regarding cultural, political and legal rules. But this may exclude those who are regarded as not being able to share in this: Aboriginals in Australia are a case in point.

In all societies, women of different groups are encouraged to reproduce the nation differentially and some are encouraged to 'grow and flourish' whereas others are seen as undesirable. For example, in many Western societies ethnic minority women's fertility may be seen as a threat to the nation, involving demographic and nationalist policing and ideologies and the use of depoprovera and sterilization techniques against some. Indigenous mothers who give birth to many children (termed polytechna mothers in Cyprus) may be rewarded whereas migrants and their descendants in this situation may be subjected to policies and discourses of inferiorization.

Although women are members of collectivities they are subjected to different rules and experience them differently.

As well as functioning as biological reproducers, with state policies being geared to different women in these terms, women also reproduce the nation culturally. Women may be seen as targets and agents of national acculturation. The education of women becomes a key dimension in producing loyal citizens and in some cases there have been highly publicized attempts to assimilate women into the dominant culture, such as in France through the notorious scarf affair.

As Anastasia Karakasidou (1996) points out, the education of women in the Greek language and tradition was central after the incorporation in 1913 of Thrace into Greece, in order to make women suitable mothers. She quotes as an example a 1924 report to the Governor General of Macedonia, the Superintendent of the Fiorina Educational district, who maintained that it 'was imperative to educate women and very young children who spoke no Greek'. He warned that children would come to harm if they lived in a 'foreign speaking' home environment (1996: 104).

Deniz Kandiyioti (1989), on the other hand, shows how the modernization project of Turkey, at both political and cultural levels, used the emancipation of women as a strategic tool. She also argues that because the domestic sphere represents the continuation of tradition, it becomes most subject to state discourses under situations of political change. Women are also symbolic of the nation, but modesty and motherhood are key elements of this as in the French Patria and the symbol of Cyprus as a martyred mother mourning for her loss.

In Nicaragua, the revolution was symbolized by a woman carrying a baby in one hand and a gun in the other. Those women who are regarded outside the national collectivity, unable to reproduce or symbolize it, may face particular forms of racism and exclusion. Racism against women intersects with sexism to produce particular forms of exclusion against different ethnic and class groups. Filipina maids may experience it differently from women involved in the 'porn' trade and differently from women 'brain drain' migrants from Eastern Europe.

GENDER AND THE ETHNIC BOUNDARY IN CYPRUS

In Cyprus, as in other societies, women may be seen as the direct transmitters of the 'cultural stuff of ethnicity because of their dominant day-to-day role in domestic and familial life and in child rearing. Amongst other cultural values, women transmit the values of 'good' Greek-Cypriots or 'patriots': those of sexuality, the 'work-ethic' and nationalist consciousness. The mother-nation twin is important here as is the notion of 'mother' of 'fighting men'. Women may be seen as definers of the ethnic boundary. This works in terms of the legal definition of citizenship. Only particular women can reproduce citizens within the 'national boundary'; in Cyprus those who are married to men of Cypriot origin.

However another aspect of ethnic boundary definition is entailed in conceptions about desirable sexual or gender behaviour. This works in relation to processes of reproduction of the group. For women, one of the ways of being a good 'ethnic'subject entails behaving in ethnically appropriate ways by conforming to the principle of sexual purity. For men it entails maintaining control over women. In the case of Cypriot migrants in Britain, for example, women have been the bearers, keepers and symbolic signifiers of ethnic identity and constitute one of the most important boundary markers between English and Cypriot ethnicity.

In many Western societies, migrants are feared for importing foreign cultural and moral elements, particularly if they are Muslims or Asians. This is the case in Cyprus, with many reports in the press that Cypriot culture is in danger of being undermined by undesirable foreign influences. Maids are employed mainly for their physical work in cooking, cleaning and menial child care, but public discourses show how the fear of importing foreign culture is directed at these women. There are different discourses around this, however, and tourism is also seen as a threat.

In Cyprus, eastern European women, on the other hand, are treated as morally loose or likely to be involved in drugs or the porn trade. In addition, when national feeling is strong such as during the recent events in the buffer zone between Greek and Turkish Cyprus, more obvious hostility is shown to foreign workers. The Cypriot press has made reference to foreign workers with terms such as 'we are swamped' and talking about a 'flood of foreign workers'. The failure of people in Cyprus to accept the co-existence of foreign workers on equal terms has been noted in a number of public events and has prompted the recent formation of an anti-racist group in Cyprus.

The concern with the national heritage found in public discourse is intimately linked to the dominance of the national problem in public life for a large part of the irtrtiediate Cyprus past. Therefore new migration is in tension with the present phase of the national problem with its imperatives with regard to the use of ideas of 'national identity' in pursuing broader human rights with reference to a solution to the Cyprus problem. In other words, economic interests legitimize foreign workers whereas nationalist discourse sees them as undesirable.

This also relates to how globalization and Europeanization figure in Cypriot political discourse, with Cypriots increasingly seeing themselves as European with their initiation into the European Union and negotiations about entry. This requires the reformulation of Cyprus as containing multiple ethnicities and new forms of European citizenship; as such what is posed in Cyprus is the challenge of an increasingly ethnically and culturally diverse society, over and above the ethnic divisions between Turkish Cypriots and Greek Cypriots. However, to locate women at the intersection between economic and ethnic processes is not enough and it is important to consider them as active agents and in terms of their links to social networks, households and families.

WOMEN AS SOCIAL AGENTS

Some attempts to gender migration have tended to overemphasize the role of structures and constraints and at times have produced an impression that women are victims of circumstances. Agency is conducted in given structural and institutional contexts, but as Anderson and Phizacklea (1997) point out, the narratives of women migrants, whilst referring to the enforced response to economic hardship, also talk about migration as an escape route from patriarchal structures as well as a motivation towards economic improvement for their families. Therefore, women are not just passive receivers of social processes.

Women's agency can be explored in terms of household strategies and the formation of social networks. Although many women suffer from social isolation, friendship groups and other informal networks serve to provide important social and other support. There is no doubt that national and local contexts provide particular conditions for the enablement of migrant women's agency. The national and local governments within each country will determine their ability to find a fertile environment for the pursuit of their aspirations in the new migration setting, as Orsini Jones and Francesca Gattulo argue in this.

Nor are the links between migration and gender relations always negative. Many approaches to women and migration examine the extent to which migration may serve to counter patriarchal forms of social control. This relates both to women's social power and to the relationships between men and women; what may be regarded as both the public and private social realms. Literature on these issues has not produced simple answers to the effects that transnationalism and migration have on women. Thomas Faist (1998) writing about Turkish migrants in Germany says:

> While corrmunal reciprocity undoubtedly furthered the economic success of Alihan residents, it also cemented gender relations controlled by patriarchs of extended families ... relatively immobile women, most of whom stayed behind in Turkey, shouldered the transnational life style of Alihan men.

This example is one where men have been the main actors in the transnational sphere. However, with women migrating, there may be changes in the distribution of power in the family: for example, there is some evidence that the new economic and social responsibilities of Filipina women serves to give them a more powerful role in their families. Bhachu refers to the transformative powers of migration on Asian women. In the case of Filipina and East European women, migration involves women running away from their allotted place. For example, Escriva in this discusses the avoidance of Somalian women of men from their own group as does Walker when discussing South African women.

Analysis of migration also needs to take into account women's hopes in terms of the concerns quoted in Buijs's: the remaking of homes, the effects of individual circumstances, the growth of independence, the pleasure as well as the pain in the crossing of boundaries. The multi-faceted and complex nature of women's position does not permit us to see migration in simple terms as either leading always to a loss, or always to a gain, in social status. The migration experience impacts differently on different groups of migrant women, in terms of the role of state and labour market practices and the way women have responded to the challenges they face. Nevertheless, migration may give women more autonomy and control over economic resources than in their country of origin.

Issues of Ndifference' and diversity are now central dimensions for all feminist research as well as research on ethnicity and racism. The differences between Filipinas, who are predominantly Catholic, and Somalian, Sri Lankan and Albanian women who are Muslims indicate the importance of religious identity in relation to processes of 'othering'. The former not only tend to have a higher income than the latter, but they are regarded as more desirable domestic workers. However, irrespective of differences, most women suffer by being divided from their families and being compelled to live in an isolated nuclear family unit imposed by Western norms. Moreover, they shoulder the responsibility for supporting their families back home, a camion feature of the burden placed on migrant women.

Independent wage labour has a strong impact on the opening up of choices for women although in practice socially learnt constraints may limit the exercise of these choices. However, even with changes in economic power, there may be pressure on women to maintain customs of the group, for example the pressure or desire to marry husbands or brides from the homeland is quoted as an example of the retention of cultural traditions in Buijs.

Some of the forms of agency may therefore be contradictory. Migration sometimes indicates a willingness to cross class boundaries in a downward direction. This is the case for some Russian or Bulgarian women with university degrees working in Greece and Cyprus as cabaret artistes or as domestic cleaners and waitresses. Escriva shows in this how many domestic maids have experienced downward social mobility with migration, as many are highly educated and have university diplomas. Despite this, most of the women she researched saw the migration experience as positive because of improved welfare provision and educational opportunities for themselves and their children.

As Atsuko Matsuoko and John Sorenson say, talking about Eritrean women in Canada (1999: 238):

> the redefinitions of gender roles among the diaspora population most centainly were shaped by practical contraints that to loss of economic control over the househoide by some men, more financial independence for some women, legal prohibitions against formerly accepted practices, the absence of other family members and alternative media images.

It has also been argued that Iranian migrant and refugee women have greater possibilities to find jobs and this 'provides women with the feeling of self. Hollands, writing about refugees in the Netherlands, suggests: 'Refugee men tend to refer to the past in which they were something, whereas women refer to the present and future where they might become something.' Moreover, Bhattacharjee has seen the sites of family, ethnicity and nation as sites of gendered struggle where women challenge the status quo. This might imply that such challenges are most effective in the migration setting when the institutional apparatus for specific patriarchal controls via these forms is absent. Qrsini Jones and Gattullo, for example, also highlight the potential of inter-ethnic communication, in the context of enabling local structures.

Indra also suggests the potential for feminist transnational alliances. In other words, there are possibilities for escaping oppressive social codes and a basis for solidarity with other women. Such processes, however, can go hand in hand with the persistence, albeit in a transformed way, of gendered social relations that serve to subordinate women, as well as racialized social relations. Assumptions that the migration of women leads to more egalitarianism, as a general principle, given the discussion above and the predominance of domestic work and sex related activities in migrant women's lives, may therefore be questioned.

Access to citizenship is a crucial issue relating to the experience of southern European minorities, including women who are excluded on different terms from full citizenship, and the provision of legal and social rights could resolve some of the difficulties such women face, rebates on citizenship in relation to minority or racialized groups entail looking at civil, political and social rights. Citizenship can be defined as sets of rights and responsibilities but these must also be seen in a less narrow way than political rights and include social rights.

The classic work of T.H. Far shall have been the starting point of many feminist critiques and developments of the notion of citizenship. It has been argued that Marshall's idea of citizenship as entailing full membership of the community assumes a homogeneous community: how is the latter to be defined? Who constitutes the membership and who defines the boundaries? Who are its representatives? Who is able to speak within it? Moreover, the notion of citizenship in terms of individual rights (still very far off for migrant groups in southern Europe anyway) raises problems for the attainment of rights for groups who experience ethnic, race or gender discrimination.

Perhaps the most central aspect for migrants in the new migrations (given the large numbers of undocumented) is the right to enter, or, once having entered, the right to stay. The racialized nature of border restrictions is indicated by the differential rules relating to different categories of individuals on the basis of European membership (the freedom of movement within the European Union) and ethnocentric rules found in many countries. Cypriots and Greeks born abroad, for example, are permitted entry to Cyprus as they are treated as potential members of the nation state. Black nationals in Britain are restricted, on the other hand, through changing patriality rules or the informal policing of borders.

The notion of citizenship, recently much debated, therefore needs to pay attention to inclusions and exclusions of entry, as well as settlement. Furthermore, inclusive models of citizenship require a split between notions of nationality (and therefore ethnic and national belonging) and ideas about relations to the state or polity and to the society more generally. Thus issues are raised about civic entitlements, rights and obligations, which may be divorced from nationality and notions of national belongingness and identification.

The political dimensions of participation, the social dimensions of social entitlement and the national identities and sentiments attached to these therefore need to be disassociated. The European project of consolidation is dedicated to containing migrant populations as well as reducing the number of people that might eventually have to be recognized as having legal rights to some form of citizenship. Undocumented workers, however, pose no such problems and can be confined to the least desirable and lowest paid jobs within the large unregulated sector of many southern European countries.

Moreover, instead of being encouraged to develop policies of social inclusion for new migrants, southern European countries are being urged to follow the increasingly powerful European Union (EU), which wants them to secure and control the southern frontiers of Europe. This goes hand in hand with specific forms of ethnocentrism and xenophobia in each country. Allied to economic interests these produce a situation whereby large numbers of people are subjected to increasingly unacceptable conditions of human existence. The legalization of these workers has begun in some countries but is patchy and uneven.

Moreover, the desire on the part of other states to join the EU and the negotiations around entry, for example in the case of Cyprus, is pulling them in two opposite and contradictory directions. On the one hand, there is the impetus toward the recognition of interculturality with the breaking of national borders and the potential impact of this (for Turkish Cypriot and Greek Cypriot rapprochement in Cyprus for example); the development of multiculturalism is one side of this.

On the other side, is the need to develop policies in harmony with the powerful countries of the EU that involve the policing of the borders of Europe against undesirable 'others'. Many of those already in these countries are illegal Ymdesirables' and yet are needed by the economy. Turning a blind eye to these may no longer be possible and threats of deportation and state violence are issues that may very well come to the fore increasingly. However, even if issues of illegality are resolved, there still remain broader issues of citizenship that will need addressing, issues that still remain unresolved within Europe as a whole.

This chapter has tried to show that migration needs to be located in terms of the globalization of labour, as well as the continuing bonds with ethnic and national territories and identities, on the one hand and gender relations on the other. Any discussion of migration and its relationship to the economy and to ethnicity requires looking at the issue of gender and ethnic difference; it must also attend to women as active agents within these processes rather than treating them as passive victims. This is quite an agenda to gender.

2

Mothers' Rights to Equal Rights

Since the collapse of the Soviet Union, human rights groups have expressed considerable concern about post-Soviet women. Arguably, this is because most glasnost-era discussions of the Soviet Union's democratization paid little attention to its impact on women. But this is not the only reason. Despite considerable effort on the part of international women's rights programs, the region's nongovernmental organizations for women are themselves new, inexperienced, and relatively weak. They are finding it difficult to cope with the demands of the current transition, which has exacerbated previous social, political, and economic problems and created new ones like unemployment, inflation, and homelessness.

It is estimated that post-Soviet women's rights organizations constitute less than one percent of nongovernmental organizations active in the former Soviet Union. Not only are there too few women's organizations to effectively meet the needs of local women, but those organizations that do exist are small and inexperienced at working together. Lack of coalition building experience has hurt some of the women's movement's biggest campaigns. For instance, many women in Russia and Ukraine were concerned when women lost political representation in Russian and Ukrainian parliaments after the demise of Soviet-era quotas.

They formed a variety of women's parties. However, so far, these women's parties have failed to elect any of their candidates and their influence has arguably declined at least in part because of rivalries. In Ukraine, at least four separate women's parties have formed in the last decade, each short-lived and weak. The current weakness of post-Soviet women's activism is the consequence of preexisting weaknesses that have long been stressed in Western accounts of socialist states' treatment of women: the absence of a Western-style civil society of nongovernmental organizations (NGOs), exacerbated by state paternalism and lack of contact with the international women's movement. In order to explore how these factors left post-Soviet women unprepared for community activism, my analysis will focus on how changes in state policy limited Soviet women's access to three sets of crucial collective action resources: nongovernmental women's organizations, collective action frames, and coalition-building opportunities.

There are many other factors that influence women's community activism; however, the ability to establish nongovernmental organizations, develop effective collective action frames, and gain experience in coalition building have repeatedly emerged as important dimensions of successful collective action. Thus, a focus on these dimensions constitutes a useful (if imperfect) starting point for making cross-national comparisons about globalization's consequences for post-Soviet women as activists, as well as for assessing how other factors have affected local activists' domestic capacities for collective action.

By discussing women's community activism prior to the introduction of market reforms, or perestroika and briefly examine the kind of organizations and collective action frames that women community activists developed during the final years of Soviet rule. To analyze the collective action frame that has been encouraged by the NIS-US Women's Consortium, a U.S.-funded organization designed to foster post-Soviet women's leadership through cooperation between U.S. and post-Soviet NGOs and conclude by suggesting some reasons why the ultimate success of such transnational partnerships depends on whether they promote or impair domestic coalition building between older and newer activist networks.

WOMEN'S COMMUNITY ACTIVISM PRIOR TO PERESTROIKA

Observers have tended to view the Soviet Union through two opposing perspectives. Party leaders and official Soviet women's activists claimed that the Soviet state had emancipated women from traditional forms of patriarchal exploitation, and enabled women to enter all traditionally male-dominated spheres of society. The Soviet Union's critics saw it as a paternalist one-party state in which both men and women were atomized and powerless, and in which the party monopolized resources for collective action. Both perspectives present a distorted view of Soviet women's capacities for collective action.

Though the Soviet Union was one of the first countries to make gender equality and women's rights important political goals, claims that Soviet women had attained full political equality with men are overstated. In reality, their progress was slow. The Soviet leadership carefully recruited women into official organizations such as the Communist Party and other secondary associations, and as the country industrialized, women's access to these and other resources for collective action gradually expanded. As the country became more urban and more industrial, Soviet women and other Soviet citizens also gradually developed a certain degree of political influence, within limits set by the party leadership. Most of these changes occurred during the post-World War II era.

During the early years of Soviet rule, the party strove with little success to integrate Soviet women into state-building projects. Initially, these efforts were coordinated through local branches of "Women's Departments" [zhenotdely] of Communist Party organizations coordinated through a Women's Department (or zhenotdel) of the Communist Party's Central Committee founded in 1919 at the urging of Aleksandra Kollontai. The Women's Departments trained a cadre of local women activists, recruited local women into the party, and directed community relief work among orphans, wounded soldiers, and the homeless. But Soviet leaders quickly closed Women's Departments when they became channels for local anticollectivization protests. In 1930 the Central Committee abolished the Women's Departments, and merged their branches with local Communist party organizations.

After World War II, the party consistently targeted women in its recruitment drives. In the 1960s and 1970s, Soviet women entered the party in greater numbers, but their role in the party remained relatively limited. The proportion of women party members which for decades had remained low, very gradually rose to one-quarter by the late 1970s. Official Soviet statistics on party leadership show that by 1980, women had also achieved a certain kind of political influence as party leaders at the local level, where they constituted half of all people's deputies and a majority of judges.

Women activists also began advancing through the system of Communist Party and state-controlled secondary associations. There were several reasons for the party's efforts to recruit more women and to pay greater attention to their welfare. One of the most important was declining birthrates and an increasing incidence of one- and two-child families. Party leaders feared that steady declines in the postwar birthrate would, in decades to come, create serious labour shortages. In an effort to reverse this trend, a variety of measures were taken to investigate and formulate solutions to problems that Soviet women faced. Women party members and academics were appointed to state agencies and commissions that investigated issues related to childbearing.

These investigations determined that many women would not have more children because they lived for years in overcrowded dormitories or apartments, came home from work to face a stressful "second shift" of household work (unshared with their husbands) made more difficult by chronic shortages in housing and consumer goods. State leaders made some effort to use trade unions to relieve some of the pressure on women workers. Groups called Women's Councils [zhensovety] were periodically revived within trade union organizations in order to help women gain access to day care and vacation passes for their children. Because the councils were concerned primarily with using existing trade union resources to help women workers to combine work with childbearing, their contributions to Soviet women's material gains were limited.

Women's Councils were politically weak, and there continued to be no women in the Politburo and few women in decision-making bodies. How did Soviet women fare in terms of their control over indigenous organizations, the development of a collective action frame, and opportunities for coalition building among groups with ideological differences? Soviet women were officially given considerable attention. They were treated as an interest group with a common identity -"working mothers."

They were encouraged to have more children. In order to help them to combine work and motherhood, women were mobilized into official women's organizations. To some extent, this allowed women to develop organizational resources through which to articulate grievances within the workplace. However, these organizations were not intended to help women engage in collective action in other realms.

SOLDIERS' MOTHERS COMMITTEES AND MATERNALIST ACTIVISM

Soviet women first began to engage in independent, locally based collective action in the late 1980s, during the Soviet Union's brief experiment with market reforms. In the mid-1980s Mikhail Gorbachev introduced perestroika, "restructuring," or market reforms, and glasnost, "openness," or political liberalization. During the first years of reform, Gorbachev gave women's issues considerable attention. Like earlier Soviet reformers, he promised to help women combine motherhood and work (e.g., by creating more part-time positions and alleviating housing shortages). He also pledged to promote more women to positions of authority.

More important still, Gorbachev revived the Women's Councils, and placed them under the jurisdiction of the high-profile Soviet Women's Committee, which represented Soviet women internationally and thus, had ties to international women's groups from whom the country's activists had been isolated for so long. Gorbachev thus increased women's activists' access to new collective action frames and created opportunities for new international coalitions.

These reforms had some results. Women's Councils expanded their membership rapidly. By April 1988, there were reported to be 236,000 Women's Councils, with a total membership of 2.3 million. Women's Councils formed in workplaces throughout the country, to investigate and discuss solutions to their members' concerns. Contacts with international women's activists also increased, leading to new, more critical treatments of domestic problems. Not only did these developments broaden the realm of public debate to include a variety of formerly taboo issues such as abortion, contraception, and even feminism (which party leaders had long cast as a bourgeois ideology), they also emboldened women activists to engage in collective action outside state- and party-controlled channels.

During 1989, a year when glasnost protest activity began to spill over from state- and party-controlled channels throughout the Soviet Union, women activists formed dozens of direct action protest groups. A handful of women (located primarily in Moscow) experimented with feminism and tried to adapt it to Soviet women's problems. The vast majority of these protest groups was unconcerned with this largely foreign ideology, and brought together local mothers who sought to force state agencies to provide relief and assistance to their children.

Soldiers' Mothers Committees organized and carried out the first such women's protests to capture the support of the public and receive considerable attention from the Soviet leadership. These committees were initially founded in 1989 by mothers of conscripts who had died in peacetime military service as a result of hazing. At that time, Soldiers' Mothers groups staged a series of public demonstrations and hunger strikes through which they sought to draw attention to the system of hazing and to pressure the party leadership to reform military service. These protests achieved sufficient moral authority in the publics eyes that Gorbachev met with its representatives to hear their concerns.

Beginning in 1989, women activists also formed many other new women's direct action groups to force other state agencies to reform their treatment of women and their children. Independently or with the assistance of local Women's Councils, such "maternalist" activists established dozens of new community associations that sought state protection or assistance from Soviet state agencies to mothers of large families, single mothers, mothers of disabled children, disabled mothers, and other categories of needy mothers.

Also in 1989, non-Russian women began to form new national women's associations that embraced a nationalist variant of maternalist activism that sought to recognize the role women played in national identity formation. These groups tended to utilize organizational resources from the system of secondary associations (chiefly, professional unions and academic institutes) that the Soviet state developed to administer areas of education and culture. Nationalist women's activism of this type was concentrated in the western Ukraine, the Baltics, and the Caucasus, where national sentiment was rising.

This wave of community activism had complicated effects on women's capacity to use glasnost freedoms to gain greater control over indigenous organizations, successfully develop a collective action frame, and build coalitions among groups with ideological differences. For the present discussion, it is important to note first and foremost that the most effective attempts to seek control over community organizations united local networks of needy women who embraced fairly conservative Soviet definitions of women's rights and pursued fairly short-term goals, principally, increased state assistance to their children.

Rarely are such community groups interested in, or able to pursue, coalition building that might increase women's political power. Typically, such groups form self-contained networks or work in relative isolation. Associations of Mothers of Large Families that began forming in 1989 now exist throughout the Newly Independent States. In Ukraine (which Western women's rights advocates would later claim had only three women's NGOs in 1994), such an organization formed in 1993.

As of 1996 (the most recent year in which a comprehensive survey of Ukrainian women's NGOs has been conducted), 25 local chapters of this NGO had united under the auspices of the All-Ukrainian Association of Large Families, based in Kiev. This organization has engaged in a wide variety of activities. It cooperates with a variety of state agencies and advocacy groups for women, children and the disabled, and conducts regular meetings, independent research, conferences, and public service work to bring attention to the rights of children and families.

Similar organizations have also proliferated in Russia, although many outside Moscow and St. Petersburg work in relative isolation from each other (perhaps because of the country's size), and conduct activities primarily in conjunction with local successors to Soviet Women's Councils. In Kalingrad, an organization was established in 1990 that sought to help mothers of large families by providing assistance, advocating the preservation of state benefits, and raising public awareness about large families. It claimed 600 members in 1998.

A second such organization is Home (Dom), located in the town of Olenegorsk, Murmansk oblast, established in 1989, with 250 members. A third community group, Women Together, of Novosibirsk, was established in 1994 and claims 300 members. Hundreds of such organizations have formed throughout the NIS by formalizing preexisting informal networks of mothers whose children had received particular types of aid. Only rarely have these mothers' associations' merged two welfare constituencies to create a stronger group.

One relatively rare example is Orange Tree of Leningrad Oblast, which was established in 1991 with the goal of mutual support of mothers with many children and single mothers. In 1998, it claimed 260 members. As important as these groups may be for needy women, they have limited political goals and capacities, and hence a limited impact on the policy-making process. Ethnocultural women's associations originally sought to revive women's commitment to national languages and cultures and claimed to have no political goals.

However, many were closely affiliated with organized movements for national sovereignty that during the final years of Soviet rule called for independence. These types of groups, in mobilizing support for national sovereignty, enjoyed considerable political influence. In part as the result of the new conditions of independence, some of these groups have been able to form large federated national associations with dozens of local chapters. However, they have achieved their success primarily by building coalitions with nationalist groups that were not focused on women's rights and that have lost vitality since achieving their goal of independence from the Soviet Union.

Although national revival movements have subsided, a number of nationalist women's groups have survived independence. Two examples are the Ukrainian Women's Association (Zhinocha hromada), affiliated closely with the Ukrainian movement for independence (Rukh) and the Ukrainian Women's Union (Souiuz Ukrainok), both of which were established in 1989 to restore national traditions and are run by wives of prominent nationalist leaders. These two organizations have prospered and achieved a sizable mass membership of locally based chapters affiliated through a national association based in the capital.

In 1996, the Ukrainian Women's Association claimed 15,000 members, and the Ukrainian Women's Union claimed 11,300 (Women's Information Consultative Center 1996). Both lost some members as new feminist women's NGOs have formed. And neither they nor the new feminist groups have had much success in their attempts to advance women's issues in the political arena. Indeed, the share of women in Ukraine's parliament is lower than it is in Russia's. The success of these groups will depend on their ability to build coalitions. So far, efforts to build such coalitions have foundered.

As these examples suggest, it not true that Soviet-era

secondary organizations failed to become channels for Soviet women to engage in collective action. Nonetheless, Soviet-era resources have been insufficient for women to develop political power in their own right. Soviet women activists used both institutional and noninstitutional channels to increase their control over local organizational resources. The strongest protest activity was motivated by maternalist claims, which foreign and domestic observers have often argued had a depoliticizing effect on women.

When glasnost first allowed women community activists to engage in independent collective action, they utilized this discourse of motherhood to elaborate a "maternalist" collective action frame to make new political demands. Soviet women thus turned "maternalist" activism against the state. Groups of soldier's mothers, welfare recipients, and non-Russian cultural activists tried to wrest from the party and the state control over areas that had long considered the jurisdiction of women. But opportunities for coalition building have declined as the result of this sudden decentralization of state power. Many new community organizations either don't know of each other's existence or are prevented by ideological differences and new political borders from common initiatives, and this might be seen as an important limiting factor on glasnost-era women's community activism.

In short, when the Soviet state loosened long standing prohibitions on nongovernmental associations, the gains for women community activists were mixed. While Soviet state organizations quickly gave rise to certain kinds of independent women's community activism, nonetheless, the official, federated Soviet women's associational structure created through Women's Councils collapsed, and this organization ceased to be able to coordinate activities that might have translated greater agenda-setting independence into increased political power. As a result, glasnostera organizations remain nodes of community activism, but their efforts to coordinate women's collective action have been fairly local, and even at the local level, community activists have been seriously hampered by the state's incapacity to make concessions in a time of economic crisis.

POST-SOVIET WOMEN'S ACTIVISM

Perestroika and glasnost were intended to stimulate the USSR's flagging economy and inspire greater confidence in the country's government. Instead, they soon unleashed a dramatic wave of protest against party and state hegemony. In one republic after another, the Soviet state lost control. Separatist movements arose and demanded greater local control over economic and political affairs for the Soviet Union's republics. Those pressures contributed to the Soviet Union's collapse and led to the reconstitution of its far-flung republics as independent states, many of them quite unstable.

Local independence movements stressed the inability of Moscow-based reform to understand and be responsive to conditions in their republics, and advocated that local leaders develop their own policies. However, since independence, the locus of control over post-Soviet economic and political reforms has moved from Moscow even farther abroad. The International Monetary Fund (IMF) now sets the pace and decides the nature of reforms with support from foreign lenders who constitute a major source of funding to post-Soviet states: the World Bank, the European Union (EU), the European Bank for Reconstruction and Development, and the governments of the United States, the United Kingdom, Germany, and Canada.

These foreign donors have worked closely with one another to put pressure on local aid recipients to increase the pace of mass privatization and economic restructuring, and of course, to increase foreign trade and investment. What effects have these macropolitical shifts had on resources for women's community activists? It is important to note that donors have made repeated efforts to stimulate the growth of civil society, and in particular, to empower local women's NGOs. The U.S. Department of State and the U.S. Agency for International Development (USAID) have focused considerable attention on developing a unified strategy for civil society building.

In the words of an early report that set the agenda for future Western partnerships in Russia and Ukraine (the largest post-Soviet countries and the first priority for Western assistance), "facilitation of private voluntary action and the strengthening of civil society institutions is necessary to generate a successful transition to democracy". In short, U.S. policy has targeted coalition building between American NGOs and local post-Soviet partners as a policy priority. This approach to democratization has created several unintended problems that have weakened preexisting local women's groups. First, it fails to acknowledge the important role that local state agencies and governmental organizations can play as local nodes of civil society-building activity (thus ignoring the organizations that trained many Soviet women's activists).

Second, it gives priority to transnational exchanges between local organizations and U.S. partners, rather than seeking to strengthen domestic ties between the dozens of small women's groups that formed during the Soviet period. Third, in practice, rather than building on well-networked local organizations such as the Women's Councils as nodes of women's community activism, it leads to the creation of new women's groups able to appeal to the particular interests of Western foundations and other intermediaries who act as gatekeepers for Western initiatives. These new women's groups often have little practical knowledge of other local women's organizations or access to the local political process. Their success also subtly shapes the kinds of activities preexisting nongovernmental groups must engage in to win ongoing financial support.

The US-NIS Women's Consortium is an instructive case for understanding some of the reasons why Western aid and Western activists have not, as yet, built effective local foundations for post-Soviet women's community activism. The Women's Consortium is the largest coalition of American and local post-Soviet women's groups to have formed through U.S. civil society partnership programs. As of September 30, 1998, 216 member NGOs and 11 individual advisers belonged to the consortium. Of these, 93 were women's groups from 26 cities across Ukraine, 2 were from Belarus, 4 were from Moldova, 2 were from Armenia, 1 was from Azerbaijan, 1 was from

Uzbekistan, 91 were from Russia, and the remainder represented the United States.

This is a smaller coalition than the Soviet-era network of Women's Councils, and few of the coalition's initial members originated in older activists networks. As a result, many have not been able to coordinate their activities with these more experienced potential allies. The Women's Consortium was initially formed in response to a USAID invitation to the Winrock International Institute for Agricultural Development, an Arkansas-based nonprofit with field offices in Brazil, India, and the Philippines. Winrock had received numerous federal grants for development work, but had no prior ties to the Soviet Union and had never established a women's advocacy group.

A self-consciously feminist representative of Winrock, Elise Smith, first traveled to several post-Soviet cities on a USAID-funded tour intended to identify local partners for USAID partnership programs. Smith had time only to meet briefly with a small handful of the organizations that had formed during glasnost. On the basis of their promises to join, Winrock successfully applied for two initial grants: a $95,000 grant from the Eurasia Foundation, and a $750,000 grant from USAID, both intended for leadership training programs for local women.

Few of the consortium's U.S. advisers and staff had ever worked with grassroots community groups, which most proponents of civil society see as the foundations of democratic life. They typically had previously worked in U.S. development agencies or other official Soviet-U.S. exchanges (e.g., Peace Links, Friendship Forces). A few of the consortium's advisers had taken part in official exchanges sponsored by the Soviet Union's official women's organizations.

Others had recent experience working full-time either with the U.S. Embassy or federally funded organizations that had only recently established programs or chapters in Moscow (e.g., the Peace Corps), or with American nongovernmental organizations that had received sub-contracts from larger federally funded organizations to undertake projects in the region after the Soviet Union's dissolution. Still others had experience working with high-profile, professionally staffed, single-issue U.S.-based organizations like Planned Parenthood that had developed and maintained chapters in developing countries and were being encouraged by the federal government to expand into the former Soviet Union.

Conspicuously absent were representatives of the small ethnic or religious community-based women's service organizations that were staffed by local volunteers and relied primarily on face-to-face fundraising and more closely resemble grassroots ideal-types of community activism. Indeed, far from belonging to a face-to-face community group that post-Soviet women's activists might emulate, many of the high-profile activists the consortium enlisted in the project had been participants in large international development projects that had worked primarily with women in developing countries. They found it hard to support the interests and objectives of the glasnost-era welfare rights mother's groups and nationalist women's associations that existed outside Moscow.

The local post-Soviet partners who became active in the consortium were from similarly elite circles. For example, one of the primary Russian figures in the consortium's work in Russia was Elena Ershova, who in the first years of the consortium's existence succeeded an American staff member to become the consortium's Moscow coordinator. A 1950s graduate of Moscow's elite Institute of International Relations (the training ground of the Soviet Union's developers of foreign policy), Ershova worked for the Communist Party organ Kommunist from 1957 until 1968. She then wrote a kandidat thesis on the American peace movement for the Academy of Social Sciences of the Central Committee.

Upon completion of her degree, Ershova left party work for a position as a researcher at the USA-Canada Institute of the Soviet Academy of Sciences, an elite think tank where she and other politically reliable scholars worked on the American New Left and on second-wave feminism- topics that were off-limits to most Soviet citizens. Until glasnost, she was also a consultant to such official organizations as the Soviet Peace

Committee and the Soviet Women's Committee. Several other Russian activists prominent in the consortium also held positions at the USA-Canada Institute and were, like Ershova, scholars rather than community activists. They had knowledge of feminism and could frame their concerns in terms familiar to American activists.

Initially, relatively young, highly placed local women with strong ties to local academic establishments were the only prospective members who expressed interest in the consortium's invitations and were encouraged to join. Few members of local community women's groups founded during glasnost joined the consortium. This was at first surprising and frustrating to the consortium's American employees, who had hoped to mobilize more classically grassroots women's groups in the former Soviet Union.

Yet they felt little enthusiasm for the local women representing the Associations of Mothers with Many Children and nationalist women's associations who attended public meetings organized by the consortium and spoke to consortium staff about the political functions of motherhood. These activists' goals seemed to subordinate women and so did not mesh well with the consortium's preexisting agenda to strengthen women's leadership in post-Soviet societies. As a result, the consortium's local members and partners in the former Soviet Union are mostly new groups that are not typical of the first small autonomous women's protest groups that formed during glasnost.

It has helped to fund a series of important local women's ventures modeled on Western women's NGOs. These range from rape crisis centers to business incubators and gender studies centers. All of these are, of course, institutions that did not exist in the Soviet Union, are sorely needed, and without question have made a genuine contribution to post-Soviet women's rights. Nonetheless, with few exceptions, because the consortium's agenda was based on strengthening women's leadership, most of its initiatives have been oriented toward highly educated professional women who might become future leaders. Its programs failed to support more classically grassroots community organizations that formed prior to the consortium.

Local members of the consortium are a select group who have been and remain better positioned to compete for Western funding than to develop local sources of financial support. The consortium teaches a relatively small number of women how to compete for Western grants. These local partners then run campaigns for women's rights that are modeled directly on U.S. or western European styles of activism. Through the consortium's influence, a handful of new post-Soviet women's groups have become integrated into transnational networks. They rarely work co-operatively with preexisting local women's groups, whose solutions are often hostile to feminism and whose focus is on maternalist causes.

As a result, deep ideological rifts have formed between a small feminist community and broader networks of community activists. Invariably, Western funding can undermine local alliances and inhibit badly needed local coalition work. Indeed, one of the greatest current obstacles to domestic coalition building has been the clash between the "maternalist" collective action frame that local post-Soviet activists tend to adopt, and the feminist collective action frame that foreign advocates use and encourage in their post-Soviet partners' funding proposals. International organizations that have established independent programs in the region soon encountered a frustrating dilemma: their mobilizing strategies frequently presuppose a type of women's rights activism that is absent in the region, particularly at the grassroots.

Western conceptions of women's rights that focus on political empowerment and independence were and remain alien to the broader population. They are also far from the collective action frame of women activists who joined glasnost-era associations and who are often unable to identify with international organizations' objectives. Hence many more seasoned activists have had little or no access to new Western resource bases, and their organizations have struggled to exist during the economic crisis that began after the Soviet Union's collapse.

Indeed, the new women volunteers and activists who became involved in Western outreach efforts were quite often not the same women who had previously managed organizations created from above by the state, such as Women's Councils and state agencies concerned with maternal and child welfare. Rarely are Western initiatives likely to attract the wives of prominent politicians or political activists who now run nationalist women's associations. Instead, their local partners tend to be small groups of young women in their 20s with close ties to academic and political elites and above-average receptiveness to Western literature- feminist writings in particular.

In short, the post-Soviet women's groups formed with the assistance of American partners are distant from many preexisting women's community groups and are also much smaller in size, tending to draw their membership and leadership from a small, relatively elite stratum of women with fairly close ties to Washington and Moscow state-based programs and agencies. Clearly, civil society as it currently exists in the former Soviet Union has brought little relief to the local women community activists who sought greater state protection for their children.

It is also far from having met the objectives of transnational women's activists who arrived to help post-Soviet women develop a capacity for feminist activism. Women's organizations have been particularly hard hit by the institutional rearrangements that the Soviet Union's collapse has entailed, and women's NGOs now constitute less than 1 percent of all post-Soviet NGOs. To what can this sad state of affairs be attributed? By asking whether the current weakness of post-Soviet women's activism results primarily from globalization or if this weakness is primarily the consequence of preexisting weaknesses that have long been stressed in Western accounts of Soviet women.

In order to determine an answer, my analysis focused on changes over time in women's access to three sets of resources needed for collective action: control over indigenous women's organizations, the development of a collective action frame, and opportunities for building coalitions among women's groups divided by ideological differences. The analysis suggests that a tentative answer can now be made. The relative weakness of post-Soviet women's community activism is a byproduct of increased dependence on foreign activists and causes; this is a direct (albeit unintended) outcome of U.S. policy, rather than simply an unintended consequence of a weak local tradition of community activism.

The centerpiece of foreign policy on civil society has been to establish transnational partnerships of local and foreign NGOs and to cultivate future leaders. Women's activists' prior dependencies (on the party and state leadership) have been replaced by ties to Western activists and causes that strive to teach local activists Western strategies for conducting community initiatives. Consequently, nearly a decade of Western assistance has taken local civil societies one step forward (increasing possibilities for international coalition building), but two steps back (decreasing local control over women's NGOs and action repertoires).

The weakness of local women's NGOs is not simply a continuation of a long history of powerlessness. An examination of access to three sets of collective action resources suggests that during the Soviet era, women gradually developed control over indigenous women's organizations and elaborated an effective collective action frame based on mothers' rights. Increasing access to these first two sets of resources created a capacity for decentralized collective action that manifested itself in a variety of new forms of women's activism and in a proliferation of new women's NGOs.

However, recent post-Soviet political instability (caused by the Soviet Union's collapse and the impact of subsequent market reforms and globalization) has indeed prevented these new forms of collective action from translating into increased political power. But this is not simply the result of globalization, as the USSR's demise brought an end to preexisting coalitions created through official women's groups. The subsequent shifts in political and economic life have tended to create great challenges for women's community activism. In other words, ironically, Soviet women activists increased their access to certain kinds of collective action resources, but their opportunities for another kind of important collective action declined considerably.

An unintended benefit of globalization has been increased Western support for post-Soviet women's activism, manifested in greater access for women activists to new public and private sources of aid and assistance from Western women's advocacy groups. Unfortunately, increased possibilities for Western coalition building have failed to compensate for the real loss of locally based coalitions. Very few of these ventures have been able to build on the wave of women's community activism that began in 1989. Instead, many Western initiatives have encouraged the formation of new partnerships between U.S. women's groups and local post-Soviet groups.

Not only has this coalition-building strategy led to the formation of new, typically feminist groups oriented toward U.S. agendas and dependent on Western public and private support, it has failed to encourage (or at least, has delayed) the formation and strengthening of cooperative ties between these new groups and the older activist networks formed during glasnost. This coalition-building failure can be attributed in part to a mismatch between the collective action repertoires that local "maternalists" adopt and the feminist one that transnational feminists view as legitimate. Thus, Western policies have stressed an approach that creates considerable unintended negative consequences for post-Soviet women's activism.

A number of new Western-funded civil society building initiatives seek to provide continued relief and support to post-Soviet women's NGOs. According to the most comprehensive recent survey of post-Soviet women's groups to date, 63 percent of Russian women's organizations that responded report that they derive financial resources from Western foundations, while just under a third receive support from their government.

This trend has been observed throughout the region, although in the Caucasus and Central Asian regions Western outreach efforts have largely failed to generate women's activism. This suggests that the region's activist networks may become increasingly divided, rather than being strengthened by increased contact with Western women's activists. This cannot fail to prevent women from sustaining local community initiatives, regaining their lost political influence.

In sum, globalization and the policies intended to soften its effect on post-Soviet societies have had complicated effects on women. The Soviet Union's transition from state socialism to free-market capitalism abruptly overturned a corporatist political system within which women's rights activists and organizations were becoming an increasingly important interest group. Even though men monopolized positions of authority and influence, Soviet women were represented politically by activists who were given access to policy makers through institutionalized political channels.

Official governmental women's rights activists and glasnost-era maternalist organizations have been fatally weakened by the dissolution of this corporatist system, but nonetheless, it does seem to be the case that they have a stable, perhaps even growing niche, among the region's women. New post-Soviet groups are small, rarely cooperate with one another, and rely heavily on Western sources of short-term support. Increasingly dependent on outsiders, post-Soviet women's rights activists and organizations remain poorly positioned to use the political system to revitalize the local infrastructure of women's organizations that might have helped shield local women from the disastrous effects of globalization.

Western initiatives have introduced complementary approaches to the local activist community. The new women's rights activists differ in composition, size, and primary basis of affiliation from the previous generation of Soviet-era women's activists. Women's groups have become more numerous, more overtly political in their demands, and in fact may now have started to develop a broader membership base (although many membership figures that post-Soviet women's groups claim are suspiciously large and may include lapsed members from the Soviet era). However, the activist community remains divided over ideological issues.

There is obviously one possible way out of this dead end: increased local coalitions between older activists who came of age before or during the glasnost eras, and younger activists who have gravitated to Western initiatives. In the short run, this may not be the strategy taken. U.S. women's activists who work for Western foundations and initiatives are often impatient with the Soviet-style women's advocates who run local successors to Soviet Women's Councils, which they see simply as bureaucratically run, mass-membership organizations that are not responsive to their members' needs and requests. But this characterization is only a half truth that obscures the fact that these organizations were anchored in valuable networks of activists who were familiar with local conditions and integrated into preexisting local and regional associations and organizations.

It is worth considering more explicitly what the costs are to leaving the "maternalists" out of Western initiatives. At least in their network ties, these older activists remain far better suited to working within the local political system than foreign-funded groups tied to international agendas. While Women's Councils were also tied to party agendas, these official Soviet women's organizations represent an enormous resource pool of trained leaders and networks of career activists throughout the Soviet Union. Unfortunately, former party members and former party-controlled organizations bore little or no resemblance to the style of activism Western funders (in particular, women's rights advocates) expected to find.

As a result, preexisting activists and organizations instead fell into disfavor with reformers, who provided the building blocks for integrating women activists. Although Western funders and advocates never came to see local Women's Councils and other locally based groups as capable of acting in their behalf, these groups continued to become important bases for community activism during and after glasnost. Thus it seems that the effectiveness of Western initiatives might be greater if they placed priority on building domestic coalitions rather than international partnerships. This is an important point to stress.

Coalition building with external advocates should not be pursued to the exclusion of other strategies for increasing local women's control over other collective action resources. Post-Soviet women who do not fit the leadership profile that Western funders adopt are badly in need of bargaining power to increase their influence over policy making. Prior to glasnost, an absence of democratic freedoms prevented local Soviet women from using official women's associations and local organizational resources to develop the commitments, skills, and resources necessary for effective community activism.

Once democratic rights were introduced, these women's groups began to develop new strategies for influencing policy, but they were not far along when the Soviet Union's collapse destroyed a significant share of their previous resource base. Rapid "shock therapy" reforms promoted by the IMF, the World Bank, the EU, and Western governments threaten to undermine existing women's organizations by moving the locus of policy making and funding further beyond their access. As a result, older activists with an understanding of the rules of local politics were at first largely bypassed by Western funders in favor of more radical women's groups of younger activists, many of whom embrace feminism and Western understandings of rights.

Although these new women's groups are much easier for Western observers to identify with, they are less effective in mobilizing public support than are older activists. It may be difficult to build bridges between new feminist groups and older networks of Soviet activists, but greater local control over organizational resources and collective action frames will ultimately give local women greater future opportunities for effective and sustained collective action, and this, after all, has long been the objective of Western advocates.

3

Alternatives from a Gender Perspective

In a context that includes the fall of the Soviet bloc and a deep crisis of the New Left, participants in the so-called New Social Movements (NSMs) develop and enact practices in the realm of civil society, as opposed to the traditional political arena. Turning away from the totalizing narratives of class-based movements and political parties, contemporary movements "abandon revolutionary dreams in favor of radical reform that is not necessarily and primarily oriented to the state". Researchers have heralded the NSMs as creating alternative ways of "doing politics" and expanding the public spaces for discourse.

In a similar vein, various researchers treating Latin-American social movements have begun to turn their attention to the "internationalization" of political mobilization. These scholars have built on NSM theory to analyze transnational social movement networks or "webs," examining "the intricacy and precariousness of the manifold imbrications of and ties established among movement organizations, individual participants, and other actors in civil and political society and the state".

These networks operate within an increasingly global world in which for the first time the core activities of the world s dominant institutions work in real time as a unit and in which global economic restructuring has repositioned states, making them more dependent on foreign investment. At the same time, increased transmigration and the promotion of emigration by some sending states have forged "transnational subjects" as well as the reinvention of states' role in the "new world order".

The globalization of capitalism and transnational capital accumulation strategies have resulted in the establishment of free trade zones (FTZs) in regions throughout the world. Conditions in the assembly factories of these zones are extremely harsh, and a largely female labour force labors long hours, frequently earning less than subsistence wages. The growth of the "sweatshop industry" has prompted new organized resistance initiatives on the part of marginalized people. Like the economic processes that they address, such political initiatives often transcend national borders.

In the pages that follow I analyze the practices of the Network, a coalition of women's organizations within the transnational antisweatshop movement that acknowledges and even works within existing political and economic structures. This chapter critically examines the "self-limiting radicalism" that makes up the Network's strategic orientation.

What do these practices tell us about how power and resistance operate within the contemporary "global system"? Rather than evaluating the Network's practices in terms of a standardized notion of transformative potential, this chapter explores the conundrums that result from these practices and the political openings to which they give rise. This analysis, then, leads beyond narrow interpretations of transformative resistance toward a more nuanced approach to opposition that is critical, but also calls attention to the points of impact and influence of these women's practices.

In addition, this case calls for a more cautionary view regarding the emergence of an increasingly "global" civil society as embodying a strong liberatory potential. If it is true that civil society is increasingly being brought together on a global scale, then it is also true that, as Alvarez and her colleagues point out, this "global village" is neither happy nor homogenous. Unequal access to power and resources are still prevalent, and there are still winners and losers, as groups compete heavily with one another.

But who are these winners and losers, and when and under what conditions are transnational political strategies successful? What kinds of obstacles impinge upon these strategies? This chapter will use the case of the Network to shed light on these questions and to tease out the complexities of what M.P. Smith and Guarnizo term "transnationalism from below." First, however, I will turn to a review of the ways in which Central America has been affected by the globalization of capitalism that will set the context for the discussion that follows.

IN AN AGE OF GLOBALIZATION

The past two decades have witnessed impressive shifts within the international economy. The globalization of capitalism, characterized by flexible accumulation strategies, dramatically increased mobility of capital, a shift from manufacturing production to that based on information processing, and the relocation of manufacturing jobs from First World nation-states to low-wage countries in the Third World, has seen the emergence of the transnational corporation as a key player. These changes have brought about the formation of a "global system".

An international economy of sorts has existed for centuries, and since the years following World War II, foreign investment in multinational production has represented an important accumulation strategy for industrialized countries (particularly the United States). Nonetheless, the current moment has distinct characteristics. As Rouse (1995) puts it, "a dialectical relationship between the national and the multinational has been giving way to one between the national and the transnational".

Instead of large multinational corporations manufacturing at various national sites for self-contained markets, corporations are distributing a single production process among sites in different areas of the world and are using rapid telecommunications to coordinate simultaneous production across geographical locations. Indeed, the rapid flow of capital, goods, people, and images across national boundaries, which communications and information technologies have made possible, is what has put the "trans" in "transnational".

The integration of Latin-American countries into the global economy has been accompanied by sweeping political transitions. The 1980s and early 1990s witnessed the demilitarization of many Latin-American states as military dictatorships gave way to electorally appointed neoliberal state regimes. Central America has seen particularly dramatic shifts in the political sphere with the end of civil wars in Nicaragua and El Salvador, the signing of the peace accords in Guatemala, and the opening of Honduras from a military dictatorship.

In accordance with their neoliberal orientations, Central-American state regimes have enacted legislation to attract foreign investment, and governments have cast their eyes on FTZs as a way to provide desperately needed jobs. The transnational apparel industry plays off this need for employment by selling its operations to the host country that offers the most benefits for the lowest costs. The apparel industry is one of the most globalized industries in existence. To more easily access the burgeoning U.S. market and avoid import quotas, Asian-based transnational corporations have recently located production in Central America and the Caribbean.

Making use of traditional systems of domination in a search for an ever cheaper, more docile workforce, transnational capital accumulation strategies specifically target young female labour markets. This reliance on a feminized, superexploited labour pool has prompted some to herald women workers as the "paradigmatic subjects" of the international division of labour. Policies implemented within this era of globalization of capital have devastated organized labour.

With their high degree of mobility, transnational corporations displace one group of workers only to integrate another more vulnerable sector, thereby pitting groups of workers against one another. In many cases the feminization of labour has displaced a male, unionized workforce. On the other hand, trade unionism has entered a crisis because it has privileged class exploitation as the exclusive site of domination.

Both the movement's failure to address the unique concerns of women workers and, indeed, the sexist practices of union organizers themselves have contributed to a delegitimization of the movement in the eyes of many in the new workforce. Struggles based on other oppositional formations, not necessarily defined by class consciousness, such as feminist/women's and antiracist movements, have represented alternatives to "modern" modes of opposition.

Like modern oppositional movements, such struggles occupy sites of contradictions generated by globalized processes. These contradictions "produce new possibilities precisely because they have led to a breakdown and a reformulation of the categories of nation, race, class, and gender, and in doing so have led to a need to reconceptualize the oppositional narratives of nationalism, Marxism, and feminism". Organizers of maquila workers have been at the forefront of such initiatives by implementing new transnational forms of political organization, mobilization, and practice.

These new modes of opposition recognize a "new" laboring subject, constituted by multiple, intersecting axes of domination. Creating and taking advantage of a globalized political space through localized grassroots initiatives, the collective practices of women maquila workers' movements have blown apart a simplistic notion of a global/local duality. The words of Mary Tong, the director of the Support Committee for Maquiladora Workers, sum up the idea behind such initiatives: "Solidarity among workers should cross the border as easily as companies move production".

When the Network formed in September of 1996, I was in Nicaragua conducting ethnographic research with the Women Workers' and Unemployed Women's Movement, María Elena Cuadra (MEC). Leaders of this group were key in spear-heading the formation of the Network, and the participant observation I conducted with the MEC exposed me to the processes involved in the Network's formation and constitution. From 1996 to 1997, I attended three international meetings of the Network, which took place in Guatemala, Nicaragua, and Honduras. In addition, in June 1997 I traveled to San Pedro Sula, Honduras, to visit Network members and the communities in which they work.

As a guest of the Network, at each meeting participated in the various activities that occurred in conjunction with the semi-annual meetings of the Network delegates. These included media events, training workshops, meetings with state agents and representatives from other organizations, as well as social activities such as meals and receptions. I conducted nine intensive, semistructured interviews with members of the Network. In addition, being housed with members and sharing meals and unscheduled time led to countless informal discussions with participants.

Based on my experiences with the Network and interviews with its participants, this research provides an in-depth picture of transnational politics. It contributes to an understanding of the ways in which social structures in an age of globalization shape the organized resistance of marginalized people and how these social actors respond to the new opportunities and limitations of the contemporary moment and shape the political terrain upon which oppositional struggles take place.

The Network formed in 1996 after a meeting in Mexico organized by a group of women's organizations along the northern border. At this meeting both the Mexican and Central American groups decided to establish separate regional networks of women's organizations that work with issues pertaining to the maquilas. Funded by a Canadian nongovernmental organization (NGO), the first meeting of the Network was held in El Salvador with representation from autonomous women's groups from Nicaragua, El Salvador, and Guatemala. Subsequently, a group from Honduras and two other groups from Guatemala joined the coalition. Founders describe the Network's purpose:

> Given the situation of discrimination and super-exploitation in which women maquila workers live as a result of the process of globalization of the regional economy and given the lack of proper spaces and conditions that permit them to make demands and proposals and stake claims regarding their rights as women and as workers; we have come together in order to analyze, generate and contribute by means of this organization a space which could serve this purpose.

(Red Centroamericana de Mujeres en Solidaridad con las Trabajadoras de la Maquila 1997, 1)

The Network meets every six months, and the role of host country for each meeting rotates. Meetings are attended by two or three appointed representatives from each organization belonging to the coalition. The events that occur in conjunction with the internal meeting are open to foreign visitors as well as maquila workers from the host country, members of the hosting organization, and other invited guests. The Network is completely dependent upon financial support from international NGOs. Most of its funding has come from Canadian and European NGOs and solidarity groups.

The general organizational term "network" is used to denote umbrellalike organizations that link diverse groups. Although every network is different, the general idea behind this organizational form is to allow diverse groups to organize around certain basic principles or issues. Thus, each organization within the Network is autonomous, and in the words of one participant, "The Network is not over and above (encima de) any one group." The loosely formed structure allows organizations with diverse histories, affiliations, perspectives, and priorities "to share and coordinate efforts in the search of alternative proposals in confronting the problem of the maquilas and to improve the conditions of women workers in the Central American region" (Red Centroamericana de Mujeres en Solidaridad con las Trabajadoras de la Maquila 1997, 1).

Though the Network takes part in regional and international campaigns and activities, each organization must decide how best to implement these activities in their home countries. The idea is for each group to be able to address the specific issues facing the communities in which they work. For example, in Guatemala a large number of minors are employed in maquila factories. Not only are these children superexploited and exposed to extremely harsh work conditions, but they are too young to receive social security benefits in the form of medical coverage. The situation of these child workers is a major concern for the Guatemalan groups, while in Nicaragua and El Salvador child labour in maquila factories is not as predominant.

Organizations that make up the Network all work with communities where large groups of women are employed by maquila factories, and the principal organizers of all the groups have had substantial experience in popluar movements, particularly in trade union federations. The majority of the Network organizations formed as a direct result of gender-based conflicts within an organization of the Left. For example, the MEC formed as the result of contradictions and conflicts within a Sandinista trade union confederation (CST). Organizers, who formerly held leadership positions within the confederation's Women's Secretariat, either left or were ousted after a series of conflicts culminating in a dramatic coup in which the Executive Council refused to appoint the candidate elected by the women of the various federations as the next director of the Secretariat.

The Association of Women in Solidarity (AMES) split from the Syndical Federation of Food and Agroindustry (FESTRAS) in Guatemala after male leaders changed the federation's political orientation and strategy. The union cut off support to the Women's Committees that had formed to organize women in the maquilas. In addition, union leaders replaced the committees with a Women's Secretariat to which they appointed leaders, making all projects proposed by this Secretariat subject to approval by the male leadership.

The Women's Committees had been nearly the only ones in Guatemala to successfully organize female maquila workers. After FESTRAS cut support to their efforts, basically casting off all organizing efforts in the maquilas, the leaders of the women's committees decided to form an autonomous organization. Members of the Network see the formation of autonomous women's organizations as necessary in order to work for the particular concerns and needs of women maquila workers. Organizations' relations with feminist organizations and feminism have varied.

Some organizations of the Network have embraced typically "feminist" approaches to issues such as domestic violence and reproductive health, and many groups openly identify as feminist; others remain suspicious of feminism, however. These women base their criticisms on the privileged class position of feminist organizers as well as what they perceive as a lack of consideration of class issues; feminist organizational practice in Central America has never been "of the masses," they say.

Most of the women hold extremely ambivalent and complex positions regarding unionism-at once highly critical of the traditional labour movement for its rigidity, corruption, and sexist practices, while acknowledging that in many cases "the first political organizing experience for [Central-American] women was in unions." Rosa María, an organizer from Guatemala, describes the culminating meeting that resulted in her and her compañeras' leaving the federation to form AMES: "They told us, 'Look, compañeritas, we're sorry, but we are going to restructure in this way.... And if you want to ask for authorization for your projects, fine. If not, you will have to leave.'" Like many of the Network's members, despite her vehement critique of unionism, Rosa María has mixed feelings:

> I still believe that syndicalism is the only mechanism that truly represents the workers. Now, that unions have not properly involved women is another matter...[otros cinco pesos].... So, perhaps we are not against unions, as such. We are opposed to methods and attitudes, but we are not against the ideology of the unions. We have lived in the flesh the attitudes of the men and have a different expression.

A common experience among Network organizers within the union movement was exclusion from decision-making power. Manuela, from El Salvador, contends, "First they [union leaders] would tell us that yes, they wanted to talk [about gender issues], then they accused us of being divisionistas." Network members criticize unions for leaving out women maquila workers from their agendas. They contend that it is only now that it is "fashionable" to work with this sector that the unions are turning to maquila workers.

Still, Network members are highly critical of unions for continuing to apply the same methods in the maquilas as they had in traditional industrial settings in past decades and for failing to incorporate a "gender perspective" into their strategies for organizing this predominantly female sector. Though some Network participants maintain active and friendly dealings with particular unions, in many cases relations with the labour movement are extremely tense, and even hostile. Some union leaders have accused the women of the Network of betraying syndicalism.

Particularly in the cases in which the women's organizations' split from the labour movement was conflictive and hostile, some union leaders actively tried to subvert the efforts of the Network within the FTZs. For example, leaders of the CST have denounced the MEC or its strategies in public several times and have engaged in clandestine efforts to undermine its organizing initiatives. In this manner the Network is an alternative to union representation, and is also a means to make visible "the social and labour reality of women."

The organizations that make up the Network see the coalition as incorporating a "vision for addressing integral problems associated with the women of the maquilas and of developing processes of collective leadership." The organizations of the Network, then, are not just concerned with traditional labour issues. Network members work to empower women and improve their daily lives in all sectors of society. Their programs and strategies cut across the public/private divide by addressing women's social position at home, in the workplace and in society in general.

The organizations of the Network run programs for maquila workers on domestic violence and sexual abuse along with those connecting workplace violence on the shop floor with the larger issue of women's position in society. The groups of the Network also devote a great deal of effort to creating educational programs to teach women about their labour, human, and civil rights. Organizations administer revolving credit programs for maquila workers to use to improve their homes, and job training programs for workers and their daughters.

One Honduran organization even established workshops for maquila workers to learn how to sew their own clothes.

Ironically, though these workers labour all day at sewing, the piecemeal way in which labour is organized in the factories means that these women lack the skills for sewing an entire article of clothing from start to finish. Workers' low wages and the fact that many are the sole breadwinners in their large families makes sewing their own clothes an important economic strategy. In addition to such community-based programs, the organizations of the Network address women's role in grassroots politics and describe one raison d'être of the Network as being a means to make women visible within popular organizations. In the words of one organizer, "Now we are giving a face to our work. We have always been there, but now we want to receive recognition."

ORGANIZING IN THE INFORMATION AGE

The increased importance of the production, manipulation, and control of information has become a defining characteristic of the global system. Within the world economy, as competition is played out among transnational actors, information technologies make possible the extremely flexible, decentralized, and customized strategies of production coordinated among multiple locations. In the garment industry such extreme flexibility is reflected in "just-in-time production" strategies and the increasingly shortened fashion trends.

Control over information, however, is not only crucial for economic competitiveness. As grassroots politics has "gone global," social actors increasingly are engaging in "information politics" in an effort to achieve goals of social justice. Wielding information as an instrument of power, social movement organizations can transmit knowledge or information through diffuse transnational channels (often using the media and telecommunications technology) to reach other international organizations and "foreign reference publics."

Through these linkages international actors and institutions can then pressure state institutions or nationally located actors to bring about change. The practices involved in such politics include negotiation, lobbying, media campaigns, and electronically disseminated action alerts. New Social

Movements and other nonstate actors depend on information to challenge institutions and influence change through persuasion and changing perceptions and values. In the struggle to improve work conditions in the assembly factories of Central America, the important role of information is immediately apparent.

There is little or no publicly accessible data regarding the characteristics of maquila workers, pay scales, benefits and production quotas. In addition, regulation of this industry by state or other institutions is almost nonexistent. Most maquila factory managements blatantly disregard state labour legislation. And regulating state agencies such as ministries of labour have been both unable and unwilling to enforce local laws. Thus, simply keeping track of what happens behind the closed doors of the maquila factories represents a crucial project for organizations interested in improving work conditions.

By definition, a "network" as an organizational form is characterized by the flow of information and services among members. At their semiannual meetings members of the Network share reports on the latest changes and issues regarding the maquila industry in their country. They also circulate materials that they have developed for use in workshops and training sessions with workers. The host organization for each meeting coordinates the event by e-mail, fax, and telephone. Indeed, the establishment of communication technology (including telephones) was one of the coalition's first priorities.

Members recognize the importance of communication within the Network, but also that communication by e-mail and fax matches the rapid mobility of capital within the Central-American region. Thus, members can warn and inform each other about factory conditions and relocations. Another goal is to create documentation centers in each of the organizations that would hold databases and libraries of information regarding the activities of the transnational corporations, the labour conditions within maquila factories, and the occurrence of human rights violations. The primary strategy of the Network has been to launch national, regional, and international campaigns to raise public awareness regarding the situation of maquila workers.

The goal of one major campaign has been to pressure maquila factory owners to sign a "code of ethics" agreeing to uphold workers' human rights and complies with local labour laws (with particular reference to those laws that specifically apply to women). The lobbying and negotiation involved in this type of strategy have become the new tools of the trade for grassroots oppositional groups, marking changes in the political landscape of the Central American region. Negotiation and lobbying as political tactics require certain conditions-political spaces that allow dialogue and the participation of civil society.

The context in which organizations of the Network negotiate is different from union negotiations in "national" workplaces or those that would take place as a resolution to armed conflicts. In the latter situations, although negotiators from oppositional groups do not come to the table holding equal levels of power as their adversaries, they do hold an important trump card-the threat of a strike or violence. In the new transnational context, oppositional negotiators no longer hold this bargaining chip. Whereas in the heyday of unionism, force in numbers was the key to power at the negotiation table, in the new context of weak labour and high mobility of capital, information becomes the key commodity.

In order to engage in information politics, members of the Network devote a great deal of effort to monitoring conditions within the FTZs. State agencies like ministries of labour have proved to be extremely incompetent and ineffective in monitoring complaints of labour code violations, frequently turning a blind eye to violations within the FTZs in order to protect the interests of foreign investment and the only growing employment sector in most countries in the Central American region. As Keck and Sikkink point out, nonstate actors gain influence by serving as alternative sources of information, but to be credible the information produced must be reliable and well documented.

Needless to say, obtaining reliable information regarding shop floor conditions is not an easy task. Conditions from one factory to the next within the same FTZ can be very different. This is especially a problem in countries like Honduras, in which, at the time of this publication, there are 11 FTZs with more than 200 factories, employing approximately 100,000 workers. To make matters worse, working conditions vary considerably from production line to production line, depending, among other factors, upon the supervisor for that line.

Many workers themselves do not know if they receive payment for overtime hours or how such payment is calculated, and pay rates are determined by a complicated system of piece-rate wages sometimes combined with base pay scales which vary from factory to factory and frequently change. Unlike union representatives, members of the Network do not have access to workers on the shop floor and must devise strategies for obtaining information from outside. For example, MEC organizers have created a network of promoters, maquila workers who represent the MEC within their factories. They meet once a month in the MEC's office to report on recent changes within their factories to impart such information as the latest brand names being processed in production lines.

In addition, an MEC organizer visits the FTZ weekly and meets with workers at a spot outside the entrance to the zone. This organizer has a long history of experience as a union organizer and community activist. She and another MEC organizer reside in the same barrios as a great number of maquila workers. They also visit maquila workers at their homes and have family members who are employed in the FTZ.

Promoters collect pay stubs and brand tags from workers as well as social security statements, and copies are archived in the MEC's documentation center. In addition, they act as liaisons between movement organizers and workers who have suffered violations of their rights and wish to file complaints at a ministry of labour, referring workers with grievances to the MEC's office and putting them in contact with MEC organizers. The organizations documentation center also keeps a record of these cases and their results, as well as any information from the media regarding the activities of transnational corporations and state agents.

NEGOTIATING NATIONAL AND TRANSNATIONAL SPACES

In their lobbying efforts and public awareness campaigns, the groups that make up the Network work to open and take advantage of different political spaces. Their strategic orientation regarding the maquilas is encapsulated in a campaign slogan: "Jobs, Yes…but with Dignity!" Thus, the Network does not call for the removal of the assembly plants, as this would leave women workers with no means of generating income. Acting as interlocutors for the women of the FTZs, Network organizers' commitment to improving women's daily lives makes them sensitive to testimonies like that of one Nicaraguan maquila worker: "I want my job and value it, because even though it tears me apart and exploits me, with my job I am able to feed my kids."

Such "radical reformism" or "self-limiting radicalism," as Cohen and Arato (1992) term it, is not particular to the Network. Scholars have noted it as being characteristic of New Social Movements. This orientation acknowledges institutional structures and seeks to work within them for change. In the words of one Network organizer, "Our people are tired of these confrontational methods. We need to propose alternatives." So, unlike the oppositional movements of "before," the immediate goal here is not to seize the state or even to replace the capitalist system.

The focus instead is to work "where the women are" to improve their daily lives given existing political and economic conditions. Network organizers themselves are very conscious of the limited range of their strategies. As one member put it, "We are asking for the minimum. We aren't even questioning the exploitation of workers. If the goal of the code of ethics were to dismantle the system of capitalism we would be fried."

In its implementation of the campaign, the Network's strategy has been for individual organizations to negotiate at the state and local levels. The Network organizes press conferences, and the local media spread the message of the campaign. The international character of the Network has not only drawn local media attention, but has added weight and legitimacy to members' negotiations with state agents and transnational capitalists.

It seems clear that the Network's strategic use of the media has contributed to increased public visibility of the issues facing maquila workers. Network members also report that shop-floor violence has decreased in some Central American countries. As part of the campaign "Jobs, Yes...but with dignity," Network members have met with state agents, factory owners, managers, and FTZ administrators to present their code and ask for support and have addressed governing bodies like the National Assembly of Nicaragua. In a landmark victory for the Network, Nicaragua's minister of labour, Wilfredo Navarro, was the first state agent to endorse the code of ethics, which he signed on February 1, 1998.

Later, he adopted it as a ministerial resolution, which all factory owners in the Nicaraguan FTZ eventually signed, symbolizing their agreement to comply. In some cases factory owners have granted Network members access to certain factories and have entered into negotiations to allow the Network to monitor factory conditions. Despite the Network's relative success in calling certain state agents and factory owners and administrators to the negotiating table, the political tools that the Network has chosen have also posed problems. For instance, the Network's negotiation techniques are borrowed from the business world and are designed to reach an agreement at any cost between relatively equal adversaries.

It is questionable, then, that negotiation in and of itself can be an effective instrument for bringing about changes in social structures. The marginalized position of oppositional groups means they often come to the table making minimalist demands with little room for "cutting a deal." Similarly, mediation techniques require mediators to remain impartial. Some of the women of the Network have questioned if this is an appropriate tool for social justice.

COMPETITION AND CONFLICT IN THE GLOBAL SYSTEM

The Network's strategies at the transnational level have been vaguer, and some groups have met with obstacles in implementing a transnational effort to bring about their objectives. While the Network's strategic orientation has enabled the coalition to open political spaces, at the same time its "self-limiting radicalism" has impinged upon options available to it and the effectiveness of its strategic practices. For example, the Network's strategy regarding the maquilas means that organizers must be extremely careful in their lobbying efforts not to pressure the factories to the point that they relocate production.

This greatly limits the Network's ability to engage in the kinds of political maneuvering that have been successful for other transnational advocacy networks, such as international boycotts in the case of the Nestle corporation. Other transnational networks have found the global media to be an important tool for implementing strategies of "information politics". For some groups of the Network the global media has been a useful mechanism for exerting pressure, while for others it has been a double-edged sword.

For example, it was an international media campaign regarding the Kathy Lee line of garments that helped spark the development of the U.S. Apparel Industry Partnership's Workplace Code of Conduct and pressured the Honduran factory KIMI into allowing an independent monitoring team, which included members of the Network, to monitor conditions there. On the other hand, the experiences of other members of the Network demonstrate the difficulties and unpredictability involved in employing the global media.

In November 1997 the New York-based National Labour Committee (NLC), with the help of a solidarity organization in Nicaragua and the coordination of the Sandinista textile union, organized a visit of reporters from the television program Hard Copy to the country's only free trade zone. In a three-part series reporters used hidden cameras in entering the garment assembly factories (maquilas) of the FTZ to expose the working conditions. To add more shock value to the series, reporters exaggerated some claims, reporting that a barbed-wire fence surrounded the zone to keep the workers inside, and those minors as young as 13 were employed there.

A national uproar ensued when a local television affiliate picked up the segment and broadcast it in Nicaragua. Public opinion was split. Supporters of the maquilas, including neoliberal state agents, pointed to Hard Copy's dealings with the NLC and described the report as a plot by U.S. unions whose jobs are threatened by offshore production. Meanwhile, the Sandinista labour movement called for the ouster of the foreign-owned factories. The headline of an editorial by former Sandinista Minister of the Interior Tomás Borge, in the oppositional newspaper La Barricada, read "¡Que se vayan!" (essentially, "They should leave!"). Borge clearly articulated an extremist, "all or nothing" position: "The benefit received by the country is insignificant. Our national dignity is of greater value".

In response, more than 350 male and female workers marched on the Ministry of Labour calling for the factories to remain in operation. The Sandinista media portrayed this as workers being manipulated by the free trade zone corporation in order to protect their jobs, while supporters and neoliberal state agents cited the march as evidence that Nicaraguans supported the FTZ. Sandinista union and party leaders exchanged accusations of "national betrayal" with state elites, and each camp struggled to use the issue to demonstrate their representation of true "national" interests. The Nicaraguan media also approached the leaders of the Nicaraguan members of the Network, the MEC, for their views.

"We felt like a sandwich," said one MEC leader. Organizers chose to remain silent rather than have their views distorted in order to fit within the binary frame that the public debate had adopted. Thus, the more nuanced position of these women-that they wanted the factories to remain in the country but to respect the human and labour rights of workers-was effectively excluded from public discourse. All the workers who appeared in the Hard Copy segment were fired after the report aired in Nicaragua. "Are they going to give these people work?" an MEC organizer wondered of both state agents and the Sandinista labour movement.

Network members have met with other barriers in enacting transnational strategies. For example, the Network plans to enter negotiations with international organizations and present its code of ethics to the Central American Parliament and the International Labour Organization (ILO) asking for political support from these institutions of "global governance". However, members have found it difficult to gain access to them as well as to other transnational political spaces such as summits of Central American ministers of labour or Central American presidents. When the ILO held a conference in Nicaragua, only representatives of the labour movement and the media received official invitations. One representative from the MEC finally found a way to attend, but only after searching through her personal networks of old friends from the labour movement; they were able to secure an extra invitation for her.

Similarly, in 1998 when the Department of Labour met in Washington, D.C., to discuss the sweatshop issue, human rights groups, trade unions (like UNITE) and student groups were there, but women's organizations were left out. The Network has also sought to establish alliances with other regional and transnational networks in order to gain access to transnational political spaces, but has faced obstacles. For example, Inciativa Civil para la Integración Centroamericana (ICIC [The Civil Initiative for the Integration of Central America]), a network of Central American NGOs, was eager to meet with representatives of the Network.

Members were disappointed, however, when ICIC's invitation to "join us" (no autonomous women's groups belonged to the initiative) indicated that the organization hoped that the Network would be a "women's branch" along with the "women's wings" of the other organizations in the initiative. They were not invited to join other members of the initiative at the 1997 summit of Central American presidents but instead were invited to participate in a "women's forum" to be held in Guatemala. Another difficulty pertains to support for the Network's campaign on the part of solidarity organizations from the North. So far, all of the Network's funding has come from progressive NGOs from Canada and Europe.

But the coalition has not yet determined how best to use the support of solidarity groups and individuals from the north. That is, the Network has issued no clear message regarding how international individuals and groups can best support its efforts. Thus, the international component of the Network's campaign has been based almost entirely on the dissemination information about work conditions and the code of ethics through transnational channels, using the Internet and linkages with groups from the North. The only thing that the organizations of the Network have clearly articulated is that they do not support consumer boycotts.

Again, this somewhat compromising position regarding the maquila factories greatly limits the amount of pressure that the Network is able to exert on factory owners, who can easily relocate production if the political arena becomes too heated. Coalition organizers acknowledge that the real power resides not in the factory subcontractors, but in the so-called "mother" (matriz) companies, transnational corporations like the Gap and J.C. Penney. The fear here, however, is that under boycott pressure, these companies will simply turn to other factories for their production needs-once again leaving the workers jobless. Indeed, this fear is not unfounded, as there have been several cases in Central America in which boycotted companies have withdrawn contracts from subcontractors, resulting in the shut-down of these factories.

Relations with Northern-based solidarity organizations pose other problems. Due to their greater access to material resources, such "global agents" have considerable influence over the shape that transnational corporative initiatives will take and who will be involved. The Hard Copy report reflects the continued orientation of many of the Northern NGOs that make up the solidarity movement toward the traditional organizational strategies of the labour movement. Network members have experienced other tensions with international NGOs that have exerted indirect and direct pressure for organizers to include unionist language and strategies in the campaign for the code of ethics.

One Network member expressed her frustrations with individuals in such Northern groups who continue to be extremely invested in the ways of "before" and to espouse a limited vision of unions as the only truly appropriate organizational model for protecting workers' rights: "They have all these theories about the transformation of society, but...this is a process. It is step by step. It's not true that we are going to change the whole world-the whole economic system-from one day to the next." Ironically, in many cases Network members have encountered more opportunities for political alliances within certain state institutions than within the transnational labour movement.

Northern-based organizations such as the NLC have demonstrated a willingness to ally themselves with local trade union federations in working to establish independent monitoring teams within FTZ factories. Autonomous women's organizations, however, have been excluded from most of these transnational initiatives, reflecting a narrow vision of what constitutes a "labour organization." The tense relations between the unions and autonomous women's groups and the exclusion of women's organizations from independent monitoring groups have prompted the Network to pursue alliances with NGOs that have teamed up with corporations themselves to define standards to protect workers' rights and certify companies who meet these standards.

For example, the Council on Economic Priorities Accreditation Agency (CEPAA), a Northern-based NGO, accredits qualified organizations to conduct audits of factories and certifies companies and contractors who successfully pass the independent inspections. CEPAA has been vehemently criticized for excluding unions and other labour organizations and for its vertical decision making, based in the North (Clean Clothes Campaign 1998).

The advisory board of the CEPAA consists not only of representatives of human rights organizations and NGOs but also of people from various corporations. Critics claim that CEPAA's (SA 8000) auditing system does not obligate companies to disclose the full names of their suppliers and subcontractors. Thus, a company could be certified while still subcontracting to uncertified suppliers.

Though linkages among local groups across national borders continue to represent a highly significant and powerful form of oppositional mobilization, clearly there is much complexity involved in "transnationalism from below." Returning to the question posed at the beginning of this chapter, what do the practices of this transnational network tell us about how power and resistance operate within the "global" system? The Network's "alternative" strategies have at least been effective in calling state and local public attention to the situation of women maquila workers. As one Network member stated, "If there is something that has to be recognized, it is the space that we have come along opening up."

On the other hand, the Network's efforts to fully enter the transnational political arena have met with obstacles. Unlike human rights networks and other oppositional groups, such as the Ejercito Zapatista de Liberación Nacional (Zapatista National Liberation Army) of Chiapas, Mexico, the Network has had little success with influencing the global media and using international public opinion to pressure transnational corporations; instead, it has focused on localized negotiations and the use of local media. In addition, the Network has had difficulties engaging international supporters and NGOs within the campaign for "Jobs, Yes…but with Dignity." How can we explain participants' limited ability or willingness to access and operate at this transnational level?

In Keck and Sikkink's terms, the challenge that confronts the women of the Network is implementing effective "accountability politics" around the issues of women workers in maquila factories. Who should be the target actors of the Network's efforts to hold transnational corporations accountable for human and labour rights violations? In the current context of global capitalism, it becomes unclear whether the most effective lobbying strategy is to focus on state or global institutions or national or global civil societies. The Network's self-limiting radicalism, which has at least opened spaces at the state and local levels, impinges upon efforts to gain material leverage within national and transnational institutions.

Given that the overall goal of the organizations that make up the Network is to improve women's daily lives, the nature of the issues pertaining to female maquila workers-work-related issues involving both class and gender social structures-combined with conditions in the global economy and within a transnational political landscape do not lend themselves very well to the types of strategies that other transnational networks have found to be effective. For example, in the case of human rights violations in Argentina, human rights networks used information politics to target specific governments which in turn exerted pressure on the Argentinian state. Boycott strategies have also been effective for other networks. When political actors, however, adapt such practices to fit the complex issues facing women maquila workers, these strategies lose much of their material punch.

If Keck and Sikkink's assessment of transnational politics is correct, then the problem in engaging international public opinion to exert pressure becomes formulating a clear and direct "causal story" regarding who is responsible for the situation of maquila workers. Large companies like J.C. Penney can easily point to subcontractors who can just as easily blame individual supervisors for rights violations. Likewise, assigning blame to the state can be difficult, especially when protesters call for factories to remain in production. State actors can, and do, throw up their hands in the name of "competition in the global economy," claiming that they must make concessions in order to maintain the jobs generated by maquila factories.

Other actors have stepped forward to fill the void left by noninterventionist, neoliberal state regimes-NGOs, labour organizations, and others. However, salient contradictions have arisen within the various initiatives for establishing mechanisms for holding corporations accountable for labour and human rights violations. Gender blindness continues to be a problem within the transnational antisweatshop movement. Voluntary corporate codes of conduct, such as the SA 8000, also pose serious problems and have been accused by labour organizations of being "the fox guarding the henhouse." North/South tensions crosscut both transnational initiatives.

The tensions experienced by members of the Network call for an analysis of the power relations that occur within transnational organizing initiatives. In particular, a gender-blind analysis of the initiatives making up transnationalism from below provides an incomplete picture of power and resistance in the global system. The experiences of MEC organizers show that the transnational political terrain is highly gendered. Just as in the case of national politics, gendered structures of power and hegemonic definitions of the public/private split construct certain political spaces as male domains.

We see this in the exclusion of autonomous women's groups from various political spaces-networks of NGOs, independent monitoring teams, institutions of global governance like the ILO, or transnational forums like international meetings of Central-American presidents. In addition, the case of the Network points to the continued salience of power differentials even within the "new" era of globalization. The Hard Copy example reflects internal power dynamics within transnational political strategies, highlighting the importance of asking "Who controls information?" when viewing transnational political efforts.

Who decides that an issue will receive "international" attention? It is important to recognize that all players do not have access to a transnational public sphere or to the global media. Because of power differentials within transnational political initiatives, local agents who manage to gain access to the global media can lose control of the information, which can lead to adverse results. Consider, too, the union officials, who despite the crisis of labour movement are willing to devote considerable efforts to destroying and undermining the work of the women of the Network. They stand in stark contrast to the state agents who, in some cases, have actually been supportive.

All these examples lend risk nuances to the idea of transnationalism from below which reveal these processes as complex, multilayered, and rife with power differences. Finally, this research calls attention to the importance of not dismissing the efforts of groups like the Network as being merely reformist. Instead of rating the Network's transformative potential according to some narrowly conceived definition of transformative potential, the case of the Network points to the need for an expanded analytical focus. A shift in focus to consider not only the Network's strategic orientation, but its democratic and feminist vision as exemplified in organizations' work at the grassroots level, allows for a deeper analysis of the implications of its practices.

The feminist vision of the groups that constitute the Network reflect the idea that the personal is political, and the training and educational programs that these groups bring to the maquila workers bridge the public/private divide by making connections between what occurs on the shop floor and what occurs in the home and community. Thus, as in the case of women's gender politics in a variety of contexts, the Network's vision and work politicize the heretofore "private" or apolitical and challenges hegemonic definitions of the public/private split.

Turning attention to the processes that have led to the constitution of the Network also sheds light on significant implications of its practices. Members' development of a gender/feminist consciousness based on gender and class experiences led to their breaking with male-dominated popular movements to establish autonomous organizations. Thus, the formation of the Network has involved a process through which women have become more visible in grassroots politics and have articulated alternative conceptions of what constitutes political claims and who are legitimate political subjects. Such alternative conceptualizations indicate a shift in ways of "doing politics."

The women of the Network draw from a rich, cumulative oppositional history as political actors in order to negotiate the constantly fluctuating political landscapes of the global system. These social actors reconfigure and reinvent political practices in response to changes, shifts, and openings within national and transnational political arenas. An indepth study of these actors' practices calls for the recognition of a continuing and creative process generated from below.

Political agents draw from a collective oppositional experience to formulate and remold strategic practices in order to fit particular conditions in the current transnational context. This is an ongoing process. Thus, there is reason to believe that the strategies used now by groups of the Network will not necessarily be those used in the future, as changes and transformations continue to occur within national and transnational political spheres. The minimalist demands that MEC organizers make now could very well be a necessary step that must be taken before larger demands can be articulated.

In assessing transnational politics, then, it is crucial not to overlook these aspects. Employing a gendered analysis that recognizes such microlevel processes, rather than adhering to a more traditional and outcome-oriented model of what constitutes social transformation, brings to the fore important complexities and provides a more complete picture of the inner workings of the so-called global village.

4

The Challenges of Transnational Feminist Praxis

The complex processes of globalization and resistance highlighted in this demonstrate the contradictory array of possibilities for our collective future. This politics of possibilities has two faces. One vision of this future foregrounds the oppressive consequences of global capitalism and military conflicts that constrain the achievement of economic justice and peace throughout the world. The other reflects the possibilities for resisting imperialism and for achieving equality and justice for people around the globe. The case studies in this collection highlight this latter vision and focus attention on the challenges and possibilities of a transnational feminist praxis.

The former vision is crystalized in the September 11, 2001 terrorist attacks and the subsequent bombing of Afghanistan. The events of September 11 have jolted people in the United States and around the world to contemplate possibilities of continued attacks from the global network of terrorists as well as to prepare for a global war against terrorism. These events give urgency to the call for a transnational feminist praxis informed by a rich understanding of grassroots feminist analyses of peace building and organizing across differences and across national borders.

Transnational feminist praxis foregrounds women's agency in the context of oppressive conditions that shape their lives. Although the primary justification for the U.S. retaliatory bombing of Afghanistan is to destroy al Qaeda, concern has been expressed about women's oppression under Taliban rule. For example, in an address to the nation on November 17, 2001, U.S. first lady Laura Bush highlighted women's loss of freedom in Taliban-controlled Afghanistan. However, missing from the dominant media and government discourse on women in Afghanistan is an acknowledgment of their role as political actors and political analysts.

No mention is made, for example, of the Revolutionary Association of Women of Afghanistan (RAWA) that was established in 1977 to fight for human rights, adequate health care, education, and economic justice, and for democratic and secular rule in Afghanistan. The case studies highlight the role of women in helping to shape a future free of the oppressive features of globalization. The authors profile the challenges of resistance to the oppressive economic and political regimes as well as the possibilities for solidarity across class, culture, and national borders. In this I focus on the contradictory politics of location and neoliberalism as they constrain women's effectiveness as international political actors.

GLOBALIZATION AND THE POLITICS OF LOCATION

The dominant discourse on economic globalization stresses the speed of communications and financial transactions that seem to render local economic activities and face-to-face transactions obsolete. However, as Saskia Sassen argues, "many of the resources necessary for global economic activities are not hypermobile and are, indeed, deeply embedded in place." In fact, she explains, "global processes are structured by local constraints, including the composition of the workforce, work cultures, and prevailing political cultures and processes".

Sassen, along with feminist geographers and Third-World feminist analysts, emphasizes the importance of place and locale in exploring the dynamics of globalization as well as articulating strategies of resistance. In fact, as Vandana Shiva notes, localization can provide "the countervailing citizens' agenda for protecting the environment and people's survival and people's livelihood".

Localization involves "subjecting the logic of globalization to the test of sustainability, democracy and justice" and "reclaiming the state to protect people's interest". Local resistance strategies developed in response to oppressive forms of globalization may not necessarily offer effective counterhegemonic alternatives. Many scholars have written about the limits of locality-based struggles. For example, David Harvey notes in his discussion of the environmental movement that "particularistic militances-fighting an incinerator here, a toxic waste dump there, a World Bank dam project somewhere else, and commercial logging in yet another place" do not provide the grounds from which to challenge the global processes that generate environmental degradation.

He argues that a transnational movement must move beyond "narrow solidarities and particular affinities shaped in particular places...and adopt a politics of abstraction capable of reaching out across space, across the multiple environmental and social conditions." In a related vein, Leslie Sklar points out that "[t]he knowledge that workers, citizens, churches, and other concerned groups all around the world are monitoring their activities clearly encourages some TNCs [transnational corporations] to act more responsibly than they otherwise might be doing".

Contributors to Women's Activism and Globalization recognize the limits of local struggles that fail to challenge the extralocal processes that shape them. Yet the authors also view the local as a site of politicization where activists collectively develop analyses of the complex economic, political, and social processes that contour locally experienced problems. Authors depict locality and place as sites in which women generate the collective vision of an economically, politically, and socially just world. The local is also the site where activists work toward building the just world they envision by creating "more inclusive organizations and approaches that may help them confront capital more effectively in the future".

For example, Betty Wells emphasizes the very "local" ways a small group of women built a network of activists, farmers, and consumers opposed to oppressive modes of capitalist production. As they worked together to organize Women, Food, and Agiculture Network (WFAN), they developed a vision that went beyond an exclusively economic one. Their political analysis also includes a political and social critique of the dominant processes of globalization. Their broad analysis provides a vehicle to link the issues of a variety of constituencies.

For example, they define food security as a basic human right and see it as tied directly to sustainable agriculture and environmental health and safety, thus bringing together the interests of small farmers, consumers, and environmentalists. These local sites are also highly contested places where members redefine their identities and strategies in the context of ever-changing community dynamics and international relations. Winifred Poster and Zakia Salime describe the process by which AMSSF (the Moroccan Association for Solidarity without Borders), was transformed from a small grassroots group that provided microcredit for poor entrepreneurs to a part of a hierarchical network of organizations that refocused the relationships between the leaders and clients in AMSSF.

This everchanging complex funding arrangement including relying on the Moroccan Association for Solidarity and Development (AMSED) to access financial assistance from Catholic Relief Services working in Morrocco who in turn received funding from USAID. As a consequence, they lost the autonomy to manage their clients' loans. In addition to the externally imposed tensions they encountered, leaders and clients also experienced internal tensions based on their class differences. Despite these multiple tensions, Poster and Zakia remain optimistic about the potential for grassroots groups like AMSSF to use nongovernmental organization (NGO) linkages to create transnational feminist alliances.

Optimism about the significance of women's local activism in the context of economic globalization is reflected in Jennifer Bickham Mendez's analysis of the Central American Network of Women in Solidarity with Maquila Workers. The Network has raised the consciousness of local and state officials about the problems faced by women maquila workers. Network members have also experienced a deepening in their gender consciousness that led them to create autonomous women's groups and challenge male-dominated social movement organizations. As a consequence, women have gained greater visibility in local politics and legitimacy as political actors.

To further complicate our notion of the "local," it is important to point out that many of these sites for building alliances and political strategies may not be co-terminous. Drawing inspiration from Benedict Anderson's notion of "imagined community," feminist scholars stress the myriad of ways that women who may never meet can draw strength from each other and organize across differences. Solidarity across "often conflictual locations and and histories" derives from "the political links we choose to make among and between struggles".

The Internet has facilitated the process of organizing across specific locales and further illustrates how the global lands in place. What may appear distant and remote is brought into view through a technology that also helps promote the very conditions against which people struggle. Yet how women activists use this technology must also be understood contextually as Ellen Kole demonstrates in her analysis of WomenAction in Africa. WomenAction was developed to facilitate the participation of nongovernmental organizations in evaluating the implementation of the Platform for Action developed during the United Nations Conference on Women Beijing in 1995.

Not surprisingly, Kole found that women's groups in Africa use the Internet in a manner that differs from the way women in the western world access and use the Internet. As importantly, diverse groups of African women use the Internet in ways that differ from each other. As evident through the work of a number of authors in this collection, women have been able to create cross-class, cross-race, and cross-national coalitions that are enriched by the diversity of resources, political skill, and experiences.

Sharon Navarro details how activists in La Mujer Obrera in El Paso work across the Mexican-United States border to achieve seven basic goals including access to stable employment, housing, education, nutrition, healthcare, peace, and political liberty. Clare Weber's on the cross-national organizing between Nicaragua and organizations based in the United States demonstrates that knowledge and other resources can transfer from South to North as well as North to South when participating organizations remain self-conscious and actively work against power imbalances. In other cases, most clearly illustrated in Alexandra Hrycak's study, cross-class, cross-cultural, and cross-national alliances further reinforce inequalities across and within national contexts.

NEOLIBERALISM AND THE POLITICS OF ACCOUNTABILITY

Many of the cases reported in Women's Activism and Globalization emphasize the continued significance of the liberal claims for economic, social, and political rights. Many feminist scholars are concerned about the limits of the modernist, liberal framework for achieving political, social, and economic justice. The rhetoric of liberalism argues for a division between the so-called civic and political spheres, and between economics and politics. University of Delhi law professor Upendra Baxi insightfully points out that "the neoliberal frame, even when cloaked in 'people-friendly' global governance, is about creating…'market-friendly NGOs' that can cooperate with, and be co-opted by, but do not oppose CSOs [civil society organizations], states, and international organizations that support a neoliberal agenda".

A key dimension of neoliberalism is the framing of social, political and economic issues in terms of "human rights." After years of organizing, feminists have achieved recognition for "women's rights as human rights." However, as Inderpal Grewal (1999) warns, by globalizing women's human rights discourse, the "notion of essential gender finds new impetus". As further evidence of the limits of neoliberal discourse, the recognition of poverty as a human rights issue has had much less success on the international political stage. The neoliberal human rights frame has been criticized most harshly by activists and scholars interested in native Indian and indigenous peoples' struggles for political sovereignty and for territorial rights.

As Alexander and Mohanty explain, "there is no language or conceptual framework to imagine territorial sovereignty as a feminist demand-or to theorize decolonization as a fundamental aspect of feminist struggle". However, a group rights claim as developed through the struggles of American Indians raises another issue of "who belongs or does not belong to the group and redefinitions and representations of traditions that define the group". Yet the discourse on human rights can be an effective tool for achieving progressive goals. Drawing on the Universal Declaration of Human Rights, United Nations Secretary General Kofi Annan invited corporations to follow the Global Compact, a voluntary effort to enlist transnational corporations in efforts to improve the human rights of people around the world.

Organizations such as NUDE have used international human rights agreements like the Universal Declaration of Human Rights to pressure their government to address the concerns of their constituency. As Rachel Cichowski demonstrates, women activists in Europe have successfully advocated for the Equal Pay Principal to be adopted by the European Union and have, in turn, drawn on this principal to press for similar policies in member states that had yet to pass such legislation. Susanna Wing documents how the women in the Sahelian State of Mali have used the international discourse on women's rights to increase women's activism on behalf of their constitutional rights and their political representation.

Wing notes that after Mali began to pursue political liberalization in 1991, women succeeded in increasing their representation in the legislative seats from 2 per cent to 13 percent in one electoral season. Mary Meyer and Elisabeth Prügl (1999) stress that the significance of international documents is not that governments will quickly adopt them but that national and local groups can use such documents to hold their governments accountable. In effect, the groups can use these "universal standards" in different local contexts to further their own aims. Yet, it also remains to be seen how, and under what conditions, certain international statutes can be enforced at the level of the nation-state.

For example, Meyer raises this question in the context of the terms of the Convention on Violence against Women established by the InterAmerican Commission of Women, which also is known by its Spanish acronym, CIM (Comision Interamericana de Mujeres). As an autonomous commission of the Organization of American States (OAS), it cannot participate actively in the politics of enforcement. The human rights frame was generated in the context of violence perpetrated by oppressive military and political regimes. More recently the frame has been used to highlight injustices in western countries like the United States.

For example, the Permanent People's Tribunal held a special session in Spain on 1989 and determined that "the US government was denying the People of Puerto Rico their most fundamental human right: the right to self-determination". When Amnesty International turned its attention to human rights violations in the United States and identified abuses in prisons and jails as well as in the treatment of asylum seekers and other immigrants, they generated a great stir among U.S. officials. The organization's campaign, Rights for ALL, added the United States to a list of countries that includes such well-known violators as Turkey, China, Sudan, Indonesia, and Colombia.

Amnesty International's report emphasized the problems that female prisoners face such as sexual abuse by male guards and being placed in leg irons or shackles, both of which, according to the report, are common practices. Radhika Coomaraswamy of Sri Lanka, special rapporteur on violence against women, charged that the United States "is criminalizing a large segment of its population, a segment overwhelmingly composed of poor persons of color and increasingly female".

When Coomaraswamy requested permission to visit three prisons in Michigan, the governor of the state refused her request. This response illustrates the extent to which the human rights frame has been used to maintain a hierarchical distinction between the "Western world" and non-Western nation-states. Viewing policies and practices in Western nation-states that increase economic, social, and political inequalities in the Western world through the human rights frame reveals the colonialist, ethnocentric, and racist assumptions underlying neoliberal policy.

NGOS AND INTERNATIONAL POLITICS

In response to global economic restructuring and international trade agreements as well as neoliberal policies, women are organizing through a variety of networks, transnational organizations, as well as through traditional vehicles like the International Ladies Garment Workers Union. In addition, they have put global restructuring on the agenda of national women organizations and are organizing across borders. For example, Jennifer Bickham Mendez examines the efforts of the Network for Maquila Workers Rights in Central America.

This network challenges the effects of global economic restructuring and neoliberal politics and policies in their effort to improve the situation of women maquila workers. Women workers in the network document their working conditions and gather detailed information about how fast they work, what they produce, for which TNCs, and their relationships with supervisors and others in managerial position. This information is used for local unionizing efforts and is communicated through network NGOs to enable groups in the North to undertake public consciousness-raising.

Marina Karides analyzes transnational activism and unionizing efforts of another major sector of the informal economy, namely domestic workers. She shows how Trinidad's National Union of Domestic Employees (NUDE) has worked for the rights of domestic workers, who are primarily women, by using the global rhetoric and international agreements signed by Trinidad to make the government accountable at home.

When the government declined to address the grievances raised by NUDE, its activists wrote letters to various government ministers reminding them of their international commitment and undertook a public consciousness-raising campaign about the relationship between local and global injustices. Thus, through a form of public shaming they were able to make some changes, though to date they have not been successful in achieving all of their demands. Many of the recent analyses on the role of NGOs and transnational networks highlight the limits as well as the possibilities of these organizations and advocacy networks for progressive social change.

Sonia Alvarez raises a major concern in her discussion of what she calls "the Latin American feminist NGO boom". She notes three troublesome trends:

First, states and inter-governmental organizations (IGOs) increasingly have turned to feminist NGOs as gender experts rather than as citizens' groups advocating on behalf of women's rights. Second, neoliberal States and IGOs often view NGOs as surrogates for civil society, assuming they serve as "inter-mediatirs" to larger social constituencies. And third, States increasingly subcontract feminist NGOs to advise on or execute government women's programs.

NGO is a deceptively short acronym applying to a wide array of groups with more or less access to resources, to political influence, and to diverse membership. However, as a consequence of the processes Alvarez identifies, many feminist NGOs are transformed from advocates to professionals serving the needs of neoliberal states. Since the early 1980s, the contradictions inherent in the process of professionalization and institutionalization of feminist practice have become a focus of numerous scholarly accounts and a major concern among feminist activists.

For example, in the case of the battered women's movement, the development and expansion of battered women's shelters and rape crisis centers stand as a testament to the success of feminist political activism of the 1970s. On the one hand, battered women's shelters and rape crisis centers are now a site for organized public advocacy, community education, and crisis intervention on behalf of battered women as well as a place where incest survivors, rape victims and children, the elderly, and other abuse survivors find political allies and supportive services. On the other hand, the institutionalization of the activism against violence against women in shelter-based services and rape crisis centers has raised concerns for the continued vibrancy of the feminist antiviolence movement.

In this regard, Clare Weber demonstrates the value of transnational feminist networks for rendering visible the limits of local and national organizing against violence against women. Nicaraguan women activists who met with U.S. antiviolence activists discussed their different organizing strategies and what they saw as the limits of the U.S. approach for ending violence against women.

As Weber and other emphasize, to understand how local activists connect their organizing with transnational feminist movements, one must explore the institutional and network links among various actors at different sites. In the field of international relations, the term "civil society" is used to reference an extensive network of social interactions and institutions that mediate between individuals and the state. Global civil society is defined as a network that provides various "channels of opportunity for political involvement". Networks associated with the so-called global civil society have more or less autonomy from local, national, and international institutions of the state.

In a special issue on gender and globalization of Signs, the coeditors note the frequency by which scholars of globalization distinguish between so-called spheres of civil society, state, and multinational corporations. Feminist analysts challenge the division of social, political, and economic life into these separate spheres. The role of the military in supporting multinational corporations provides the most powerful illustration of the intersection of civil society, the state and economic institutions.

Yoko Fukumura and Martha Matsuoka detail women's resistance to U.S. militarism in Okinawa and explain the complex role the U.S. military plays in supporting global trade, destroying the local environment, and placing residents of the Pacific region in jeopardy. The NGO, Okinawa Women Act against Military Violence (OWAAMV), has been effective in its struggle against the U.S. military present in Okinawa but OWAAMV activists are concerned that once the military sites become available for local development, another battle over control of the development process will ensure.

Nongovernmental organizations are one of the main mechanisms for participation in the so-called global civil society. Exclusive attention to NGOs renders invisible the multitudinous informal ways women organize on behalf of themselves and their communities. Furthermore, as political scientists Ann Marie Clark, Elisabeth Friedman, and Kathryn Hochstetler point out, the fact that the number of NGOs with shared transnational goals has increased does not necessarily mean that a global civil society has been achieved. To begin with, these organizations are often founded and led by middle class, professional women, and have had little success incorporating poor women.

For example, Meredith Weiss, in her discussion of the role of NGOs in Singapore, describes the narrow class background of the Association of Women for Action and Research (AWARE), which she calls "the only avowedly feminist group in Singapore". She reports that AWARE, founded in 1985 by 50 members grew to approximately seven hundred members by the late 1990s. Though the most active leadership comes from educated, middle-class women, the organization remains committed to working across class and other differences. Weiss reports that the leadership of AWARE appear "quite open to input from rank-and-file members; however, since such input is seldom forthcoming, this accessibility is rarely tested".

Further complicating the politics of NGOs in the context of globalization are the relationships between Western and Northern NGOs and those in other parts of the globe. For example, constructions of feminism promoted by Western-based international feminist organizations and funding agencies often conflict with national women's movements in many locales. Differences in power and resources are also constructed in terms of a "North/South divide."

However, in their analysis of NGO participation in United Nations World Conferences, Clark, Friedman, and Hochstetler conclude that the divide between the North and the South may not be the primary source of contestation. They explain that "this divide partially overlaps more persistent divisions between the new generation of small grassroots organizations focused on local action and more professional, often larger and older, organizations with longstanding activists at the UN".

Rather than viewing these divisions as an expression of inequality among feminists in the North and those in the South, it is important to acknowledge the ways in which class and status differences frequently characterize relationships between women's groups within nation-states. Anthropologist Deborah Mindry demonstrates this in her analysis of women's organizations in South Africa. She characterizes the role of the western imperialist and racist "politics of virtue which constitutes some women as benevolent providers and others as worthy or deserving recipients of development and empowerment". Other scholars have also noted the significant alliances formed across the so-called First and Third Worlds by right wing religious groups and demoninations.

THE SIGNIFICANCE OF THE UNITED NATIONS

Many of the authors in this collection, along with others writing on transnational feminist organizing, also stress the significance of international conferences, especially UN-sponsored events for expanding women's participation in the global political arena. As Dianne Otto points out in her review of the changing relationship between NGOs and the UN, NGOs have had a somewhat antagonistic relationship with the UN and have only recently begun to fund openings for direct participation in UN conferences and other events. However, through parallel conferences and effective lobbying, NGOs have influenced official proceedings and gained more effective roles in UN deliberations.

However, Otto wonders whether the UN, with its "state-centric world view," can "rise to the challenge of reorienting its focus to be inclusive of peoples as well as states". Currently, representatives from NGOs who are consultants to UN organizations like UNESCO (the United Nations Educational, Scientific and Cultural Organization) or UNICEF (the United Nations Children's Fund) may attend their meetings as observers and make proposals with permission from the presiding officer. However, these recommendations are merely advisory and may not be acted on by the specific UN groups.

Despite the limitations of the UN structure, women's groups have used UN conferences to build a transnational women's movement and bring their local concerns to the international political stage. Eve Sandberg persuasively argues that the three United Nations world conferences on women served as a catalyst for Zambian women's domestic organizing, legitimated their activism, and provided resources and strategies for successful mobilization though these benefits accrue more to elite women than to less privileged Zambian women.

Feminist scholars also note that a focus on preparation for UN conferences often has the effect of diverting attention from the issues of most direct concern to local activists. In their discussion of the Alliance for Arab Women (AAW), Nawal Ammar and Leila Lababidy-mother and daughter who are founding members of AAW-acknowledge the significance of the UN conferences for Egyptian women's domestic organizing but also point out that [s]ince the UN Third Conference on Women in Nairobi in 1985, some nongovernmental organizations concerned with women's issues in Egypt have changed their focus from welfare work to development of empowerment skills. Reasons for such changes are numerous, but most salient has been the priority of international funding sources.

Elisabeth Friedman concludes her analysis of the impact of UN conferences on the women's movement in Venezuela by stressing that "the stage of the national movement, its sources of funding, and the politics of particular national administrations all interact with conference preparation, with quite different outcomes at different junctures."

Manisha Desai addresses the contradictions of the United Nations for "transnational feminist solidarities" in her chapter. Her description of the four phases of UN policies on women demonstrates the effectiveness of transnational organizing for the incorporation of women into the design and implementation of UN programs. Despite inadequate funding for the implementation of UN programs designed to improve women's lives in different parts of the world and the failure to gain support from nations like the Unites States for the Convention on the Elimination of All Forms of Discrimination against Women (CEDAW), Desai argues that the establishment of programs like the International Research and Training Institute for the Advancement of Women and the United Nations Development Fund For Women, and the adoption of CEDAW by the UN, demonstrate the power of women's international organizing as well as help promote the expansion of transnational solidarities among women.

The UN Conferences on Women provide further opportunities for women activists from around the world to share their experiences, learn from each other, and develop strategies to counter the intensification of religious fundamentalism, militarization, poverty and sexual abuse, and to expand women's political participation. Women's influence on the transnational political stage is further demonstrated by their leadership and broad-based participation in world conferences on the environment, human rights, population, social development.

POSTLIBERALISM AND THE POLITICS OF FEMINIST PRAXIS

In contrast to the liberal approach that is predominant in international organizing, Dianne Otto argues that a "postliberal perspective, which decenters states and stresses the importance of local participation in the international community, is allied with a postmodern understanding of power... as conceptualized as dispersed throughout the global polity rather than...centralized in the state and the economy". In shifting from a liberal to a postliberal frame, feminist scholars explore the possibilities for a transnational feminist politics that will work against global inequalities of region, gender, race, class, and sexuality and toward what Ernesto Laclau and Chantal Mouffe term "radical and plural democracy" within movement organizations and coalitions.

The postliberal approach to women's movement politics recognizes that the feminist struggle is not based on "a definable empirical group with a common essence and identity-that is, women-but rather as a struggle against the multiple forms in which the category 'women' is constructed in subordination".

The essays in Women's Activism and Globalization provide further evidence of the diversity of women's movements around the world as well as within different nation-states. Like the authors in The Challenge of Local Feminisms, we are interested in rendering visible "what actually existing women's movements have achieved and failed to achieve, of the challenges yet to be confronted together and separately". In this collection, we define "women's movements" very broadly. Referring to women's movements in the plural as recommended by Gluck and colleagues reflects a deepening awareness of how the multitude forms of women's activism throughout the world all work to challenge patriarchal hierarchies.

We also include forms of collective struggle that may not have achieved the level of a "movement." For example, Betty Wells analyzes the work of rural women who have been traditionally left out of women's movements. These women engage in local activism, offer insightful indigenous knowledge about daily survival strategies, and participate in national and transnational organizing. Revisioning women's movements to include the diversity of women's political analyses and strategies also requires us to rethink the labels used to categorize feminisms more generally. Third World and postcolonial feminists have effectively criticized the imposition of the Western feminist worldview in women in different parts of the world.

In the introduction to her edited collection, Basu discusses the widespread resistance to feminism, but she points out that many Third World critics "go on to identify indigenous alternatives to Western-style feminism". Rather than pose indigenous and Western feminism as mutually distinctive alternatives, recent analyses demonstrate the interdependence of women's movements and feminist analysis in different parts of the world. As Gay Seidman illustrates in her case study of gendered politics in South Africa, "the international flow of ideas and resources has become a basic element in local debates involving gender equity".

Victoria Bernal turns to the Tanzania Gender Network Programme (TGNP), a feminist group based in Dar es Salaam, to explore the relationship between the local and the global. She finds that the organization voices its concerns in language common to women's organizations worldwide, emphasizing that "Tanzanian NGOs such as TGNP speak an international language of democracy, human rights, and development". When communicating in their national language, Kiswahili, the Tanzanian feminists sometimes simply adopt the English terms (as in the cases of "gender mainstreaming" and "patriarchy"), leading, Bernal writes, "to what some have called 'Kiswahenglish".

However, Bernal concludes, "Neither the view of local organizations as somehow operating independent of their global context, nor the view of such organizations as mere puppets of external forces will allow us to explore the potentials and pitfalls in the globalized terrain of contemporary post-colonial political activism". In the context of increased mobility and displacement, distinctions between home/abroad, insider/outsider, and Third World/First World, have become difficult to maintain.

In her contribution to Women's Activism and Globalization, Bandana Purkayastha compares and contrasts her community activism during the latter part of twentieth century as an Indian-born woman in the United States with her mother's activism during the earlier part of the century in a rural Indian village. She argues that community activism facilitates the transmission of resistance strategies to counter the negative effects of global economic restructuring in local contexts.

Many of the lessons we have learned through more nationally defined feminist politics will continue to serve us as we expand the horizons of feminist organizing. These lessons include how to respond to problems that arise in organizing across class, race, ethnicity, sexualities, space, and religious and political perspectives; how to sustain feminist activist engagement over time; how to build and mobilize effective coalitions; how to create democratic structures at all levels of organization; and how to negotiate the politics of language, funding, representation, and social movement framing.

Along with the politics of naming, the politics of location, the politics of accountability, and the challenges of fighting against the scattered hegemonies of capitalism and patriarchy, research on transnational feminist praxis reveals a number of contradictions that require careful consideration before we pass judgment on the limits or possibilities of different political strategies, organizational forms, or social movement frames. This collection of case studies deepens our understanding of the complexities, challenges, and possibilities of grounded struggles against oppressive forms of globalization associated with antidemocratic international politics and capitalist expansion.

5

Wage Work in the Services Sector

The women in this study all worked in the personal services sector as coffee-shop waitresses, petrol pump attendants, and domestic workers, housekeepers in hotels, cleaners and assistants in child-care centres. In the context of Sarawak, such work is full-time employment, except for some domestic work, and is feminised, apart from waiting at tables and working petrol pumps. The women are employed in small enterprises with an unpredictable pay structure and no career path. In the main, the work is repetitive, dirty, and dead-end and frequently entails unsociable shift work.

They work the hardest during public holidays when others are off work. Domestic workers often complained of loneliness and isolation, naughty children under their care, long hours and demanding employers. One woman who has been in domestic service throughout her work history said: 'When I returned on a Sunday evening after a day off, the sink would be full to the brim with dirty dishes and I would have a big pile of laundry to fold and put away.'

Petrol pump attendants were often paid less than RM200 a month which was not even enough for basic survival because they had to pay for their own food, lodgings and transportation to work. It was also hot and unpleasant in the petrol stations in the sizzling heat of the afternoon. Thus women who worked in petrol stations did not stay for long. Sales assistants in supermarkets are on their feet the whole day and their wages were often cut to compensate for any shortfall in the tills. When they worked night shifts, they were afraid to go home alone at 10:00 p.m. as transportation was not provided by their employers.

Coffee-shop and restaurant waitresses suffered from long hours on their feet as they moved from table to table and many complained of insufficient rest. Most coffee-shops are small family-owned businesses which remain open for long hours. Work days of 9-16 hours were mentioned by the participants. In a local chain of coffee-shops where some of the single women worked, the conditions were slightly better. They worked nine-hour shifts and had one day off a week. They had weekends off on a rotational basis. Their employer provided two main meals a day and free lodgings above the coffee-shops.

Although beer promoters earned more than coffee-shop waitresses, they worked mainly nights and travelled out of town. Single women were therefore preferred by employers as they do not have domestic responsibilities and can work nights and bc out of town. Beer promoters frequently complained of working in noisy, smoky environments such as karaoke lounges or discotheques and sometimes suffered verbal harassment from drunken male customers. At this juncture, it must be pointed out that employment in the personal services industry is often perceived to be highly sexualised because of the nature of the work. Adkins in her exploration of the links between sexuality and women's employment in contemporary Britain studied two tourist organisations, a hotel and a leisure park. She pointed out that women's work in the service employment sector is deeply sexualised.

Women employed in this sector have to look 'attractive' and respond when male customers pay them sexual attention. She argues that the sexual commodification of women workers through their work, through the rigid requirements of their appearance and the uniforms that they have to wear, produces a sexual power relationship between male customers and female workers. Adkins emphasises that although male workers are subjected to the same requirements of appearance and uniforms, they did not engage in this sexual work and are therefore not undermined by a subordinate sexual status. She concludes that the issue of sexuality is neither marginal nor non-economic in the discussion of women and the labour market, but is central in gendering the labour market itself.

Sexualisation of the women's work in this study is explicit in some cases as in the work of beer promoters, and less obvious in others, for instance assistants in child-care centres. They often have to serve customers of both sexes. The majority of the women also work in small family businesses and therefore have to deal with employers who are family members of both sexes. In addition, domestic workers are employed in homes and therefore do not have to interact with male customers. Nevertheless, the personal services sector is highly feminised. Apart from the work of waiting at tables and working petrol pumps, the jobs included in this study are dominated by women.

At the end of the spectrum are domestic work and hotel housekeeping which are exclusively female domains. Age is yet another factor, with older women waiting at tables and housekeeping in the better establishments. This sector is also ethnicised in that most of the employees are from indigenous communities like Bidayuh, Iban and Malay to name a few. In other words, few Chinese work in this sector except as sales assistants. In waiting at coffee-shop tables and domestic work, locals are increasingly replaced by Indonesian workers, males in waiting and females in domestic work.

In other words, the work-force at the bottom of the services work hierarchy is mainly young, female and non-Chinese. Implications for such a feminised and ethnicised sector of work are that it is undervalued and therefore lowly paid. The married women interviewed in this study earned half of their husbands' monthly income despite the fact that they have the same, if not more, years of schooling than their husbands who worked in male dominated sectors. Few women in my study complained of sexual harassment in the course of their work although waitresses and beer promoters in coffee-shops, restaurants and karaoke lounges are particularly vulnerable. The only account of sexual harassment came from a petrol pump attendant, a 20-year-old respondent who told me in an interview:

> I was working one evening when a fat, balding old man drove up in his red sports car. He invited me to go for a drive with him (... pergi makan angin). I declined and he gave me his mobile telephone number and asked me to contact him. Why would I want to ring him? (Mana mahu talipon dia?)

Although beer promoters sometimes mention talking back to drunken customers, sexual harassment at work was seldom an issue which the women brought up when talking about problems they encountered at work.

Given this litany of employment woes in the personal services, I asked the women why they chose to work in this sector of employment as opposed to factory work. This is what the women had to say:

> I prefer to work in a home because I don't have to find a room to rent. I also don't have to buy my own food and drinks (... kerja dirumah orang tak payah cari bilik sewa, tak payah tanggung makan, minum.)
>
> (June, working mother)
>
> It is nice to work in a home especially if the employer is not fussy (... majikan tak cerewet). We can work at our own pace. My employer doesn't complain much. She just eats whatever I cook. We follow our own schedule (... ikut aturan sendiri) and we are not rushed. If we work in a noodle or a biscuit factory, the working hours are long.
>
> (Cecilia, working mother)
>
> I have worked in a plywood factory before and it is noisy and dusty. The restaurant here is a much nicer place to work.
>
> (Sally, working mother)
>
> Factory work is terrible. It is very hot.
>
> (Diana, single woman)
>
> Working in a factory is very hard and the pay, low. The biscuit factory at Sungei Apong pays only RM5 a day for packing biscuits.

(Judith, housewife)

People say that factory work is easy work and we are not confined in the house all the time but we have to pay our own food and rent. We have to mix with all types of people which can bring a lot of problems.

(Alison, housewife)

I don't like working in a factory because many different types of races mix together and there is much gossip and quarrel.

(Jacky, working mother)

We cannot save if we work in a factory because food is not provided. My mother said that factory girls are too free. Many are made pregnant but they don't have a husband.

(Julia, housewife)

We work shorter hours. A factory runs 24 hours a day. It can also be very dusty especially in furniture factories.

(Janet, single woman)

I can't stand the shifts in the factory. Here [in the coffee shop] we only work two shifts but my friends in the factory work three or four shifts. The first shift starts at 7:00 a.m. and finishes at 3:00 p.m. Another shift starts from 3:00 p.m. to midnight and the last shift is from midnight till 7:00 a.m. The factory runs 24 hours a day. They tell me that their eyes cannot stand it and they cannot sleep (... mata tak boleh tahan dan tak boleh tidur.)

(Elaine, single woman)

I applied twice but the factory was not ready so I started here [in the coffee shop]. My village friend stopped work [in the factory] because her section was very terrible. (Kawan kampung henti kerja kerana bahagiannya teruk sangat.) I have three more friends there and they say it is very isolating. They cannot contact the village and their family in the village cannot contact them. If the supervisor is good, then it is all right. If not, it can be very bad.

(Rosalind, single woman)

At first I was interested in factory work but my sister who worked in a children's garment factory in Johor was cheated. They say that her salary will be RM800 but she received only

RM400. Girls from Sarawak are paid less than the girls from West Malaysia who get between RM800-1000. They say that girls from Sarawak come cheap. (… gadis Sarawak murah.) She also had to pay for her uniform when they told her it was free. They held her identity card and she finally got it back when she said that she had to change into the new identity card. When she left, they wanted to sue her for breach of contract.

(Jane, single woman)

I don't like to live in hostels, so I didn't try factory work. I prefer to live with a family or alone.

(Vicky, single woman)

I heard from friends that they have very strict rules. I don't think I will be able to stand the air-conditioning especially if it is very cold and there is a smell.

(Cynthia, single woman)

It is obvious from the quotes above that the women were talking about two different types of factory work. The younger cohort of single women took factory work to mean employment in transnational electronic factories. Thus, their considerations were that of the rigour of the work regime and hostel living. In contrast, the older women interviewed saw factory work in terms of its exploitative conditions in small family backyard workshops. Therefore, their concerns were more about making ends meet.

Others felt safe as a domestic worker in a home environment where food and lodgings are provided free by the employer in exchange for the protection of living with a family. There are problems of exploitation of domestic workers of course, but women like Alison and Jacky feel that the risk of problems arising from the congregation of workers of both sexes and of different ethnicity, in the work and living conditions of a factory are far worse than those of domestic workers.

What the women in my study say about factory work makes an interesting contrast to what the Shenzhen factory women in Lee's study say about work in the personal services. According to Lee, although waiting at tables and serving in stores paid better, they were not morally appropriate for young single women living away from parental control. Such jobs in public places were associated with rendering sexual services to men while factory jobs were disciplined, regular and confined within the factory walls. In this way, women's choices of the sector of employment to be engaged in are also very much an outcome of women's construction of what is appropriate for their gender. A sector of employment is gendered not only by employers hiring policies but also by the women's own gendered constructions.

SOME EXPERIENCES OF WOMEN IN THIS SECTOR OF EMPLOYMENT

In order to reveal some of the characteristics of employment in this sector, the work histories of three women are described below. They are illustrative of the points made earlier that wages in this sector of employment ride on a roller coaster and work trajectories do not necessarily follow any pattern of rising wages. In addition, wage earning in the city often takes a back-seat during labour intensive periods in the agricultural cycle when women return to the village to help out on family farms.

However, it must also be pointed out that women's employment trajectories are also outcomes of family expectations of what are deemed appropriate jobs for women. The work history of Lisa is a case in point. Her case is unusual in that her work history as a working daughter was very much shaped by family pressures. However, as pointed out earlier in this chapter, Bidayuh working daughters have a lot of leeway in choosing their own employment with minimum interference from their parents and elders.

Elaine (coffee-shop waitress, aged 23)

Elaine is the eighth in a large family of twelve children. After eight years at school, she stopped because she decided not to be dependent on her parents ('... tidak mahu harap mak dan bapak').

Her first job at sixteen was as a domestic worker for her cousin who was a nurse. She spent three years there and by the time she left, she had a monthly wage of RM220. She had to look after two pre-schoolers aged five and three and an infant below one. It was exhausting as she often had to look after them at night as well, when her cousin was on night duty. When she left, she returned to her village and stayed for a year, helping her mother in the rice field.

She next took a job in a small market town near her village as a coffee-shop waitress. Her monthly salary plunged to RM180. The hours were long. There were only three employees and it was difficult to get days off. They worked seven days a week. She finally left after six months.

She moved to her third job in a photocopying shop in the same town. She suffered yet another drop in wages to RM150 a month. Customers would bring their documents for photocopying and she would operate the machine. It was often quiet and she left out of boredom after six months. She moved to Kuching and was in her fourth job when I interviewed her. She lived with her sister near her current place of work. Her sister is married to a tractor driver and lives in a squatter area with her husband and three children. As her employer provides meals, she buys her sister's family incidentals and pays her own way in the household. She had been working as a coffee-shop waitress for over a year when I interviewed her.

I am happy working here because it is not boring. There are different things that I have to do and I am always moving and doing something. With overtime, I can sometimes earn up to RM310 a month. I give my mother RM40 [a month]. I don't give my father any because men are clever in finding money (... laki pandai cari duit). It is good to have our own money. We can go shopping and spend on ourselves. I like living in Kuching because our experience is wide and we are free to mix with others (... luas pengalaman dan bebas pergaulan).

Although these women represent the more socially respectable rural-urban migrant wage earner, their narratives of the sociability of their environment, their sense of autonomy in earning and spending their own money and their rejection of factory work are reminiscent of sex workers in Murray's study in Jakarta (Murray 1991:125). These are attractions to a wide spectrum of women migrants and explain their acceptance of poor wages and stigma in the case of Murray's sex workers.

Monica (domestic worker, aged 21)

Monica left school after six years of primary school. She was the eldest of four and her mother wanted her to help support her younger siblings. Her father, on the other hand, wanted her to continue her education. She was scolded so often by her mother that she decided to leave home at thirteen. She spent the next eight years working as a domestic worker in six different homes. Her first job only lasted three months. She was paid RM150 a month. She ran away as her employer was very demanding. In her second job, she was paid the same wage but the employer treated her better. However, she contracted malaria after two months and had to be hospitalised for a week. She decided to change jobs as her room in the house did not have any mosquito netting and she was afraid of getting malaria again.

Her monthly wages moved up to RM170 in her third job and it lasted six months. Her parents needed her at a crucial stage of farming and she returned to the village for the next six months. A friend from the same village introduced her to her fourth job and she had a drop in wages to RM130 a month. She stayed for only two months as she and her friend (they both worked at the same place) did not get on with the employer.

She subsequently returned to work for the employer in her third job and resumed her last pay there (RM170 a month). She was happy as she felt part of the family. She stayed for the next four years. Unfortunately, her employer who was a school teacher, passed away and her husband became the sole breadwinner. He was unable to afford Monica's services and his parents moved in to help with the children and Monica lost her job. However, he introduced Monica to his friend and for the last three years, she has worked part-time there. She was paid RM200 a month for six mornings of household work a week. She also started to work an afternoon a week with another family for RM60 a month. She was able to take up these part-time jobs as she had moved in with her boyfriend, into free lodgings provided by his employer. Monica said:

> As domestic workers, we are sometimes accused of stealing and we also receive harsh scolding for breaking things. We apologise and explain that we didn't do it deliberately but we are scolded just the same. We have to replace things that we break. I would like to try a different job but I am very shy and I don't know what else I can do. I prefer to live out [not with the employer] and work office hours so that I don't have to work from morning till night.

Lisa (hotel receptionist, aged 24)

Lisa is petite, pleasant and is third in a family of four children and has completed Form 5. Her two older sisters who are now housewives in the city were also educated up to Form 5. Her younger brother is the only one in the family who studied up to Form 6.

Lisa started work when she was 18. At the time of the interview, she had worked in six different jobs in the past six years. According to her, her first job as a tour guide with the Sarawak Tourist Association was her best ever. She earned between RM700-1000 a month inclusive of tips and she worked for one and a half years. However, her parents disapproved of her extensive travelling as they felt that such jobs were not suitable for a woman and forced her to give it up. It was very painful for her to give up such an enjoyable job. She liked meeting people. She lamented the fact that she has not been able to reach the same level of earnings ever since.

She was so upset with her parents that she went to live with her maternal grandmother in the village for two months. Her second job was that of a Carlsberg beer promoter and her monthly wage dropped to RM600. Her job involved travelling to smaller towns to promote beer in various restaurants and coffee-shops. Again her parents objected to her travelling. She was forced to give it up and her wages took another tumble in her third job as a sales assistant in a souvenir shop at the airport. She earned a monthly wage of RM400-500 but had to put in long hours in the evenings, especially if a flight was delayed.

She stayed in that job for only four months and found her fourth job as a receptionist in a local hotel. Her pay took a dip to RM250 a month but she stuck it out for one year before moving to work as a receptionist in another local hotel. It was a bigger and more established hotel and her pay climbed up again to RM600 a month. Around that time, she married a Muslim. She worked there a year and decided to quit when she became pregnant and was unable to manage the 11:00 p.m. to 7:00 a.m. shift. She entered the work force again after the birth of her child and joined another local hotel as receptionist at her last pay of RM600. She had worked there for three months when I met her. Her son was two years old at the time of the interview and she was expecting her second child.

A distant cousin runs a nursery of twenty five children with two assistants and Lisa's child is there. She sees him only on her days off and in the evenings when she is working the morning shift. Child-care alone costs RM450 a month. After deductions for child-care, Lisa takes home RM150 a month. In spite of this, Lisa wants to remain in the work-force because of her abusive husband. She feels her participation in the labour market offers her some security for the future. The latest on Lisa is that she has moved yet again to become a receptionist at an international hotel.

The women's perception of wage work in this sector is not only coloured by their experiences but also by their knowledge of what awaits them in the village should they decide to return. In other words, whether paid work in the city is 'easy' or otherwise is often relative to farming and other unpaid work that they have to do in the village. We therefore have to understand what they say in the context of the requirements of their labour contributions in the village if they chose to stay.

WOMEN'S AND MEN'S WORK IN THE VILLAGE

In the agricultural cycle of shifting cultivation, the felling of trees is traditionally done by men while women clear the undergrowth. However, women nowadays also do the felling if necessary. The collection of jungle products during the felling and clearing of land for hill padi cultivation is mainly done by women. Various jungle leaves, fruits, shoots, firewood and rattan for making baskets are collected. Some of the baskets made are for their own use while others are sold for cash. The men construct paths to the farm while the women make the attap roofing for the farm hut.

The slashed vegetation is allowed to dry for two to three weeks before being set on fire. Burning the fields occurs in the dry season of August and although the decision for setting the date for the burning rests with the men, the initial decision as to which land to farm is very much influenced by the women. Clearing of the farm occurs after the burn and both men and women participate in this arduous task. Debris that is not completely burnt is gathered into a pile and burnt again. Women and men then plant secondary crops such as cucumber, ginger, pumpkin, egg-plant in areas where ash accumulates. Women are also in charge of the different varieties of padi and vegetable seeds for planting.

Padi planting occurs in late August or early September just before the arrival of the north-east monsoon in October. The men dibble and the women follow, sowing the padi seeds into the holes. After planting, weed control is the next task. Handweeding is done by women but increasingly, herbicides are used and this is done by both men and women. However, some women explain that usually men carry the heavy weedicide tank on their backs for spraying. Weeding starts from October through to January. No herbicide is used after that as it may destroy the ripening padi. Women continue to handweed between the secondary crops in the field.

According to Gerrits, handweeding utilises 13.1 per cent of the labour required in hill padi cultivation while herbicidal weed control utilises only 9 per cent of the labour requirement. In other words, women do more of the back-breaking task of weed control. Padi harvesting occurs in March or April and as the padi ripens, the men improve the farm paths in order to facilitate access to the farms as they have to carry heavy loads of padi on their backs. Women collect rattan and bamboo for making baskets and mats in readiness for the harvest.

Every household member participates in the harvest. After the major harvest, women return to harvest whatever is left behind accidentally or has not matured at the time of the main harvest. Some secondary crops are also harvested at that time. Traditionally, there are many steps in padi processing. Men are involved in the first part of treading the padi with their feet in order to dislodge the grains and the work of sieving, winnowing and drying the padi grains is done by women. However, Gerrits notes that there is no longer a strict gender division of labour in the different stages of padi processing. Guarding the drying padi grains from pets and pests is usually the work of the very old, the very young, the pregnant and new mothers. Pounding the rice in order to dehusk the padi is definitely in the women's domain.

The most labour intensive stages of hill padi cultivation are harvesting, undergrowth clearing and handweeding, in that order. Given the gender division of labour described above, it is not surprising that Geddes (1954:81) concluded, 'Although it is the basic concern of both, farming is even more an occupation of women than of men.'

They are not only the mainstay of their farms, rural Bidayuh women both young and old are mainly responsible for all household work like cooking, washing and child-rearing. Some men would cook, wash dishes and their own clothes and take care of the children, but they are in the minority in the Bidayuh village. These domestic chores were often only done by men when their wives were ill.

The arduous tasks of collecting firewood and carrying water were also the domain of Bidayuh women. Thus, women rose early in the morning between 3:00 a.m. and 4:00 a.m. in order to do the housework, feed the chicken and pigs, cook the family's morning meal and pack lunch before going to work in the fields between 6:00 a.m. to 7:00 a.m. It must be added here that women were also responsible for preparing food for the poultry. They would return from their farms between 3:00 p.m. to 4:00 p.m. only to resume domestic work once home.

Older women and older children performed child-care in order to release the labour of other women in the household for agricultural work. Although productive work in the fields was seen as having higher priority than domestic chores, women were still the ones who were responsible for the latter. A woman leader in the DBNA pointed out that although the Bidayuh customary laws (adat) were egalitarian by virtue of women's crucial contribution to food production and the household, in practice there was great gender disparity in Bidayuh society.

Men were considered the heads of households but women were the main income-earners when the prices of conventional cash crops were poor, as they sold jungle products, vegetables and secondary crops in the markets in Kuching and other nearby market towns. The traders in the farmers' markets and Sunday markets in Kuching are predominantly Bidayuh women.

> I disagree ... that there is no sex discrimination in Bidayuh society. The written adat may say so but practice is contrary to the adat... The Bidayuh who trade their goods at Sunday markets are mainly women making many of them the main bread-winner of the family. The time women spend in housework and in farming is considerable. (Drebra 1993:6-7)

There is little written about the domestic work performed by the various individuals in the rural agrarian household. Geddes (1954:81) however, provides us with a glimpse. He reported that young adolescent girls had to look after the household's poultry, releasing them from their cages in the morning and putting them back in the evenings. They also fed the pigs in the evenings. They dried the padi, helped to pound it and gathered firewood and edible ferns, leaves and shoots from the jungle. They also collected large green leaves for wrapping cooked rice for farmers who took their lunch to the fields. They caught small prawns, fish, snails and frogs in the river and helped with the cooking, and with the care of younger siblings. A young boy who had no older sister had the same chores but as Geddes pointed out,

> There is, however, a difference between days spent by boys and those spent by girls on infant care ... In the case of a girl, such a day gives less opportunity for relaxation, for she

usually still has to help with domestic duties, such as drying the padi. In the case of a boy, an infant is often merely a restriction on the scope of his play ... The lot of boys who do have sisters old enough to take care of the younger children is an easy one. Most of their days are taken up in idleness and play. To be born a boy in Land Dayak culture is usually a passport to a carefree childhood.

As for adult single women, their labour contribution to the household was no different from that of married women except that they did less child-care. Given the harsh and demanding work required of Bidayuh women in the village, it is not surprising that paid work in the city is viewed as comparatively 'easy.' For a start, single women (apart from that in domestic work) who live in lodgings provided by their employers have far less domestic responsibilities in comparison to their counterparts in the village. Similarly, married women employed in the city enjoy maternity leave and therefore have more time off work than their mothers in the village.

Although Geddes noted that child-bearing offered the only brief respite for rural women from the hard work in the fields, it was often of a short duration. Lydia's comparison of herself with her mother in the village illustrates this point:

My mother does everything my father does but not necessarily the other way around. Both my father and husband will only cook, wash dishes and look after the children when their wives have just given birth but normally they don't. My mother had the luxury of a seven-day confinement and I had 44 days.

The women that I interviewed were therefore, in the main, accepting of their poor work conditions. When I asked them what strategies they used in order to overcome problems that they encountered at work, many mentioned 'don't get involved,' 'just bear with it,' 'be patient,' 'keep quiet when towkay [boss] scolds,' 'ignore the problem,' 'just pray in our rooms,' 'scream at the children,' 'just quit.' Only one woman mentioned speaking directly to the person concerned and another said that she consulted her supervisor. Their non-confrontational stance is a reflection of their vulnerability as they are unprotected by unions, are atomised and isolated in their different work places and have few opportunities to develop a sense of workers' rights.

In addition, I found that the women in this study did not have entrenched identities as workers. They did not expect to find employment fulfilling and paid work was merely a means to earning a wage. Few would be enamoured by dirty, repetitive and lowly paid work that does not have a career path. Instead, it is the experience of city living and the autonomy that a wage afforded, however limited, which was more powerful than the employment experience per se.

Not only is this because they are the first generation of female wage earners from their households and employment is a new dimension in their lives, but also, because they have a pragmatic approach to paid work. Although some women would like to leave this sector of work for something better, a lack of paper qualifications and a limited job market means that many have little choice but to stay. Magaret who works in a retail garden shop and earns RM450 a month is on the look-out for a better paying job.

I would like to work office hours but my choice is limited. I don't have any qualifications. I only finished nine years of schooling. If I have the chance, I would like to be a tailor or hair-dresser.

Up to this point, the employment experiences as described in this chapter affect all women regardless of their positions in the life-course. However, the paths of the three groups of women in this study begin to diverge when they make a decision as to whether to stay or to withdraw from the labour market as they marry and have children. I use the word 'decision' with caution given that these women occupy the lower socio-economic strata and in the absence of a welfare state, the decision that they make can only be a very constrained one.

Once again this is a modern decision as it is a decision that their mothers in the village never had to make, as they had to farm throughout their productive lives. It is also a gendered decision as it would not even occur to men to withdraw from the labour market. It is precisely because women's employment is shaped profoundly by marriage and child-rearing that this research is set up to study single women and women with children. However, the latter group diverges once again, with those remaining in paid work and those opting to withdraw from the labour market.

SINGLE WOMEN MIGRANTS IN THE CITY

In this chapter, I discuss the choices that single women migrants have now that they are in the urban labour market. Unlike married women, withdrawal from wage work is not an option for them as it is the raison d'etre for their migration into the city in the first place. Instead, they can choose to marry or not to marry, and who to marry, if they decide on the course of marriage. This is a choice that their village mothers did not have as village women gained adult status through marriage and child-birth.

This will be elaborated later in this chapter. However, with wage work in the city, single women migrants are self-supporting and marriage is no longer a necessity but a choice. In looking at this issue, I draw upon the work of historians documenting the changes in the lives of single women urban migrants in nineteenth century Europe. Comparison between nineteenth century Europe and late twentieth century Sarawak is relevant because women in both instances were/are facing massive transformative forces although the structural forces effecting changes in Europe at that time was wrought by the industrial revolution.

In both instances, waves of young women from peasant households migrate to the city for employment. However, it would appear that the long drawn out changes in the last century in Europe have somehow been compressed and accelerated in the context of late twentieth century Sarawak. Comparisons will be made with other south-east Asian countries wherever possible, although most studies of working daughters in the region have tended to focus on their employment experiences and natal families rather than on marriage.

As in nineteenth century Europe, late twentieth century Sarawak has a large rural population which lives off the land. Just as members of a peasant household in Europe had clearly defined duties based on their age, gender and position in the family, so does a rural Bidayuh household. In what Tilly and Scott (1987) call the family economy in pre-industrial Europe, daughters who were old enough were sent out to work as agricultural labourers and domestic servants. However, the difference is that young rural Bidayuh women are not sent out by their parents and do not hire themselves out as farm hands.

In this study, they entered the personal services sector instead. Unlike English and French parents in that earlier time, Bidayuh parents do not choose their daughters area of employment nor do they have much control over their daughters' wages although there are some exceptions. In one case among the women I interviewed, Jane had more than a third of her monthly wages deducted and put into a bank account which was directly accessed by her father. In another case, Monica did not remit any money to her parents but gave something under 20 per cent of her monthly wages directly to her school-going sisters.

When discussing the changing family form during the first and second industrial revolutions in Europe, Seccombe argued that family forms and the mode of production are closely enmeshed and the transformation of the former will follow closely on the heels of the latter. In other words, a certain mode of production will facilitate the reproduction of a certain family form while impeding the development of others. He pointed out that the capitalist mode of production severed the bonds between adult children and their parents as the individuated wage could not sustain anything more than a nuclear family of parents and their children.

Seccombe further stressed that the process of proletarianisation meant that those who did not stand to inherit any productive property or a father's trade had to sell their labour as free workers in the labour market. Thus, the young left home to find employment spent their wages as they liked, married a spouse of their own choice and lived wherever they could afford. In this way, familial bonds with one's natal family eroded over time.

Tilly and Scott on the other hand, were interested in the impact of industrialisation in Britain and France on women's paid work. Although they acknowledged that changes in the mode of production wrought important changes in women's wage labour and the family structure, they were circumspect as to the speed and the extent of those changes. They argued in an earlier essay that family structures in urban areas were more a continuation of rural patterns rather than a disjuncture. They pointed out that the transformation of family relationships in the context of structural changes was more gradual and complex and involved the adaptation of traditional values in new situations.

Traditional families then, operating on long-held values, sent their daughters to take advantage of increased opportunities generated by industrialisation and urbanisation. Industrial development did not affect all areas of a given country at the same time. Rather, the process can best be illustrated by an image of 'islands of development' within an underdeveloped sea, islands which drew population to them from the ... less developed areas. The values of the less developed sector were imported into the developing sector and there were extended, adapted, and only gradually transformed.

Women in different parts of Europe had different experiences at different times of the changes wrought by the massive structural changes in the late nineteenth century. Tilly and Scott argue that an evolutionary model of change which assumes an inexorable structural force pushing all women along a single path must be abandoned. This discussion of the gradual erosion of family ties and the impact of the individuated wage in the city on the autonomy of young migrants is relevant to the discussion of the rising number of illegitimate births in the hundred years between 1750 and 1850 in many European cities.

According to Scott and Tilly, there were several reasons for this. First, the loneliness and isolation in the city added to the pressure to find a spouse. Second, as many of the young women at that time were in domestic service, marriage was an avenue of escape allowing them to become mistresses of their own homes. As premarital sex for women was premised on a promise of marriage, irresponsible suitors meant single motherhood for abandoned women. Social mores which dictated courtship behaviour in the village were not enforceable in the urban centres and many women were caught unawares when they first arrived in the city.

The increasing numbers of sexually vulnerable women in the city, removed from family protection and assistance, resulted in a sharp rise in illegitimacy. This, Scott and Tilly argue, is yet another example of the persistence of old cultural values in new situations. However, Shorter provides a contradictory view. He argues that the increase in illegitimate births in that period of European history was a consequence of dramatic changes in values. According to Shorter, young wage-earning women were exposed to individualistic and hedonistic values in the city and rebelled against parental authority.

The sudden rupture of parental control and guidance gave the young women in the city the opportunity to find self-expression through romantic love and sexual encounters. Where parents and village elders previously supervised the choice of eligible marriage partners, courtship, betrothal, marriage and the setting up of a new household, young women in the city were left unsupervised. They chose their marriage partners through 'new' notions of romantic love rather than the prospect of land inheritance, and sexual 'liberation' resulted in illegitimate births.

These discussions have relevance to my study because although there are no statistics on illegitimate births in Sarawak, the sexual exploitation of young single women migrants has been a major concern. The Ministry of Social Development and Urbanisation commissioned a state-wide study on single mothers in December 2000. In this study, three interviewees became pregnant as single working women and were deserted by their men. The interview material in my study, and my long contact with Bidayuh women in this sector of work, has led me to agree with the arguments of Scott and Tilly.

As they pointed out, the peasant values that young women brought with them to the city were reflected in the types of employment that they chose. The wage work which they entered was not a radical departure from work that women traditionally did in the home in the past. This is particularly so in the types of work performed by Bidayuh women in the personal services sector in Kuching. The sexual behaviour of young Bidayuh working women in Kuching was frequently more a consequence of village values operating in new situations than the outcome of drastic changes in values as a result of new found freedoms. In order to better understand this, I will now return to the rural Bidayuh village and discuss courtship and marriage patterns there.

COURTSHIP AND MARRIAGE IN THE VILLAGE

Although match-making by parents was common in the past, Geddes' study of a Bidayuh village called Mentu Tapuh in the early 1950s provided some more recent insights into the courtship pattern of the Bidayuh. According to Geddes, young men often looked for potential spouses from villages other than their own. A young man might visit a friend or kin in another village during a festival in the hope of finding a wife. Sometimes he might be forced to spend a night in another village on his way back to his own village after a visit to the bazaar and meet a girl in that neighbouring village.

If he decides to court her, he would find an excuse to be in the village more and more frequently and might eventually stay in the village with a relative or even with the girl's family. It would not be difficult to find villagers who would accept him into their household, as additional labour was always welcomed. Thus, a suitor's village of origin and family background would be known and his intentions tacitly understood in the girl's village.

A young woman at a marriageable age of seventeen or eighteen would have her own bed and mosquito net, although young children often slept with their parents under the same mosquito net. Her bed was placed near a door and parents sleeping in the same room would usually know when a young man visited to court their daughter at night. After many frequent visits, he would be asked about his intentions regarding marriage. In this way, pre-marital sexual activity between single people was tolerated in the village as marriage was expected to take place, and a woman would only have a sustained affair with a man that she intended to marry.

A man intending to marry a girl would give her, through her father, gifts of a sarong, a piece of cloth, a pair of earrings and a ring. If these were accepted, the marriage was approved and the man could sleep with the girl at night. In other words, premarital sex was legitimised by the suitor's promise of marriage. In a village, such a promise was not easily broken as the girl's parents and village elders could be counted on to enforce the customary laws (adat). According to Geddes, in a Bidayuh village, pre-marital sex and adultery were not regarded as very serious offences if pregnancy did not result. Men caught sleeping with single girls were fined by the girls' parents. Sometimes the fine was extracted by the village headman.

If pregnancy occurred, the sanction was marriage. If the man was already married, the man would be fined for adultery. Pregnancy out of wedlock was a serious offence as it was believed that it would bring disaster and bad luck to the whole community. Parents of illegitimate children were shamed because of this, although the children bore no stigma themselves. The father of the child was also expected to pay for the maintenance of the mother and child. If the woman refused to name the father of her child, she would be fined.

Although the customary laws concerning courtship and marriage remain largely the same, courtship patterns have changed. Nowadays, boy meets girl at village parties where an amplifier to play loud music is set up in the village 'square' for discotheque type dancing. All this would occur under the watchful eyes of everyone in the village. For Christians, Bible study and choir practice provide additional avenues for meeting potential partners. Courtship among young adults these days would include visits to the nearest bazaar, picnics at nearby waterfalls and beaches and chats on the verandah of the girl's house. The courtship period is normally short and lasts from a few months to a year. However, a pregnancy will herald a quick marriage. Indeed, it has been said that such a method has been used to circumvent parental objections to a potential partner.

BIDAYUH WEDDINGS - THEN AND NOW

Geddes also reported that at the time of his study, there were no religious rites accompanying a marriage. The bride and the bridegroom's friends and relatives gathered in the household which they would join in marriage. Village elders and the fathers of the bride and bridegroom would instruct the couple on the rights and responsibilities of marriage. Some rice wine (tuak) would be passed around to enliven the gathering and the marriage was thus publicly acknowledged.

The village weddings of the women that I interviewed retained the same simplicity. They were still simple affairs. An exchange of rings is usual but sometimes even that is dispensed with. The bridegroom frequently gives the bride small items of gold jewellery such as a pair of earrings, bracelet, necklace and a piece of cloth or sarong. Other gifts included a token sum to the bride or to her father and a sarong for the bride or to her mother. There are no hard or fast rules. Sometimes there are no gifts, just an exchange of rings. However, a small gathering in the village is the norm. It serves as a public announcement and acknowledgment of the marriage.

If the couple come from two different villages, those who can afford two receptions will have one in each village, but normally only one is held. The expenses of the reception are normally shared between the bride and the groom but the partner and his/her parents who host the wedding reception will pay more. One woman said that they had a 'cowboy wedding' (kahwin cowboy) because they did not have a reception in the village but only registered their marriage in the district office.

The simple Bidayuh weddings mentioned by the women in my study are in contrast to the Malay wedding ceremonies in Rembau as documented by Stivens, where the level of consumerism in the village is explicitly demonstrated in the gifts that the groom gives to the bride. They include all manner of modern consumer goods as well as the paraphernalia of the modern woman and cosmetics, handbags and platform shoes are mentioned. The simplicity of the Bidayuh wedding in contrast to the lavish Malay wedding in Rembau is again evidence of the adaptation of old values and customs in the face of new contexts. Many of the Bidayuh women I interviewed express very pragmatic views about lavish weddings. Jocelyn, a working mother said:

If we have a proper wedding [registered and legally recognised], we can also be happy. We don't need to go to the restaurant or hotel. A big wedding can also end in divorce. (Kalau kahwin betul-betul, bagus juga. Tak payah pergi restoran, hotel. Kahwin besar-besaran, kita boleh cerai juga.)

In early nineteenth century industrialising Europe, cohabitation was a common phenomenon and often marriage occurred only after child-bearing. As a marriage licence and the pastor's fee were expensive, many working class couples replaced the church wedding with informal marriage rites in front of a small circle of family and friends. There are parallels between the informal marriage proceedings amongst the working class in nineteenth century Europe with the marriage customs as practised by the Bidayuh women in my study.

BIDAYUH HOUSEHOLDS IN THE VILLAGE

According to Geddes, in Bidayuh villages the most important economic unit was the household where land and property were held in common. He pointed out that there was no widespread kinship system above the household level. Any village level groupings were temporary and co-operation existed for specific tasks. In Geddes' study of Mentu Tapuh in the early 1950s, nuclear families consisting of the conjugal couple and their children were found to be in the minority. Instead, the majority were extended families which included aunts, uncles, in-laws, spouses of siblings and grandchildren of the conjugal couple.

Forty years later when Gerrits did his study in another Bidayuh village, nuclear families were found to be in the majority. Perhaps it can be concluded that fragmentation of extended households into nuclear households in the agrarian rural economy began with the individualisation of landholdings and monetisation through cash cropping, and has been accelerating this century. In this study, the majority (70 per cent) of working mothers and housewives live in nuclear families. Single women have been excluded from this calculation because they mainly live in accommodation provided by their employers.

There is no fixed rule as to which household a newly married couple would join. If one of the spouse was an only child, they would join her/his household as they would inherit an established household. The youngest son or daughter had a duty to care for his/her aged parents and that would also determine the household in which they would live after marriage. Apart from such cases, they were free to choose from either parent's households. The general principle of Bidayuh inheritance is that the son/daughter who lives with his/her parents and looks after them in their old age will inherit the family home. Even if the family home was built with remittance from migrant members of the family, they have no inheritance rights to the house if they live in the city and do not look after their aged parents. In addition, a son or daughter who marries may not use the land of his or her parents' line until such a time as a child is born from the marriage. The effect is that a person who marries into a village is bound to the household of the parents-in-law, as a junior partner in a co-operative team which works, eats and lives together, because he cannot get any place to make his own separate farm. Thus the system of land tenure protects the integrity of the community by keeping a new-comer on parole until he has actually mixed his blood with the community stream.

Having children was therefore very important as the couple could then set up their own household and become full members of a village community. When a newly married couple joined a household, it was merely a transitional stage. The household became a nuclear household once again when the couple moved out after the birth of their first child. In other words, single women in the village had to marry and become mothers in order to achieve adult status and economic security.

SEXUALITY AND YOUNG WOMEN MIGRANTS

One significant difference between the Bidayuh women in this study and the factory daughters in many other countries in the region is that the former are remote from parental control. In city-states like Singapore and Hong Kong, women commuted daily from their homes. In Indonesia many factories were located in close proximity to villages and women were bussed to their work-places. When this was not possible, the women either lived in hostels provided by their employers or took out boarding rooms in nearby industrialised villages. Most of the single women in this study either lived with kin in the city or in rooms above their work-places provided by their employers. Many returned to their villages only once a month, usually after pay-day. Thus, they were able to manage their own money.

The migration of single women to the city for wage work has also upset the courtship patterns of old. With the exception of domestic workers who work in isolation from others, most of the young women worked amongst their peers in coffee-shops, petrol stations, child-care centres, restaurants and hotels. On Sundays and other days off, young female migrants would go out together with their work-mates to meet kin and friends from the same village for a meal and a jaunt in town. Churches on Sundays, the museum gardens, the Reservoir Park, the Waterfront and eateries and shops around the bus terminals in the city centre were favourite places for socialising. Young women met men from different ethnic communities, their family and employment background unknown and unfamiliar to them.

The departure of women from the village also meant that their sexual activity could no longer be monitored by parents and village elders. Although living in the city away from family and earning their own wages gave single women autonomy, the flip side was that they were also vulnerable. Pre-marital sex for young women migrants continued as in the past to be an expression of marital intent or of anticipation of an impending union. Few young women would be reckless enough to start an affair with a man without first eliciting a promise of marriage.

However, with greater labour mobility and anonymity in the city, many men deserted their pregnant girlfriends on discovery of their condition and there were no parents or village elders to force a marriage or to mete out punishment. Although there are no statistics on illegitimate births in Sarawak, it is common to hear of migrant women returning home to the village with fatherless children. City life is exciting but it also evokes fear and anxiety in the women. Stivens had similar findings in her study of Muslim women in Rembau. She wrote of 'the ideological conflict [for village folks] about the release of young labour to the wickedness of the city and the world and the fears about unsupervised, moden women'.

Low wages meant that young single mothers had no choice but to return to live for a spell with their parents in the village. Although divorce carries no stigma in the village, having illegitimate children does. The child bears no shame but the mother does. As mentioned earlier, three women interviewed in this study became single mothers. One single woman became involved with a married Iban man who had a wife and children in the village. Another single woman was living with her Iban boyfriend at the time of the interview. His family disapproved of their relationship but could not enforce any sanctions. However, not all such prenuptial cohabitation ended in illegitimate children, and many do eventually marry. In fact, pregnancy would trigger a public announcement of their union in the village of either partner. One housewife said:

I was two months' pregnant when my husband brought me back to his village to meet his parents. There were no exchanges of rings or gifts. We merely had a small thanksgiving meal (makan selamat) and invited his relatives.

Thus, the context in which young Bidayuh meet and select a partner is very different from the 1950s. However, it must be pointed out that in the village, even now, sexuality is collectively managed by the elders of the village (including the parents) and customary laws are administered in an even-handed manner to both women and men. In the city, courtship has less direct parental and community supervision and women no longer enjoy the protection of egalitarian customary laws.

They are at the mercy of impersonal multi-ethnic communities that do not have an understanding of the operations governing sexual liaisons in Bidayuh villages. Women therefore have greater autonomy but this also has its attendant risks. If urban single motherhood either through divorce or abandonment is on the rise, women's participation in the labour market becomes one of necessity rather than individual choice because in the long run, many would return to wage work in the city.

MARRIAGE PARTNER SELECTION

Low wages, mounting living costs in the city and their new found independence have fostered pragmatic values amongst single women. They send some money home but also save and spend money on themselves. They learn the value of money and the difficulties of not having any. Thus the criteria for an eligible marriage partner have also changed. A man who is a good hunter and an industrious farmer would be favoured in the village, while in the city, it is his earning capacity that would be a desirable trait. A single woman knows that marriage to a man with a steady income is not only her best escape route from a lifetime of poorly paid employment but her future living standard depends on her husband's occupation.

All the single women (with the exception of one who did not want to get married) say that they have no wish to marry farmers but prefer men with money earning potential. The most important criterion is a regular income which would guarantee financial security. Elaine, a single woman remarked, 'My mother said that I should look for a man with a salary and not a farmer.' Josephine, who is in her thirties and engaged to be married to a technician professed, 'I will never choose to marry a farmer.' A working mother said that she would advise her daughter to go for a man with '... enough income, a fixed job and not just casual employment (... cukup pendapatan, kerja tetap dan bukan kerja main-main).' Nancy, another working mother added:

It would be good if one's husband had a secure job with a pension. He could work continuously without stopping until he reached retirement. (Bagus jika laki ada kerja tetap, ada pencen. Bekerja berturut-turut tanpa berhenti, sampai pencen).

It must be pointed out that marrying well is not the only aspiration the women had for their daughters.

On the contrary, all the women who had daughters said that they want their girls to succeed academically and have white/pink collar jobs, if not professions. I did not interview many men, but one of the husbands I interviewed explained that he had enrolled his daughter on a diploma course in computer programming because such a qualification would enhance her chances in the marriage market. He felt she was likely to marry someone who had higher, if not the same, qualifications as her. In contrast to this husband's view of paper qualifications, Agnita, a working mother, saw them as quite a different kind of insurance:

I told my daughters to study hard and get good jobs because without education, you cannot survive. Nobody can steal education from you. Others can steal your husband, but your knowledge and education (ilmu dan pelajaran), nobody can steal. If someone else attracts your husband, you can still survive. These gendered views speak volumes about the vulnerability that women feel and their need for independence from men. It also shows that women want a marriage for their daughters which are different from their own.

Barbara at eighteen married a widower twenty years her senior. He has an Indian father and a Chinese mother and works as a clerk in a government statutory body. He has two sons by his first wife. Barbara has a baby boy and wants more children but her husband said that he is old and refused. She suffers daily verbal abuse from her adolescent step-son and her husband spends almost the entire weekend playing mahjong in his friend's house. She is unhappy and regrets marrying him. She has this to say concerning the selection of marriage partners in the village and in the town:

In the village, marriages are better because spouses are nearer in age and they love one another (… mereka dekat umur dan sama suka sama). In town, we want to look for someone who works in an office, a stable job and income. Look at me. I ended up with a man twice my age and someone I don't love.

Jill, a working mother commented, 'People used to marry for love. Nowadays, people marry for money.'

Agnita added:

Marriage is very dangerous nowadays if you don't know how to deal with it. Women are keen to get men with money especially when they [the women themselves] don't have good jobs.

To marry for money and not for love, as the interview material indicates, reflects an economic pragmatism which disputes any notion that romantic love was the new self-expression of young female migrants to the city. This is in contrast to Wolf's study of factory daughters in Java where she found her respondents marrying 'quickly on the basis of sexual attraction and flirtation'.

One possible reason for this is that marriage for rural Javaneses women were typically arranged by their parents and were viewed as economic partnership more than romantic liaison. In South China, young factory women migrated from their villages in order to evade marriages arranged by their parents. Sexual attraction as a basis for marriage and factory daughters' choice of their own marriage partners reflect an increase in their decision-making power. In the case of Indonesia, this is an outcome of their economic contribution to the household.

REJECTION OF MARRIAGE

Most Bidayuh women choose the course of marriage. However, some working daughters resist marriage. I encountered several domestic workers in their late thirties who have chosen to remain single. Working Javanese daughters on the other hand, do not see such a 'choice'. To marry or not to marry, is a non-question, according to Wolf because marriage is almost universal in Java. Parents marry off their daughters early as a way to control their sexuality. Among the thirteen single women I interviewed, only one, Cindy, said that she had no wish to marry. Cindy had been a domestic worker for her entire employment history. At thirty-nine she was the eldest in her family. Three of her sisters who were in their thirties were also single which is unusual. She explained why she wanted to remain single:

I don't want to marry because as a single person, I can enjoy myself if I have my wages. (Saya tak mahu kahwin. Bujang dapat enjoy jika ada gaji.) If one marries the wrong man, for example a gambler, life will be worse. Nowadays there are many divorces and separations. After one or two children, they will divorce. Listening to the sad stories of others, I'd rather not marry and enjoy my freedom.

As with the working daughters in Taiwan, Hong Kong, Singapore and South China, women can choose whom they marry as opposed to the arranged marriages in the days of their grandmothers. The women are also getting married at older ages partly through parental encouragement in order to lengthen a daughter's years of monetary contribution to the natal household. However, I argue that single women enjoyed a brief window of time and space for self-indulgence but they confronted their new found freedom with a certain measure of ambivalence.

When women con-templated marriage, they approached the process of mate selection with pragmatism and chose marriage partners who, they hoped, would enable them to leave paid work. However, marriage and children bring with them a totally different set of decisions.

6

Coping in a Country of New Immigration

As growing numbers of women are likely to opt for international migration as a means of improving their life chances, it seems particularly important that we consider how these women cope with their new lives and how the countries, where they arrive, receive them. The context for this study is the migration 'about-face' that has occurred in southern Europe since the early 1980s. Over the past two decades, southern Europe, and specifically for this study Italy, changed from being areas of net emigration to areas of net immigration, most importantly with significant inmigrations from the 'south'.

This study focuses not so much on this well-documented turnaround, but on the effect on women of international migration to a country of new immigration and on their economic and non-economic activities. Key findings of the data include altered power and status relationships between the sexes and across generations. This is exemplified in the spatial arrangements constructed within the migrant's new environment. The investigation is also a response to the general need for a tetter understanding of the role of women in international migration, concluding with the observation that these women are pivotal members of their communities in allowing them access to new forms of production.

To investigate the issue of women's participation in international migration this study relates the experience of two female migrant groups arriving in Italy at a tumultuous time in Italy's immigration history, Filipinas and Somalian women. Initially, female migration to Italy tended to be fairly limited, concerning only a few women from a handful of nationalities: mainly women from the Cape Verde Islands, the Philippines and Eritrea who were employed as domestics. Today the number of female migrants has increased sharply with a greater range of nationalities represented, yet still remaining confined to the service sector.

The findings presented in this chapter are based on my doctoral research completed in 1994. At that time, Filipinas were a regular sight in most Italian cities; they had provided unskilled labour for Italy since the early 1970s and were beginning to exhibit signs of a maturing migrant community-family reunification and diversification into new professions. However, the second migrant group at the centre of this study, Somalian women, is a more recent phenomenon, still at the initial stages of a migration process initiated by civil unrest.

Female migrants have arrived in Italy from various countries and with different migration projects, exemplified in the two groups concerned here. Indeed this study intends to show that although there are few generalizations to be made concerning the migration of women to Italy and its impact, these women are playing an active and protagonist role in contemporary international migrations, contrary to reductionist stances that portray female migrants as dependants. These women are illustrative of the need to reassess the traditional treatment of migration in gender-blind terms. There are marked gender and occupational selectivities in migration streams, a difference that deserves special consideration.

NEW MIGRATIONS TO ITALY

This section concentrates on the emergence of Italy as a country of immigration since the 1970s, drawing attentions to the fact that the economic and social isolation of this study's participants are a byproduct of naive and ineffective reception policies. International migrations to Europe have grown in size in recent years, their compositions and directions substantially altering. Significant among these alterations is the emergence of southern Europe as a destination in the new pattern of migration flows to the EU, and the equally important recognition of non-EU females as economic migrants within these flows.

The rapidity of Italy's transformation, in a little over twenty years, from a country of emigration to one of immigration has been achieved through a combination of return migration, and the influx of new (largely non-EU) migrants. The existence of irtmigration in a traditional country of emigration like Italy may seem paradoxical, but it can be explained when several corresponding factors are considered in combination. One factor is the diversion effects of measures taken in the main receiving nations. In 1973 strict immigration controls were imposed throughout the EU, enforced through border controls and national regulations.

This led to a reduction in the number of clandestine migrants in the main receiving countries and their diversion to southern European countries, added to which there may have been migrants expelled from the main receiving countries finding alternate destinations. Some observers termed this 'the development of a "buffer state" situation' in which migrants were absorbed without being transmitted further north.

The fundamental role of the 'underground economy' in Italy is another factor. In economic terms, Italy's fortunes have profoundly altered. The country once considered as an economic backwater to Western Europe has blossomed at a time when the highly fragmented and segmented nature of southern European, and especially Italian, labour markets created a sectoral shift away from heavy manufacturing to high technology and service industries. Consolidated niches have developed that demand specific labour characteristics, typified in the case of migrant workers by a thirst for 'inexpensive and flexible' labour in 'marginal' areas of employment.

The concentration of such employment in cities such as Rome, Eari, and Milan only consolidates the effects of this precarious employment, with the migrants' poor conditions at work replicated by bad housing and living conditions. 'Immigration to Italy has become a model case because of the power of the informal economy ... this informal economy (and its flexibility) needs an unorganized labour force that is willing to accept any kind of working conditions, and migrants can provide this'. The 'secondary labour force' employed in this underground economy consists mainly of young women and retired Italians and foreigners.

Significant among this group are the irregular migrants employed in mainly service sector jobs, jobs that are hard, dirty, unattractive and sometimes dangerous. It would be wrong, however, to make the assumption that the migration phenomenon in Italy consists almost entirely of non-EU migrants. Four out of the ten largest migrant groups in Italy are from West European countries and the US. Italy is attractive to non-EU migrants for a number of economic reasons: it is also relatively easy to enter and moreover is geographically proximate to North Africa.

The country is still very open to entry with a tourist visa and the geographical proximity of Africa and Tunisia in particular, makes Sicily and the Mediterranean ports easy to enter. Cultural proximity through a colonial heritage has also attracted particular national groups such as Eritreans and Somalians, with many people in North African nations having some knowledge of the Italian language. Also important is that Italy is the centre of the Catholic faith, with missions from Italy to Africa and Asia (relevant particularly to the Philippines) acting as a means of forming interest in Italy and extending the information networks that facilitate migration. However, besides those flows originating in Africa and Asia, the political developments in Eastern Europe have created a potential new source of migrants that have also found Italy easy to enter.

Yet another factor explaining the influx of migrants into Italy is its uncertain national inmigration policies. For some time it has been suggested that southern European nations have not been prepared to deal with large-scale immigration and that national legislation is inadequate. Perhaps it can also be speculated that inmigration is far behind in political urgency in a country that has other problems and issues to address, and this can, to a degree, explain the non-intervention of the government. When crises have occurred, these nations have not been ready to deal fully with the situation; they have instead resorted to ad hoc policies. For decades, these southern European countries have had to deal only with emigration and adopt policies that protected these emigrants' rights.

Yet today, they are forced to a–dopt similar policies to those of the former countries of immigration. This has meant confronting clandestine inmigration; a difficult task when there are political and moral contradictions to be overcome and at a time when the political and economic situation of Italy is very different from that the northern European countries were faced with in the 1970s. Political ambiguity in relation to immigration matters and the difficulty of finding a way forward may explain the reluctance to impose European immigration reforms, which until the Schengen agreement of 1989 remained implicit rather than explicit.

The result to date has been residual gaps in the national legislation that allow individuals to slip through the net and into the underground economy. Because of its physical location, a thriving 'underground' market, and the insufficiency of legislation governing the inflow of migrants, Italy earns its reputation as an unguarded and unpredictable backdoor to the rest of Europe. It is a predicament compounded by the transitory nature of many migrant flows to southern Europe.

FEMALE MIGRANTS IN ITALY

How can one explain the concentrated presence of non-EU female domestic workers in Rome? In the early stages of immigration during the late 1970s the tertiarization of the Italian economy generated mainly white-collar, female-typed jobs filled by Italian women who, with a heightened feminist consciousness, have preferred them. The incoming migrants, particularly the female migrants, have satisfied a demand for work that comes not from the productive system, but the redistribution of income where families from the 'middle-classes' have rediscovered a function for migrant labour not readily available from Italian nationals.

This development would seem to indicate a similar experience to the northern European countries' past demand for migrants through industrialization and changing labour relations, yet Italy's employment demand is configured in a significantly different manner. The functions of labour migrations have altered, with a preponderance of female migrants confined to the service sectors. These immigration flows are no longer for quantitative rebalancing of labour markets where there is a need to supplement the shortfalls in native labour, but there are qualitative rebalances, required to ensure flexibility of the labour market in areas where particular duties and qualifications experience a shortfall.

Meanwhile, structural unemployment in countries such as the Philippines created a surplus population, which finally migrated in the desire for income and a better standard of living. The immigration of Somalian women was for distinctly different reasons. The onset of their move from Somalia coincided with the outbreak of civil war in their country. However, the move also coincided with the introduction in Italy of the Martelli Law in early 1990.

Respondents stated that the regularization opportunities presented in this law, the fact that Somalia was once an Italian colony, coupled with the economic opportunities available in Italy, were together strong incentives for choosing Italy to go to. Indeed, it is fair to say that the exile itself was caused by civil unrest, but that the prolonged stay in Italy, even after the unrest had abated, was due to the need for economic security in the wake of hardship incurred in exile.

Such economic determinism only goes part of the way to explaining why it is that, in a country such as Italy where the supply of domestics is larger than the demand, more women still migrate. I suggest that in addition to the economic attractiveness of Italy, both the existence of 'facilitating conditions' in Italy (intermediaries such as the Catholic Church and strong personal networks) and a 'culture of migration' within certain migrant groups have continued to facilitate the migration of female migrants to Italy. I would also suggest that the overrepresentation of women in the domestic care niche is perpetuated because of sexist and racist stereotypes. Indeed, 'Filipina' and 'domestic help' are synonymous to many. (As indicated by Lazaridis, the synonymy of 'Filipina' and 'domestic help' is also widely encountered in other southern European countries such as Greece).

The Italian employers interviewed in this study supported this hypothesis, going so far as to state that in the hierarchy of domestics available, Filipinas were the 'domestic of preference'. The migration of women to Italy is also being fuelled by a new occupational demand. Evidence from this study revealed that the domestic 'home help' phenomenon is now itself being transcended due to a shift in Italy's demographic profile. The Italian fertility rate is well below the 2.1 rate which assures replacement of the population. Italy's 1.27 fertility rates are the lowest in Europe.

The percentage of the population in the over-65 group in 1991 was 14.8 per cent and by 2011 will have reached 20.8 per cent. An indicator of the significance of this for the labour force is shown in the ratio of under-15s to over 65s. In 1991 it was 91.2 elderly for every 100 under-15, but by 2011 this will be 151.7. An increase in the number of aged has future implications for the demand for those female migrants who perform 'home help' tasks, using formal qualifications in the medical professions that they are not legally allowed to perform in Italy. Those medically qualified migrants move from the cooking and cleaning to the more lucrative and professionally rewarding business of providing basic health supervision for the elderly.

The female respondents in this study are anything but a homogeneous group: they have different experiences, different cultural origins and references, personal and specific histories, and individual desires and expectations. There are those who leave voluntarily in hope of economic gain and for family reunification; there are also those who were forced to leave their homes – they are refugees or have no hope of surviving in a country like Somalia, where civil war combines with ecological disaster.

There are those women who have arrived from the large and cosmopolitan cities of Africa and Asia, and there are those that have left directly from rural villages and life in the country. There is also diversity in the lives that these women have left behind. Beside those women who have been economically active there are the housewives and those who belong to Muslim groups. Filipino migration to Italy began in the late 1970s, accelerating during the 1980s. By 1981 there were already an estimated 15,000 Filipinos in Italy, which grew to over 35,000 by 1990.

The accelerated growth of the group can be attributed not only to the burgeoning Italian economy which was undoubtedly attracting more migrants into its tertiary sector, but also the movement of Filipinos from the Gulf States, which experienced a recession during this period. Throughout the first half of the 1990s, this number grew to 40,000 and more, fuelled by the promises of the new Martelli law. The Somalian community, by contrast, is relatively new. The group's numbers were swollen in the early 1990s by refugees, adding to the modest number of diplomats and students already present in Rome, accounting for some 17,000 individuals by 1995.

Despite this numerical difference, the group exhibits a few similarities with the Filipinas. Female migrants dominate both, and both concentrate in Rome. For the Filipino group, the abundance of domestic work from the wealthy middle-classes during the 1980s created a strong pull. Rome as the centre of the Catholic faith was also a strong factor of attraction. In contrast, the Somalian women were not drawn to the Italian economy so much, as to facilities provided by the Italian government for those in exile. These basic differences in reasons for migrating and residing in Rome are central in understanding why these women hold different positions in the same economic activity.

The majority of both groups were employed in domestic work; however the Somalian women's primary intention in migration from home was flight as refugees, not as economic migrants. Consequentially, they have found their recourse to domestic work a necessity, not a goal. The Filipinas by contrast, experience a 'top of the pile'situation. They have made a career out of domestic service, and are able to command the highest wages. The income gap is also attributable to the greater experience of the Filipinas, and the preference of Italian employers for Filipinas as domestics.

For both groups, migration was seen not only as a means to short-term financial gain for the migrant, and above all for her family, but also as a long-term fulfilment of goals and dreams. That the migrant women would have to endure hardships and considerable sacrifice was seen as unavoidable but a worthwhile price to pay. Amongst both groups residing in Rome, future economic aspirations were prevalent but not exclusive: migration is understood and experienced both in relation to economic settlement and in relation to personal and family achievement, and for some this included a cautious movement towards self-determination and autonomy.

MEANS OF COPING

The information gathered during the study goes some way toward an explanation of how the women's ability to 'cope' is a direct product of the support networks that they develop on their arrival. In a general sense, the evidence leads to recognition that the insertion of these women into a domestic work setting, coupled with the separation from family, has imtiediately created a barrier to negotiating integration in their new setting. The unskilled migrant faces a complex and problematic situation on arrival in a country such as Italy: how to rebuild the familiar in order to be able to cope with the unfamiliar?

This study moves toward the general conclusion that although migration has the potential to improve the status of women through economic wealth, this is often at great personal and fanilial cost with individuals preoccupied with ideas of dislocation and loss. The relationships that are then formed in their new host country are central in the women's ability to 'cope' and move towards a hopeful future.

These wider relationships provide sustenance and refuge but may also reinforce traditional gender relations. Such social dependence can hinder the potential for liberation that economic independence might bring. These relationships have also quickly marked the position of women within their new environments. Paradoxically, the 'Western' environment itself may perpetuate and exaggerate the image of the women as 'home makers', consigning them to 'traditional' economic roles within the service sector.

The consequences of migration are many. There are numerous indications of the relative social isolation of these two groups of women working in Italy, yet female migrants are more than isolated women. If the assistance that the church and voluntary agencies supply and the personal networks were to be excluded, female migrants would have had to learn to fit into Italian society themselves. Indeed, there is a pervasive assumption that these women, who are earning a wage and supporting themselves, are gaining independence. Yet the moral obligation to provide support for the household is rooted strongly, and the individual finds herself to be a vital member of the household, more so abroad than at home, remitting most of the earnings from her employment. Such economic exile is vital to fulfilling the expectations made of them.

How to cope with this uprooting is a dilemma the unskilled female migrant is faced with in a country such as Italy, which has largely failed to provide adequate legislation or social provisions for new migrants. It is worth commenting that while the re-conceptualization of Italy as a country of immigration has been recognized in academic terms, critically the Italian government at the time of this study (early 1990s) had failed to make adequate provisions for the application of legislation such as the Martelli law. As a result, not only is the economic integration of foreign workers difficult in the labour market, but other forms of reception from voluntary organizations, such as the Caritas, are the only means of recourse for new migrants.

The INfertelli law, introduced in February 1990, required the establishment of reception centres for new migrants and refugees; however, three years later only two municipal reception centres existed in Rome. As many of this study's respondents pointed out, it is now too late for initial reception facilities. For many migrants the situation has developed further. A housing solution is now required. The policy implications of this are essential. Official inmigration, reception and housing programmes are necessary, measures that should fundamentally incorporate the initiatives of migrant populations and groups such as Caritas and Saint' Fjgidio, ideas which may not conform to the ideas of policy makers.

A good example is the Caritas migrant community programmes. The centre provides health care and shelter specifically designed for women and children, and unaccompanied children, a regrettable but growing phenomenon of non-EU migration to Italy. Such targeted social programmes should extend into many other areas of migrant assistance, a move in which the migrants themselves should be involved, so that they can be relevant to the needs of all migrants. One such means is to support migrants' information networks.

THE ADVANTAGE OF PERSONAL AND SOCIAL NETWORKS IN COPING

Throughout the study that this chapter is based on, the role of personal networks in the migration process was established. These networks influence the direction, content and timing of migration flows, provide initial social and housing requirements, and also allow the individual to build a support system that may alleviate some of the loneliness and hardship of family separation.

Both the Filipino and Somalian female migrant workers operate within social networks that have been described in terms of concentric spheres, the inner core consisting of close relatives, to which there are binding obligations. Around this there are graduated spheres, one of more distant relatives, one of fellow countrymen and friends, and one of persons who are not specifically obligated to the individual but who may be called on for their services (migrant traffickers, religious organizations, the state). These relationships are the focus of support both before and after migration.

The network acts as an organizing force, perpetuating the migration flow and assisting in subsequent adaptation to life in a host country. It is the crux of an individual's ability to 'cope'. If women are involved in their country of origin with activities outside the domestic unit, the situation is manageable; this is because there is a set of domestic relations that cushion the effect on the women in these extra-domestic activities. But this is far more problematic when the individual leaves that local environment in search of waged employment, and where the reciprocity of help and services are absent on initial migration.

The major problem facing these new migrants, therefore, is how to reconstruct this support network; there are strong obligations to home in the country of origin, which sometimes make it difficult to generate independent networks abroad. The migrant is a fragile thing, she is unsure and a scared creature, with an initial reaction to group together for security in the hope of finding a sort of ethnic identity, before atterrpting to be subsumed into the host society so that she has a degree of self assurity and confidence. Encompassed in this is the need to merely find a job, to achieve what they came here for, to send money home, in effect just to survive in the host nation.

There are few thoughts of actually recognising themselves as a woman and a woman with rights etc. or displaying those feminine instincts that would be expressed in their own country. There is little thought of an education process or independence. The extent, to which a woman is 'successful' in her migration and retains her sanity, depends on the extent to which she can balance these conflicting demands. In the case of refugees from Somalia and migrants from the Philippines, social networks were the main source of accommodation and assistance in finding employment. In a country such as Italy, with a problematic housing situation and no effort being made for placing migrants on waiting lists for public housing, the recourse to friends and family is a necessity, not an option.

The strength of these personal and social networks also plays a decisive role in the impact of migration on the adaptation and status of migrant women. Not all the outcomes from this support are necessarily positive, however. Not only is little independence gained because of the economic obligations to remit money home, but also the strong social networks encountered on arrival in Italy leave little chance for encountering other lifestyles. In the case of the Filipinos, the Catholic Church is the dominant form of assistance. However, provisions from the Church have followed the Catholic tenet of assistance and charity. Such intervention is not conducive to self help but encourages the continued reliance on charitable assistance for the mental, physical, social and economic health of the individual.

The Catholic organisations are more concerned with being there to act as their salvation, as their crutch, and through this there is nothing given back in return (from the migrants), and the migrants get used to having everything done for her/him, and of living within this false institutionalised structure. Through this there may also be abuse of the system. It is a sort of control through which the migrant is not exposed to any kind of independence, and then is reliant on the church. By migrating and working abroad, the Filipino migrant women at the centre of this study became the main source of income for their families, yet it is questionable whether there has been a corresponding shift in economic control.

In fact, the slight asymmetry of economic roles between men and women in the household, in favour of the women, does not seem to have produced the same change in their political and social ability to make decisions for the family unit. Similarly, the Somalian women were almost exclusively the only wage earners for their household, yet decisions over the use of that income are relinquished to male members of the household. The strength of personal and social networks, coupled with a desire to be close to the social norms of the community from which they derive all kinds of support seem to be partly responsible for this outcome.

There were other indications of the social isolation of the women. Most of the women interviewed had no Italian friends or friends from other national groups. These social networks have yet another aspect to them. Not only do they initiate migration and support the migrant in her migration - they also encourage further migrations. This migration of non-EU women, primarily stimulated by the rapid growth of the Italian economy, is fuelled by its own momentum. It is a process that is already so prevalent that it has, through information networks, generated its own mythology and oral traditions.

Indeed, migrants are often depicted as wide-eyed, naive newcomers, arriving at a large city overwhelmed by the unfamiliar nature of their destination. In fact, the majority of those who move are following a well-worn path previously travelled by family and friends. The fundamental role of these networks is to reduce the risks associated with migration and assist in the individual's efforts to 'cops' away from home. There are other ways in which these women rebuild a form of security similar to that available through networks. Many of the women involved in this study were able to build a new form of security and express in spatial terms their challenge or reaffirmation of gender and occupational roles.

BUILDING PLACE AND IDENTITY

How do you cope in an unfamiliar built environment? You build an environment that is familiar. We are born into relationships and an identity that are always based in place; there are indications however, that these migrant women consciously and unconsciously display the dialectical process of reconstructing and rebuilding 'new' female identities through the use of place. Space becomes not only a physical territory, but has a social and psychological dimension.

Examining the interplay between social relations in the household and the workplace mediated through space is an important way of understanding migrant women's resistance to unequal gender and social relations. For many migrants, security and peace of mind are obtained through a continual investment in an idealized perception of the country of origin; for those who are refugees, culture becomes a symbol of what has been lost and sacrificed. Music, religion, ritualized daily routines and places of meeting are means of retaining a collective identity, whilst the reception of this spatial display from Italian society may reinforce stereotypical images of the migrant phenomenon.

This situation is further complicated when relationships of age, gender and ethnicities are introduced. This perception is particularly valuable when these relationships are contextualized within the already spatially defined 'us' and 'them' association a migrant has with the state. Different spaces have been used to confront the changes which migration has brought to otherwise familiar lifestyles in the absence of adequate Italian reception and housing policies. MDst public spaces in Rome have a spatial definition that incorporates ethnic demarcation (the separation of different national migrant groups), gender demarcation (women in one area and men in another, whilst in the same public space), and a more subtle spatial demarcation built around distinctions between areas of origin (the Philippines or Somalia).

The distinctions between these areas are not always rigid, especially if the population in a public space at any one time is small, and then there may be some mixing, but when there are many people in one area, such as a Sunday or Thursday afternoon at Termini, these distinctions become clear. These spaces have become social maps. Termini, the piazzas and Eur station are all public spaces where transport routes converge, and as such there is maximum accessibility for the migrants. In general these public spaces are used because of a lack of provision from the 'Commune di Roma' of any meeting or leisure facilities for migrant groups.

So what does this mean for the women? With specific reference to the Filipina group, the need for places to meet other than such public areas is necessary to mask the divisions and negative aspects within the cortmunity, largely accelerated through the continual arrival of Filipino men. When I asked the current labour attache to the Philippines in Rome 'Whatare the main problems you feel the community in Rcme is facing?' he replied:

The main thing is that there is nowhere for them to meet [the Filipinos] constructively, for them to use their time well. There are just areas like Termini and that are not good, they can't spend their time productively and then they get into trouble. They lack a Filipino club with space, where they can gather and exchange ideas, where they can play sport, play videos and hold parties. This is a great need.

Public spaces in the eyes of the community leaders and the Church are accruing negative images for the community as a group, through their association not only on Sundays as areas where large community groups meet, but also because of what is seen daily as the preponderance of male migrants. The men, it is said, give the rest of the community a bad name through their drinking, their gambling and womanizing. However, it is due to the social constraints exercised at the church that not only the men, but also the women, go to such areas. Here they are away from the watchful eye of the priests and sisters where 'the lighter side of life' can be enjoyed, and relationships can be formsd that may be frowned upon in the Church areas.

This distorted image of the migrant phenomenon as largely male is compounded by the specific employment opportunities available for migrant women in Rome. An unemployed mass of migrant men is created who have largely joined these women, and who, through gathering at public spaces such as Termini and the piazzas, are perpetuating an image of the migrant phenomenon in Rome. As such, the use of public space is increasing the complex set of assumptions and attitudes used in reference to migrant women, due to this image of the migrant phenomenon as male, non-white, unproductive and uncontrolled. These are images unlikely to lead to the adjustment of migrant and national groups, or acceptance by Italian society, as frictions with the host society are likely to increase.

Through the examination of space and gender, it is shown that although place is often the way in which gender and power relations are defined, it is also through the lack of alternative space that public areas are used for this expression.

Secondly, intolerance and racism are developing in part due to the absence in the Italian public mind of any visible state control of migration to Italy. The consequences of this in the recent political climate are strong anti-migrant policies towards both economic migrants and refugees.

It is this local confusion of reactions, of who these women are, what their function is, and how they can best be assisted in their adjustment to life in Italy, which is both the result of this distorted image of the visible male migrant as the economic actor and of the misconception that the invisibility of women may mean that they need no help in adjusting. Both groups of women, Somalian and Filipino, indicated that local government organizations, trade unions and voluntary organizations, were little able to attend to or recognize the specific concerns of these women (issues such as domestic violence, pregnancy and hospitalization, counselling for the emotional distress caused by migration and for Somalian women the issue of infibulation).

The absence of large numbers of Somalian women in public areas is in fact due to their concentration in private accommodation. The drastic changes that have occurred in their lives as a result of their exodus from a civil war, combined with the feelings of being uprooted, may have instigated a search for tradition and an attempt to reconstruct familiar lifestyles within the private space. In this sense, the women themselves do gain power in the gender relations, as they themselves become a source of continuity and comfort for the rest of the community. Such strategies to cope may, however, leave a patriarchal system intact, although this may paradoxically be a source of support for the women in the absence of a certain future.

The aim of this study thus far, has been to identify and explore women in international migration and how they are able to cope with the changes that these migrations bring to their lives. It seems fitting to conclude by considering how, what is an undoubtedly fluid situation may develop. Return migration is an important aspect of international migration, because it may be said to represent the last stage of the migration process and the attainment of the ultimate migration goal. Data from this study suggests that a migrant's return is not necessarily the end of the migration phenomenon for either herself or her household. The obligation to financially support a household may continue beyond the initial migration.

Findings gathered from the Filipinos clearly suggest that the nature of Filipino migration is changing. Besides a process of family formation, what I have termed an 'intergenerational, sequential migration' is occurring. Lack of desire on the part of early Filipino migrants to unite their family in Italy but a high degree of importance placed on the income generated for the family through remittances has created a new pattern of family migration. The Filipina who has been a migrant for up to twenty years and is now in her fifties or sixties will have supported her fanily in the Philippines through remittances, allowing her children to finish school.

As the family has not been united in Italy and as the mother has reached her time for retirement, her daughter enters Italy to replace her mother as the main provider of a family income. As such, there is a replacement of migrants, which is likely to continue sequentially in the future, unless the Philippine economy becomes more prosperous or Italian irrmigration restrictions are strengthened. Given the higher ages and longer history of migration from the Philippines, this replacement phenomenon is confined to the Philippines. This cross-generational migration is being accelerated by the falling average age of the Filipinos migrating to Italy.

During the 1970s, when the first large wave of Filipinos arrived in Italy, many of the women were in their 30s or 40s. Since about 1985, unemployment and economic deterioration in the Philippines have pushed younger women, including those graduating from college and university, into migrating. It used to be that it was the mother who migrated leaving her children behind. Now, the children convince the mother to retire in the Philippines whilst the grown-up children themselves migrate. This turn-around has meant that, unlike their mothers, who had children before they migrated, these women are migrating early in their reproductive life, delaying a family. This might indeed have great significance for future generations as the phenomenon could carry on indefinitely across future generations.

EMERGING EMPLOYMENT PATTERNS

Men are increasingly joining the female members of their households in Italy. For the Filipino men, this is due to the reduction in economic opportunities in the Gulf States where many of them have previously migrated. The Somalian men are moving from the exile locations they had held proximate to Somalia (often in Ethiopia or Kenya), and on to Europe, having become disenchanted with the prospect of return to a war-torn Mogadishu. Charmed by news of a burgeoning economy in Italy, these men expect to find opportunities awaiting them in Rome. This is not the case.

Domestic service is distinctively biased towards the employment of women only. The women are then the only means of access these men have into the productive economy. One Filipino (Josie) described how this new migration has proved profitable for the Filipino men and begun a new economic trend:

Many of the men who come here have a technique of getting a job. They have to find a girlfriend to find a job; this is why so many marriages are in trouble in the Philippines. If a man spends some time with his girlfriend whilst she is doing her job the employers get to trust him, and then after a while the girlfriend leaves for another job. He will then take over the job. This is a way of getting around the reluctance of the Italians to employ men in the domestic sphere.

Finally, as previously suggested, seme Filipinos in Rome are renegotiating their economic position in the Italian labour market. The domestic work sector is not only poorly paid; it is also an unskilled sector of the economy in which you find many highly qualified women. Given the opportunity, therefore, those individuals who are frustrated with such a situation are moving into an area of employment not satisfied by national labour supply, an area of employment that allows the use of their skills and qualifications as health workers, nurses and doctors. Some Filipinos (termed assistensas) who were employed as domestics are taking charge of the care for sick and elderly members of a household instead of the normal domestic work tasks.

However, these assistensas are often administering medicine and undertaking medical procedures without the required authorization from Italian authorities, and, as such, are putting themselves at risk legally. This process is a vital step in the adaptation of the group. Although the women may remain in social isolation, not yet managing to achieve emancipation and integration into the host society, their economic activities have begun to exhibit signs of maturing through a movement into areas other than domestic work. There is also evidence of stratification within the group legally resident, longer established and betterqualified Filipinos move up into the assistensa category, creating space at the lower end of the domestic sector for other groups.

Recently arrived Filipinos, Filipino men, arrivals from countries not traditionally associated with the domestic service market, such as Somalia and Poland, all compete to fill this vacant spot. The main effect of this has been to reduce the overall cost of domestic work and produce a hierarchy of domestic labourers. The recognition of assistensa activities as well as the recognition of a demand for them must be of priority in future Philippine and Italian negotiations of bilateral agreements. Not only may these new activities be important in the stabilization of the Philippine community in Italy, but they may also be the key to one area of Italian social services that has shown a demand for qualified medical staff.

As such, the provision of educational training that supplies the women with the necessary linguistic abilities to exercise their skills within the social services sector would release a latent pool of labour. This study evolved out of an interest in female migrants, their objectives, their dreams and their means of coping. A few concluding points sum up this exploration. It was recognized that these women, when acknowledged, had usually been relegated to consideration as 'dependants' or else studied as 'the women left behind', I have pursued a movement towards refuting this 'invisibility'; the women are focal members of their economic household.

Meanwhile, in studying female migration, it has been common to emphasize that the problems faced by migrant women are compounded by being women, migrants, and often racially distinct from the national population. In the course of this study, the context of Italy as a new country of immigration with delayed legislative formation has been shown to exacerbate these factors with the effect that female migrants are overlooked in the scant reception facilities that exist in urban Italy. Indeed it has been suggested that what remains is a situation whereby female migrants are faced with dilemmas of coping on their own.

Personal and social networks are of prime importance in enabling these strategies of adaptation, whilst the built environment provides migrants with the arena for change. Beyond this, the recency of immigration has had both retrospective and prospective aspects. This is a complex interdependent relationship only touched upon, but which opens discussion into the impact of international migration on female migrants. Of course, it is also recognized that not all the changes deriving from migration, especially into a country of new immigration, would necessarily be positive changes for the status of the women involved.

To conclude: from the moment one delves into the field of female international migration, one begins to realize the paucity of research focusing exclusively on female migrants and the complexity of the phenomenon. The recency of immigration to Italy is interesting given the emerging recognition of female international migration and the presence of some migrant flows in Italy that are almost exclusively female. Such an opportune moment provides an almost perfect situation in which to examine the effects that gender-specific migration has on female migrants, especially amongst those who are still at the initial stages of the adaptation process.

7

The Status of Migrant Women in Spain

Almost all existing literature on immigrants and migration flows from developing countries to Spain has been written during the 1990s. The unexpected and rapid increase in the numbers of newcomers during the late 1980s and early 1990s surprised social researchers as much as the general public. But while migrant men - especially of African origin - were visible within the Spanish landscape, women have remained invisible to the public and in the eyes of some social scientists dealing with migration issues. As usual, it has been women researchers who have been interested in revealing the female realities that remained hidden.

The second half of the 1990s has been especially fruitful in producing contributions to the issue of gender and migration. Apart from my own research on Peruvian women in Barcelona, other research has or is currently being conducted on Moroccan, Dominican, Filipino women in Madrid and Barcelona, which are the main locations where migrant women are concentrated. These early contributions offer a very general view of the migrants' situation. The focus is placed on numbers and figures rather than on qualitative aspects. Some of the work mentioned above has analysed the experience of a specific migrant group, or compares it with other groups.

Others have concentrated on the incorporation of women in the labour market of the receiving society. Very few scholars have looked at the sphere of social and family relations in the country of origin and destination. They stress the socio-economic discrimination migrants suffer due to being both women and migrants. In these studies, in parallel to men's work, the economic aspect of migration beocmes a central issue. The difference between those writings focusing on men (the term /nigrant usually implies men) and those focusing strictly on women, is that the latter focus on women's status. Indeed, the question of women migrants' status has preoccupied international researchers for a long time. In Spain this is a recent issue - as new as the immigration phenomenon of the last decade.

In what follows I will firstly describe policy and administrative measures adopted by the Spanish government to control non-EU immigration since 1986. These measures shape the composition and character of flows in terms of their feminization, country of origin, and labour orientation. Secondly, by concentrating on the position of migrant women we address one of the major questions about female mobility: do women benefit from it in terms of a rise or maintenance of their social position? Examples will be given from research on migrant women in Spain, focusing on the experiences of Dominican, Moroccan, Peruvian, and Filipino women - which are the most important groups numerically.

CONTROL, COMPOSITION, AND CHARACTER OF FLOWS

Southern Europe can now be recognized as an area that receives migrants after several decades of being a source of emigration to central and northern Europe. In fact, from the 1950s to the mid-1970s there was a negative migration balance in Spain, which became positive in the late 1970s. This change in migration patterns is the result of, on the one hand, significant numbers of returnees, and on the other hand, international migrants, from other European countries and from Asia, Africa and Latin America. Factors influencing the shift from a country of emigration to a country of immigration include the following:

a. Political and socio-economic changes such as democratization and the economic growth of Spain, making certain work activities and conditions less attractive to nationals,
b. Free entrance of foreigners as tourists until the early 1990s - poor implementation of the 'foreigner's law' of 1985.
c. Closure of neighbouring European countries' borders to third country migrants,
d. Since 1993 the introduction of a quota system for domestic and agricultural services,
e. Opening and promotion of Spain internationally in the fields of culture, information and economy: for example the Barcelona Olympic games and the Universal Exposition of Seville in 1992; the purchase of telephone and electrical companies amongst others in countries like Peru, Argentina and so on; and the building of many hotels and tourist sites in the Dominican Republic,
f. Geographic proximity, especially with Morocco acting as a door to Europe for migrants from the rest of Africa,
g. Colonial camon history, cultural-linguistic links, especially with Latin America, and
h. Rise in emigration from sending areas, especially because of the acute political and economic crisis in parts of Latin America and Africa.

MIGRATION POLICY

The economic and political integration of Spain into the European Community in 1986 played a major role in the process of regulation of foreign migration. On the one hand, it opened the doors to European goods, capital and people, while on the other hand, it closed them to non-European Union citizens. A 'foreigner's law' was adopted some months before integration. It gave the guideline for border control.

The terms of this law were determined by what Borras (1995) calls the cross-roads of Spanish policy on foreigners, namely: (1) its membership of the European Union; (2) its strong links with Latin America; (3) its geographical proximity to the African coast. Two further influences might be added: firstly, the low birth rate (in 1995 the lowest in the world at 1.2), and the high life expectancy (of about 78 years) that prevail in Spain, and secondly the segmented and precarious labour market.

The granting of EC membership to Spain and to Portugal in 1986 represented the end of a long quest for recognition within the economic and political structure of a united Europe. Spain had made tenacious efforts to join the First World Western bloc, but previous efforts during Franco's regime had been unsuccessful, mainly due to the lack of democracy and protection of human rights. Yet many researchers cormient that Spain's integration into the EC in fact coincided with increasing tendencies towards violation of the human rights of Spain's many foreign residents and of prospective migrants.

Since the 'foreigner's law' of 1985 was enacted a year later, foreign migrants have been required to obtain a residence and work permit in order to become legal citizens. To obtain these permits a formal work contract is necessary, and this is often impossible in a dual labour market society, in which migrants perform marginalized activities. Such regulations mean that migrants are forced to violate the law by using fraudulent contracts and other nominal papers. Other restrictive measures regarding irrmigration from non-EU countries include limiting one-year permits (types A and B) to a particular activity and geographical area, and discretionary measures such as making the granting of a permit contingent upon the state of national labour demand, and family reunion dependent on the economic and social conditions of the petitioners.

Historical links with latin America are reflected in the sarE 'foreigner's law'. Latin American as well as Filipino and Equatorial Guinean migrants receive: (1) preferential residence and work permits; (2) easier renewal of permits and the issuing of longer and more flexible permits; (3) no visa requirement to enter the country (with the exception of nationals of Cuba, the Dominican Republic and Peru); (4) a faster application procedure for the granting of Spanish nationality.

Proximity to the African coast prevented Spain from making its immigration policy too open. Economic and demographic contrasts within the Mediterranean region, together with the conflict of ideologies of religion and culture, have given seme researchers and many other European citizens the impression that migration from this area to its immediate northern neighbours will continue and even increase. Whether a myth or a reality, this helps explain why Moroccans do not enjoy the same preferential treatment as Latin Americans, despite sharing historical and colonial links with Spain.

The formulation of immigration policy in Spain has been influenced by national and European interests in terms of restriction rather than social integration. Ihe fear of political leaders and the general populations of an 'avalanche from the Third World' have promoted defensive positions. In this climate, social workers and other organizations attempt to influence and guide governmental procedures towards some positive initiatives. The extraordinary regularization process of 1991 was the result of such action. It was carried out after the publication of several reports by social scientists and Caritas on undocumented migrants and was an urgent administrative measure, introduced some years after the Spanish 'foreigner's law' of 1986.

It tried to regularize as many undocumented migrants as possible but also appeared to have the effect of attracting new migrants into Spain. Statistical data from the Spanish Ministry of Labour and Social Security indicate that at the end of 1991 and the beginning of 1992 just over 100,000 non-EC workers obtained their first one-year work and residence permits through the regularization process. Permits were restricted to a specific occupation and geographical area. Moroccans received the vast majority of these permits (48,240), followed by three Latin American nationalities: Argentinians (7,405), Peruvians (5,664), and Dominicans (5,517).

Men clearly outnumbered women among the Moroccans, but they were roughly equal to women among the Argentinians and Peruvians, and a clear minority among the

Dominicans. Work activities were mostly located in the service sector. Agriculture and construction were in second and third position, but accounted for far fewer jobs for migrants. Geographically similar numbers of permits were granted in Madrid (35,267) and Catalonia (32,648), with Andalusia (11,033) and Valencia (7,471) appearing in third and fourth place respectively.

The regularization process was brought to an end in 1993, with many second permit renewals and fewer permits given for family reunions. Most difficulties were experienced by agricultural and construction workers, because of the obvious constraints in obtaining a contract when the work is seasonal and temporary, and because of a rapid decrease in construction sites after the boom preceding the events of 1992 - the Olympic games in Barcelona and the World Exposition in Seville. The central government decided it was time to introduce a quota system that granted a maximum of 20,000 new work permits to non-EU nationals a year.

Applications were supposed to be presented at the Spanish embassies in the countries of origin but the 1993 and 1994 quotas were put to use regularizing migrants already working in Spain rather than newcomers. The majority of the work permits were granted, in descending order, to the nationals of the Dominican Republic, Peru, Morocco and the Philippines. Domestic service was by now the most significant sector of migrant employment.

The 1995 quota specified those activities in which migrants would be granted permission to work. These activities were limited to domestic service (Filipinos, Dominicans and Peruvians) and agriculture (Moroccans). But after some months of pressure from migrant associations and other non-governmental agencies, the obligation to present papers at the countries of origin was abolished. A change of government in March 1996, when the Democratic Socialists headed by Gonzalez lost power to the right-wing Aznar, provided an opportunity for migrants and other social actors to question the future development of the policy.

Firstly, a new regularisation process was launched for the current year. It included many restrictions, such as the requirement of living with a close relative in Spain or having had a work and residence permit at an earlier stage and since becoming undocumented. This second extraordinary regularisation was rather unsuccessful: only 24,000 applications were approved, more than a half of which were residence permits for family members, compared with the over 100,000 approved in 1991. Second, starting from 1997 the quota was again implemented.

Having been fixed at a low number, 15,000 permits, it was increased to over 24,000 authorisations at the end of 1997. In the same way the 1998 quota increased the number of authorisations to 28,000 (9,154 in agriculture and catering, 1,069 in construction, 16,836 in services, and 941 others). Finally, for 1999 30,000 authorisations were granted. Asylum seekers are perceived as a pressing problem in many European countries. In order to avoid the possible future abuse of asylum and refugee applications by migrants, changes in regulations were introduced in 1995 to strengthen control mechanisms in the processing of applications and to speed up handling times.

Common ways of entering the country are to overstay on a tourist or student visa or to enter illegally via camion borders. More recently legal methods such as quotas for work - managed by friends or relatives from Spain - and residence permits via family reunion processes are used. For the undocumented, crossing the border may be very risky, as in the well-known case of Moroccans, although it can be made easier by passing through other European neighbouring countries that do not demand a visa from particular groups of non-EU nationals, such as Latin Americans.

THE PROFILE OF MIGRANTS

Non-EU migrants in Spain are composed to a large extent of Moroccans and Latin Americans, and to a lesser extent of other African and Asian nationals including Filipinos, Chinese, Senegalese-Zambians, and Pakistanis. These populations are generally concentrated in specific geographical and occupational areas. For instance, Moroccans are concentrated along the Mediterranean fringe of the Iberian Peninsula, whereas Latin Americans are found only in a couple of cities, mainly Madrid and Barcelona. Recent migration flows to Spain are still predominantly male, although women count for an important percentage in the big urban areas (53 per cent of all migrant workers in Madrid).

This is not very different from the situation in the European cities of central, northern and Western Europe, which have longer immigration histories. The particularity of the south (Spain, as well as Italy, Portugal or Greece) is that these women often report migrating 'independently', and not through the traditional family reunion process - where the man migrated before and later brought his wife and children to the host country. On the contrary, most recent female migration to southern Europe was started by women and followed by other women of the family or neighbourhood.

Indeed, the solo migration of women from Latin America or East Asia has been profusely reported in international literature. This solo migration is not the same as movements headed by African women which are also important. Despite the widespread image of female subjugation, many women migrate alone, mainly for work purposes. While Dominican females dominate their community composition, Peruvian women have been steadily increasing in proportion over the last five years. Moroccans are still relatively few but are also increasing while becoming in 1997 the largest group in terms of numbers of women before Dominicans and Peruvians. Also among Filipinos we find a majority of women and Chinese migrants are increasingly female.

We can differentiate among groups according to their labour incorporation. African, south- and west-Asian women are less economically active and usually married. Latin American and East Asians are more economically active and single, except for the case of longestablished Filipinos. But being single does not mean having fewer family responsibilities. The vast majority often send money home (to parents, brothers and sisters, children, even the partner).

LABOUR MARKET INCORPORATION

While men are employed in a range of activities like agriculture, construction or commerce, women are employed mainly in private houses, cooking, cleaning and/or caring for children, the sick and the elderly. They are rarely self-employed. Most have settled in the largest Spanish cities. Having no statistical information about the level of education of women, we may distinguish between those within higher education - Peruvians and Filipinos - and those who are less educated - such as Moroccans and Dominicans. However, we may find women with different levels of education in each group.

Education also determines labour market incorporation. There is a substantial number of nurses and teachers among Peruvian and Filipino women. They frequently take jobs involving some caring beyond pure cleaning. As qualitative work shows, similarity between Spain and the Peruvian and Dominican languages is also an advantage for labour market insertion and promotion to other working areas within the service sector, though it is not so much the case in Barcelona where the Catalan language is generally used.

Apart from those activities that have been rejected by the native population, the jobs taken by recent labour migrants are limited to insecure jobs (temporary contracts and seasonal or irregular work) and poor working conditions (including salaries below the legal minimum wage and dangerous work without appropriate security and health measures). There is often a difference between the experiences of documented and undocumented migrant workers in the labour market, the latter being those who do not hold a valid work permit.

These workers are potentially subject to greater exploitation because of the lack of a contract (as a guarantee of fixed work hours and salary), lack of social security entitlement and lack of union protection. The everincreasing number of undocumented migrants is related to the creation and perpetuation of a dual labour market, in which the native population and even some legal migrants are relatively advantaged compared to undocumented newcomers. Domestic workers, in addition, suffer isolation in the work place. Foreign women are found mainly as livein servants, generally having no more than one-and-a-half days off a week.

SOCIAL INTEGRATION

Many migrants to Spain have settled in the large urban areas, which were also targets for internal migration between the 1950s and 1970s, rather than in the rural areas from which Spanish emigration took place. Moroccans engaged in agricultural labour are the only exception to this. The diversity of national identities in Spain reveals current international immigration flows to be continuations of the internal migrations of earlier decades, with similar social and cultural barriers to integration, as in the case for Catalonia.

There are two other factors that helped to create new and sustain old Spanish discriminatory attitudes and behaviour. The first is the continuation of high unemployment rates among the Spanish population, which are especially acute in the case of women. Over the last few decades unemployment has become one of the major concerns of the country. The second is the persistence of racist images generated in Spain and reinforced by racist experiences of other neighbouring European countries. These images are very much linked to an historically rooted anti-Islamic discourse. But there are also other racist discourses, for example those concerning Latin Americans, defined as inferiors by the colonial tradition which opposed native-born Spanish descends to overseas-born original Spanish.

The racist colonial experience and the anti-Semitic and anti-gypsy campaigns of previous centuries, resurface from time to time and set the scene for current expressions of racism. The legal and political regulation of irtmigration together with its social response will affect the demographic evolution of migrant populations and the possibilities for social integration (as opposed to segmented assimilation). However, we need to observe how this operates differently according to sex: whether women enjoy less benefits from the migration than men or not, and how this has influenced their status. We will concentrate here on the last issue: the status of migrant women.

THE STATUS OF MIGRANT WOMEN

Feminist research has widely questioned the traditional treatment of women within social structure and stratification studies. Such studies have generally used a gender bias that marginalized women within the analyses. Much work on social mobility, class identity and action continues to treat married women's class position, as derived from their husbands. Certainly, the gender dimensions of class have not been questioned until quite recently. The participation of women in the industrial labour market was seen as marginal, and their social position was seen to derive from gender rather than class. Against that conception, feminist approaches of the 1970s and 1980s, as that of Crompton, recovered the Weberian term of 'status' and gave to it a broader content than it had been given by previous authors.

According to this position, status includes an important gender dimension (Moore 1991). Sexes have been historically divided in two gender categories where being the male has a positive connotation and being the female implies subordination. So, traditionally attributed feminine cultural practices (such as ways of dressing and speaking) receive a low status. They are connected with the conceptual division of nature and culture, the latter being a male domain.

This is reflected in the sexual typification of occupations: first, the division between the domestic (private) and the public spheres in an industrial society produces the view that domestic activities are not regarded as 'work'; second, even in the 'public'sphere the incorporation of women within paid work reflects subordination and marginalization and the performance of 'appropriate' female jobs with lower social recognition and rewards. For international migrant women other aspects need to be added to gender and class in the configuration of their status: nationality and ethnicity. It has been argued that migrant women experience discrimination in host societies in terms of the articulation of gender, class and ethnic relations.

The ethnic dimension includes the phenotypic, cultural (religion, language, etc.) and national characteristics of identification. Gregorio (1995) presents a dual schema in which migrant women in receiving societies are inserted as one of the opposite pair in the four mentioned spheres:

Even in those cases where women may achieve legal status through naturalization, for example, and also adopt cultural elements of the host society, there may still be 'physical' and/ or 'cultural' difference which does not allow migrant women to reach a better position in the occupational and social scale. This relates to the intersection of racism and sexism. It is often the case that qualified migrant women are forced to take unskilled feminized jobs and are poorly paid. For feminist Marxist discourse, such women play the role of a sub-proletariat, which facilitates native women's participation in the 'male' labour market. This is the case for much of the theory on the dual labour market and the position of migrant workers within it. Other authors, like Fortes and BSrocz (1996), attribute this downgrading to a disadvantaged context of reception, in which migrants, independently of their human capital and class background fall into lower social positions.

Connected with the study of status in host societies is the parallel consideration of migrant women in sending areas and within their own ethnic group and/or family in the country of destination. We should not forget that international migration today is very much a phenomenon of transnationalism. Migrants develop a continuous and fluid relationship between origin (s) and destination (s) through their periodic travelling and communicating. The migration process may change, therefore, the status of (migrant) women in both contexts, that of both the sending and receiving countries. To characterize and measure gender inequality, the main factors may include the following:

1. Economic indicators of status, that is, possession of and control over resources, including knowledge, time, money and material goods;

2. Political indicators of status, such as the ability or power to make decisions: this includes the decision to migrate; to participate in the labour force; to control the distribution of income from work; the ability to exercise control over other people; and being the mobilising force behind the migration of family members;
3. Social indicators of status include prestige, respect or estean accorded to women (these indicators reflect differences in socio-cultural norms and attitudes between the country of origin and that of destination).

The above help us to analyse the roles and status of women as determinants and consequences of international migration. As INSTRAW (1994) suggests, the status condition is basic for understanding those processes, including sex-selectivity in the migratory decision within the family context. In suttmary, Lim (1995) identifies the following issues of study around the status question:

1. Implications of sex selectivity, that is, the distribution of migrants by sex, or by sex and other variables such as age, marital status or country of origin, for the political, economic and socio-cultural contexts in which the status of women is embedded.
2. Influence of gender relations on the motives and potential for the international migration of women.
3. Similarities or differences between the determinants of international migration for men and women and their causes.
4. Extent to which and manner in which laws and regulations controlling international migration are not gender-neutral.
5. Selective impact by sex of labour market dynamics in both countries of origin and destination.
6. Relative importance of international migration per se as a mechanism generating or restructuring gender asymmetries given the change in social environment that migration usually entails.
7. Relative vulnerability of migrant women, that is, whether being female and foreign in an alien environment leads to the 'double discrimination' and 'threefold or fourfold oppression' of migrant women.

Some examples of these will be given with regard to the Spanish context in the following section. Existing literature on inmigration in Spain has only recently concerned itself with the position of non-EU women. loe (1997) has dealt with it in a recent work, that summarizes factors contributing to the specific social trajectories of migrant women. This presents shaping factors in the country of origin, in relation to the migratory project, and in Spain, in terms of their sphere of influence, either social or individual.

The only problem is that the category 'women status' is specified in the table as the only factor of influence in the country of origin, whereas we consider the status of women in a broader sense affecting not only origin but also the migratory project and destination - Spain in our case - as well as personal dimension of migration. This 'feminine'status, as discussed previously, is socially constructed - mainly in terms of a subordinated position in gender relations which intersects with other elements such as class and ethnicity - but is individually adopted.

In terms of determinants of migration there is a tendency to think that women involved in solo (autonomous) migration, which is a very common form in Spain, are more independent than non-migrant women. However, the decision to migrate can be determined partially by family and friends, and is therefore not a total free choice. Women's migration may be part of a family strategy to survive or to maintain and increase their social position and improve their living conditions. In this sense, the study by Ribas (1996) on Filipinas in Catalonia refers to a high level of education among Filipino migrant women - higher than that of men - as a sign of high status. Nevertheless, poor employment conditions in the Philippines affect their status as the family is not able to reach or to maintain a certain level of consumption. So, migration is a response to a number of factors:

1. In the short term, the survival of the family.
2. In the medium term, education of children, brothers and sisters.

3. In the long term, the rise of status and social position. For the Filipino working class the aspiration is to become white-collar workers and achieve an 'occidental' way of life.

This pattern of behaviour is also to be found among women from the other three most numerous nationalities in Spain. Therefore, women tend to shift or postpone their own aspirations in favour of the other members of the family, or they are just limited within the family frame. Moreover, research shows that depending on the timing and circumstances of emigration (whether married or single, with or without children) we find differences in the migration project. The information collected from my own fieldwork study in Barcelona gives examples of this.

There is linkage of female migration, not so much to expectations of climbing a career ladder, but to the career and survival of others: children, parents, brothers and sisters, even husband. This is a special characteristic of those married Peruvian women and/or women with children. In these cases, they might experience a loss of professional and social status. This may not be seen as a central problem, since a first objective when migrating - as already mentioned - was related to the welfare of others. Nevertheless, even married women, with longer residence, begin questioning their actual situation and seek more autonomy and power:

> As women in Peru we are in the background without so much freedom as you have here in Spain. I alone had to confront my husband. Till now he does not accept it, I am fighting against that 'macho' mentality. They are used not to do anything at home, they say 'that's women's affair' but for earning a life we have both to work outside. So, women play both roles, outside and inside the house. They, on the contrary, only have to study and work. Moreover, if you get free as a woman you become a prostitute, if you go out to work, the same as here, in Peru I was told to be a whore. Here it is different, it is better for women.

Apart from family circumstances at origin and at destination, the receiving society has a big impact on the way women insert in the labour market and the society. As women may be able to regularize their work in domestic service, they may achieve a higher legal status than male migrants, who usually lack stable jobs. Since the establishment of work quotas in 1993 most permits have been granted in the domestic sector, where women are over represented. Furthermore, because those women tend to be migration pioneers, men are often protected and supported financially by their female relatives.

However, in terms of autonomy, authority and power in work and over resources, and therefore also in everyday life conditions, men experience less constraints and more freedom than women. This has been especially reported in the case of solo Dominican migrants in Madrid by Gregorio. However, migration may give women more space for autonomy and control over personal and economic resources than before departure. Indeed, this is especially the case with solo migration, when numbers from a particular origin are small. Moreover, the ethnic group or community contributes to the control of women.

For this reason, many women may avoid contact with male members of their ethnic group, as reported in the case of Moroccan women in Madrid. As loe (1997) also remarks, domestic service (the most important activity among women) may offer greater stability to migrants in so far as they are registered in the National Health System by their employers. However, there is also the stigma and lack of social recognition that they suffer in domestic work, as it is a sector without the same legal rights enjoyed by other workers (for example, there is no right to unemployment provisions), the quasi-servile relationship established sometimes with employers, or the social isolation from the long working hours, especially in the case of live-in maids.

The same authors have suggested that migrant women have been able to partially fulfil the migratory project (working in Spain, sending remittances to the families, escaping unbearable situations in the country of origin, and so forth) but in the medium and long term what is perceived today as an opportunity may become a constraint.I have suggested in relation to Peruvian migration that for women with a medium-high level of education there is a downward process of deskilling through the performance of 'manual tasks'. Required skills are related to social services such as caring and attending. Many women have a degree in teaching or nursing.

Serving in private houses is seen as a demeaning activity, as in Peru this is poorly regarded and poorly paid (work for indigenous women migrating from rural areas). But over time it has become regarded more positively and even accepted as one of the best forms of employment, especially when the return myth is sustained. That explains why some women prefer to stay for longer periods as live-in maids rather than live-out: the expenses are less and there is a guarantee of protection in the house.In this regard, there are four types of occupational trajectory singled out in the literature following loe (1997) which take place in the first period of migration:

1. Experiences of downward mobility: this has been described in the case of Filipinos and Peruvians.
2. Reproduction of occupational level with higher income: the case of some women who worked as domestic servants in the country of origin or in an intermediate country.
3. Relative promotion: from inactivity or occasional activity (in terms of formal labour market) to wage employment.
4. From studying to housework - change between different forms of economic 'inactivity'.

As in the case of Peruvians, continuing to live in as maids is canron among those who have not experienced a downward mobility and have not reunified their families. Live-out and per-hour cleaning jobs are the norm among those who have been in Barcelona for more than three to five years, who have experienced a relative downward mobility with migration and/or have brought their family members to Spain and wish to live with them. Other activities may be found more rarely, but especially among those who have formed close relations with Spanish people; these could save some money. Finally, catering is extremely rare among Peruvian women, with the exception of those working for a family business in a Peruvian restaurant.

Only in the case of Argentinians do we find a similar occupational schema to that of EU foreigners in Madrid. All other nationalities are strongly represented in low-status jobs, the Filipinos and Dominicans being those who experience a greater decline in occupational status. Not surprisingly, there is a correlation between greater feminization of migrant groups and the achievement of lower working status. This assumption fits with the schema presented above in reference to the manifold discrimination against migrant women because of unequal gender, class and ethnic relations.

One controversial issue remains on the correlation between occupational status and gender. One opinion is expressed by Ramirez, who argues that Moroccan women in Spain gain autonomy and power within the family because their new role generates resources in contrast with their very poor labour market position in their country of origin. More autonomy and power are signs of a better female position. However, there is not an absolute break with the traditional female roles assigned by the members of the country of origin. Gregorio on the other hand, in her analysis of Dominican migration to Madrid, describes three stages for women's migration, leading to a not-sooptimistic evaluation of the migratory experience:

1. The flow of solo'women migrants has its origin in the reproduction of gender inequalities which characterise their society of origin.
2. Once in Madrid they reproduce their gender roles.
3. Finally, not every change is experienced as positive. Their labour incorporation in Spain and the frame of social relations are denigrating from the women's view. The labour niche for them is the domestic service, whereas social relations with native Spainish people involve discrimination and rejection.

Replying to this, Gallardo (1995) argued that if the migratory experience was so disappointing for women, they would tend to return home more frequently than is the case for Dominican migrants. From my point of view, since the supposed rise in gender status is accompanied by a decline in the class-ethnic status at destination but not in the country of origin, migrant workers prefer to stay and work for better positioning in the labour market, for themselves and their relatives and second generation. This sustains the idea of migratory paradise for those remaining in the country of origin.

In summary, migration for women may involve a gain or a loss of status depending on a number of factors explored earlier. Migration can be understood as a gain in terms of gender because it allows women (especially solo migrants) to improve their role within the family and community through the prestige gained by moving to the First World and earning money and knowledge. They also become important to enable the migration of others. Against this, the opinion that emigrating women practice prostitution abroad is still maintained in the country of origin and also at destination, not only for Dominicans, as has generally been believed, but also for others like Peruvians, damaging the social position of female migrant workers.

The gain is also relatively diminished when we concentrate on the real power and control over resources achieved by women. For example Amanda, a 28-year-old Peruvian, who was working as a domestic servant in Barcelona for two years returned to Peru in 1994 and gave all her savings to her son's father in order to invest in a new business. However, he spent all the money improperly and had relations with other women while she was still there. So, she ended with no money and no steady partner any more, since she was not willing to share him with the others. Finally, she decided to go back to Spain for the second time.

The loss of status is very much connected with the country of destination, above all for those experiencing downward occupational mobility and with very few opportunities for leaving domestic service. The latter becomes a labour market niche for female migrants in Spain, labour marginality leads to social marginalization as foreigners remain outside national culture and domains of authority and power.

Finally, migration is evaluated by women as positive due to a gain in welfare provision, social organization and educational opportunities: 'I like the order here, the cleanliness, the people who are polite, I like that very much' (Violeta, Peruvian, 22 years old, less than a year in Barcelona). 'The buildings, streets, highways, the two-floor buses and the many cars, that I find interesting, the technology moving forward so quickly, and the people, their politeness' (Irene, Peruvian, 46 years old, two years in Barcelona). 'I like the way of life here, it is more advanced in computer engineering and all those things my boyfriend wants to further study' (Dina, Peruvian, 27 years old, three years in Barcelona).

In this chapter it has been argued, firstly, that Spanish irtmigration policies and administrative measures are shaping the composition and character of non-EU flows in terms of sex and nationality and labour orientation. Other aspects of the society of origin and that of destination should be added to the analysis in order to improve understanding of processes such as the feminization of those movements and the centrality of the domestic service market for migrant workers.

Concentrating on migrant women, the chapter discussed the existing literature and research about the position of these female workers from social and occupational perspective. We started from a theoretical frame, which explains discrimination against migrant workers in complex societies in terms of the articulation of gender, class and ethnic relations. Existing literature and research about migration is Spain are still limited, but this chapter demonstrated the range of perspectives necessary for analysing the question of women's status. Depending on the aspect referred to and the place and time of analysis we may find a gain or a loss of position for migrant women.

Another question is how women themselves experience these processes. In some extreme cases they may not be able to cope with this new situation and become mentally and physically sick. Returning home, however, may still be very difficult, as they may not have achieved the objectives assigned (by them or for them) prior to departure. A less extreme description of how migrant women react against their status devaluation is presented by Gregorio from a psychological view. MDre generally, after a period of adaptation to the new requirements - as migrant, as woman, as worker, as belonging to an ethnic group and/or nationality - women tend to feel more adjusted to the new society.

The length of time needed to adjust to the new situation and what is lost and gained in the process is something missing from existing work, since non-EU female migration to Spain is quite new. Future research will have to deal with these questions if a better knowledge of the situation of migrant women (who make up a significant percentage of migrant workers in Spain) is to be achieved. Until now, most attention has been paid to the situation of workers, whereas female dependants such as spouses, mothers, female children and girls were missing, probably due to their low numbers.

Finally, an additional area for research to focus on must be a study of the implications of migrant women's status decline or rise within (and for) the ethnic migrant group, in the society of destination, and in the society of origin. For feminist and development research, this issue is of great importance. It has to be placed very much aside from controversies on cultural diversity, which may justify the maintenance of gender and ethnic inequalities. Human migrations have occurred throughout history, bringing into play new/modified roles for people.

8

Globalization in Australian International Migration

Australian international migration has undergone a massive transformation in the last decade, in part as a result of globalization. Although Australia has long been a country of immigration with a relatively high proportion of its residents foreign-born, the nature of international migration shaping the country has undergone profound change in the era of globalization. This chapter outlines some of the major dimensions of this change in international migration. The links between globalization and migration are complex and two-way but there can be no doubt that processes which have accelerated international exchanges of goods, information, ideas, trade and finance and led to an internationalization of labour markets have been associated with shifts in Australian migration.

This change has had a number of components which have increased the complexity of the international migration influencing Australia. The changes examined include the increasing significance of skill-related migration compared with other forms, increasing non-permanent migration, the increasing nexus between temporary and permanent migration, the increasing movement of Australians out of the country, the significance of student migration and the increasing significance of migration in influencing Australia's relationship with its Asia-Pacific neighbours. These changes have profound implications for Australia's contemporary and future demography.

Australian international migration has undergone a major transformation since the early 1990s. This has been largely a result of globalization and a response to it. While globalization has broken down barriers to, and accelerated exchanges of, goods, ideas, trade, finance and information, the effect on mobility of people has been more complex. Certainly levels of movement have increased and become more diverse, but nation-states maintain, and in some cases have strengthened, barriers to population movement, especially of particular groups.

Australia was already one of the world's major immigration countries before the onset of globalization but it is the argument of this chapter that globalization has produced a paradigmatic shift not only in the scale of international migration influencing Australia but in its nature, composition and effects. Among these shifts none is more striking than the move away from the dictum which dominated postwar migration policy, that Australia eschewed temporary-worker migration in favour of permanent settlement, toward a complex array of visa categories that embraces a range of lengths of stay in, and commitment to, Australia. Another element has been an increasing focus on skill in selection of migrants.

Moreover, while Australia has long been a significant country of emigration as well as immigration, the emigration of Australians has reached unprecedented levels. In addition there has been an increasing role played in Australia's international migration by the Australian cities most linked into the global economic system, especially Sydney. Finally migration is playing an increasing role in influencing Australia's relationship with its Asia-Pacific neighbours. Developments in each of these elements are discussed here.

MIGRATION AND GLOBALIZATION

International migration has increased in scale and complexity as both a causal factor of globalization and an effect of it. For half of the postwar era, global international migration has been dominated by movement from Europe to the 'traditional' migration countries of Australia, Canada, the

United States and New Zealand. However, almost all nations of the world are now influenced significantly by migration as a significant destination, origin or both. Australia continues to be an important global player in migration: the United Nations ranks it as having the eleventh-largest stock of overseas-born persons and with almost a quarter of its population being foreign-born, eleventh among countries in the proportion made up by immigrants.

Whereas the dominant global flow in the early postwar decades was from Europe to the 'traditional' migration countries it now is from less developed to more developed nations, the 'South-North' movement. In 2005, a third of all international migrants moved from less developed to more developed countries and more than half of net population growth in more developed countries has been due to immigration from less developed countries. The increased South-North mobility has taken a distinctive bifurcated form. First, barriers have been greatly reduced to the flow of highly skilled people between nations; this has facilitated the permanent and temporary movement of skilled and wealthy persons, especially that from South to North countries. Second, barriers have been increasingly created to the flows of people who do not have high levels of education or wealth. Hence, while there is a flow of such people in the family and refugee-humanitarian components of migration from South to North countries, the flow is greatly constrained.

(1) The expansion of South-North migration has re-ignited debates about brain drain with the increased flow of skilled migrants from less developed to more developed economies. (2) More recently, while there has been recognition of the negative effects of brain drain, it has been shown that emigration can have positive developmental implications for origin nations. These effects are due to remittance flows. (3) from expatriate communities, social and economic links developed by migrants between origin and destination countries, and return migration. However, the developmental implications of South-North migration are far from simple and are not well understood.

Other important developments in global migration include the increasing flows between non-OECD nations. These are not predominantly skilled migrants but particularly involve an increased flow of temporary contract workers, and refugees are also significant, especially in Africa. In addition, there has been an expansion in the level of undocumented migration and of trafficking, especially of women and children. This undocumented migration (as well as the legal movement) is greatly facilitated by the massive growth of the global immigration industry.

This involves a complex web of migration agents, travel providers, immigration officials, police, recruiters, and job placement agencies that facilitate international movement. Part of this industry is illegal and in some areas has been penetrated by large criminal syndicates such as the Mafia, Yakuza (Japan) and Chinese 'snakeheads'. It is now one of the most profitable and pervasive forms of international crime. Another distinctive feature of the 'new' migration is that there are almost as many women who move as men.

The Global Commission on International Migration (2005:6) have argued that increased international migration is being driven by a widening in the gap between nation-states with respect to the '3Ds': Development, Demography and Democracy. As gradients along these dimensions steepen there is a corresponding increase in the flow of people. However, the process is complex: some of the elements driving the new international migration are summarized here.

First, there is a steepening of the demographic gradients between more developed countries where low fertility and ageing have contributed to labour shortages, while in less developed nations workforces are still growing and labour surpluses are large despite considerable fertility reduction. Second, there are widening gaps in economic well-being between less developed and more developed nations. Third, there is globalization of media, which increases people's information about other places. Fourth, there is universalization of education in most countries. Fifth, there is a reduction of time and travel costs between countries. Sixth, there are activities of transnational organizations, especially companies with operations in many nations. Seventh, there is labour-market segmentation: people in higher-income countries eschew low-status, low-income jobs which open up niches for migrants. Eighth, there is the proliferation of the global migration industry. Ninth, there is the increased involvement of national governments in origin countries realizing the benefits that can accrue through migration.

Last, there is the massive growth of social networks which facilitate the migration of family and friends by providing information about migration, and help new migrants once they arrive at destinations. All this has meant that international migration has become within the calculus of choice of a major part of the world's population when they consider their life chances. The proliferation of migration networks and the migration industry have meant that international movement is being brought within reach of more and more of the world's population.

Along with the major shift in global international migration scale, patterns and diversity there has also been an associated important change in migration theory beginning with the work of Basch, Schiller and Blanc who argue that conventional theory did not adequately capture the new reality in which migrants identify and commit to more than one nation-state. Hence, transnational theory developed, focusing more on the nature and implications of the links maintained by movers between origin and destination, rather than on just the destination.

These changes have invigorated migration research and considerably informed our understanding of migration and its effects. As Boyle points out, 'It is the high intensity of exchanges and the new modes of contact that makes this an exciting new research arena'. Nevertheless there has been a tendency to dichotomize permanent settlement and temporary migration as though they are two quite separate and unrelated processes. King has noted however, in the European context, that as new mobility strategies are deployed to achieve economic and, importantly, non-economic objectives ... the old dichotomies of migration study internal versus international, forced versus voluntary, temporary versus permanent, legal versus illegal-blur as both the motivations and modalities become much more diverse.

Yet studies of mobility which directly investigate the overlapping of these dichotomies remain limited. Dunn has argued forcefully that the adoption of a transnationalism paradigm in migration study facilitates a more holistic way of understanding the complexity of mobility, its causes and effects. A criticism of Australian migration research and policy in the past is that it may have been too inward-looking and not taken sufficient cognizance of relevant developments in countries with which Australia has an important migration connection.

The shift in Australia's international migration regime must be seen in the context of a massive shift in global international population movement levels and patterns, and the processes shaping them. We will now turn to some of the major shifts which have occurred in Australian international migration, partly at least due to globalization.

INCREASED TEMPORARY MIGRATION

Perhaps the greatest change which has occurred in Australian immigration in the last decade is that whereas in the first five postwar decades Australia emphatically eschewed acceptance of temporary workers in favour of an overwhelming emphasis on settlement migration, there has been a reversal with a number of new visa categories designed to attract temporary residents to work in Australia. As a result there has been an exponential increase in non-permanent migration to Australia so that while in 2004-2005 there were 123,424 incoming permanent settlers to Australia, a total of 371,374 non-visitor foreigners were granted temporary residence in Australia in that year (DIMIA 2006).

On 30 June 2005 there were 599,629 people in Australia on a temporary basis (excluding New Zealanders), over half of whom had the right to work. Although there has been a long history of significant non-permanent flows to Australia the contemporary flow is quite different in scale, in the involvement of large numbers of temporary residents with the right to work, and in a plethora of new kinds of temporary migration to Australia. However, the bulk of Australian research knowledge of immigration remains largely focused on permanent settlement.

The link between globalization and increased temporary migration is a close one. The internationalization of labour markets, the development of multinational companies which transfer their workforce between nations, the cheapening of international travel, and the information and communication technology revolution allowing migrants to maintain close and regular contact with their homeland, have all facilitated the development of temporary migration.

Australia has become one of the world's five pre-eminent destinations of foreign students, along with US, UK, Germany and France. The massive increase in international migration of students is one of the defining elements of the new international migration and is strongly associated with globalization and the internationalization of labour markets. On 30 June 2006 there were 208,038 people on student visas in Australia and in the year 2005-06, 190,674 visas were issued to overseas students - both record levels.

Of the largest six countries of origin, five are Asian: China (15 per cent), Korea and India (9 per cent each), Japan (8 per cent) and Malaysia (5 per cent). Globally the number of foreign students in tertiary education outside of their own country doubled between 1990 and 2000 and increased by another third between 2000 and 2003. Australia, like other OECD nations (and increasingly more-developed Asian nations) has recognized the benefits of foreign students beyond those associated with developing better international links and knowledge transfer. First, they are a significant source of foreign exchange.

It is estimated that foreign students paid US$30 billion to their destination countries, and in Australia international education generated export earnings of A$10.8 billion in 2006.

Second, foreign students are increasingly being seen by countries like Australia as the 'raw material to train some of the human capital they need'. They are the next generation of skilled migrants who differ from the previous generation in that they are what Simmons (1999) describes as 'designer migrants' in that they have been specifically 'designed' by the destination country to meet its skilled human resource needs.

A second important group of temporary migrants consists of Working Holiday Makers (WHM). WHMs are foreign nationals aged 18-30 from selected, mainly European, developed countries with which Australia has a reciprocal arrangement. They can work on a temporary or casual basis as long as they do not work for a single employer for more than three months and stay in Australia for up to 12 months or in some cases a little longer. Their numbers have increased dramatically and reached 85,200 in 2001-02 and 111,376 in 2004-05, more than doubling in the last decade.

Kinnaird reports that while the economic effect nationally of WHM migration is limited, it has important effects in specific industries in specific areas. These migrants have become significant in the seasonal harvesting and tourism industries. Harding and Webster estimate that WHMs in 2002 took up the equivalent of 41,000 full-time jobs, but that 49,000 full-time jobs are created by their expenditure. One of the most important developments in Australian immigration policy was the introduction in 1996 of Skilled Temporary Visas which allow businesses to bring skilled workers to Australia for periods of up to four years. There was an immediate uptake of this visa which includes five main types:

Business visitors: these come for short periods and are in the 'short-term' arrival category. They numbered 339,424 in 2004-05, an increase of 13.6 per cent over the previous year. Temporary business residents: these come for longer periods and are best known as the '457' category. They numbered 49,855 in 2004-05, an increase of 24 per cent over the previous year. Independent executives: these enter Australia for the purpose of establishing, or buying into a business and managing that business. This category ceased in 2003 but there were still 5,200 present in 2005.

Medical practitioners: these are qualified general and specialist medical practitioners where there is a demonstrated need for employing practitioners from overseas. In 2004-05 there were 3,074 visas granted to doctors, an increase of 27 per cent over the previous year. Educational: this visa is for qualified people to join educational and research organizations to fill academic teaching and research positions that cannot be filled from within the Australian labour market. This has largely been replaced by the 457 visa.

While the permanent settlement program is highly planned and controlled by the Australian federal government the business visitor program is largely market-driven. There are minimum skill and salary levels for 457s and they are restricted to the top four Australian Standard Classification of Occupation (ASCO) levels: managers, professionals, associate professionals and skilled trades. This category of visa allows employers to recruit skilled migrants much more quickly than through the settlement program and represents an adjustment to the globalization of many skilled labour markets. In such markets workers move readily between countries on company transfer or as they seek promotion and career development.

There has been some concern in Australia that employers may misuse the program to replace Australian workers with lower-paid, non-unionized workers with poorer conditions than their Australian counterparts. Moreover others are concerned that it is used as a substitute for training Australian workers. Nevertheless it has been very successful in meeting skill shortages in a number of areas. While in Australia the focus of immigration attention remains predominantly on permanent settlement, there is an increasing realization that temporary migration is of significance when considering the effect of migration on Australia's economy and society.

Nevertheless temporary migration and transnationalism are still predominantly dealt with quite separately from permanent-settlement migration although there is considerable overlap not only in Australia but globally. The 'conventional immigrant' to Australia is a person who has applied for, and obtained, a settler visa from an overseas-based Australian embassy or consulate and has subsequently travelled to Australia. However, in 2004-05 some 32.9 per cent of the Migration Program was 'onshore' in that they were already in Australia with temporary residence visas, and successfully applied for and obtained permanent residency.

The number of such migrants has increased substantially over the last decade, reaching a record of 40,682 in 2004-05. But little is known about the process whereby temporary residents decide to apply for permanent residence, the extent to which temporary residence is perceived from the outset by migrants as a preliminary stage moving toward permanent settlement, and the extent to which they make the decision after arrival in Australia. The increasing significance of temporary residents becoming permanent residents has not been confined to Australia. Indeed in each of the traditional migration countries onshore settlers now make up a significant proportion of 'settlers'.

In the United States in 2004, 61.7 per cent of persons granted permanent residences were already in the country under another visa category; in New Zealand in 2005 the proportion was 64 per cent while in Canada in 2004 it was 15 per cent. Hence, the phenomenon is widespread but the focus in migration research remains on new arrivals, and the literature on the transition from temporary to permanent migration is limited. There has been useful work on how the overlap between temporary and permanent migration can be accommodated in population projections and estimates in Australia. There also has been examination of the option exercised by several nations in the last decade of granting asylum seekers 'temporary protection' visas instead of full refugee status and on their efforts to become permanent settlers.

One group of temporary migrants who seek permanent settlement consists of those becoming the spouses of citizens of the destination country, as Khoo (2001) has shown in Australia. The most extensive work on temporary migrants becoming permanent has been on the guestworkers arriving in Western Europe in the 1960s and 1970s. The latter experience has strongly influenced attitudes toward guestworker migration over subsequent decades, although its relevance to a dramatically changed global, political, economic, social and demographic context is limited. Links between temporary and permanent migration have been examined in the world's largest contemporary flow from Mexico to the United States, but there have been very few attempts to draw out generalizations regarding the transition from temporary to permanent migration, and fewer still which systematically relate this to migration theory.

Another dimension of the permanent-temporary interface in Australian migration has been in the refugee-humanitarian-asylum seeker area. Over the postwar period Australia has settled more refugees per 1,000 residents than any country except Canada, but most of these were 'offshore' settlers accepted from refugee camps based in foreign countries. Australia has a long established offshore humanitarian migration program which includes three elements.

The Refugee Program provides protection for people outside their country fleeing persecution. Special Humanitarian Programs (SHP) comprise the In-country Special Humanitarian Program for people suffering persecution within their own country, and the Global Special Humanitarian Program for people Who have left their country because of significant discrimination amounting to a gross violation of human rights. The Special Assistance Category (SAC) embraces groups determined by the Minister for Immigration and Multicultural Affairs to be of special concern to Australia and in real need, but which do not fit within traditional humanitarian categories. This program also assists those internally and externally displaced people who have close family links in Australia.

However, in recent years Australia has been forced to consider an 'onshore component' in this program with the increased numbers of asylum seekers arriving in the country, which may be associated with globalization processes. The number of unauthorized arrivals in the country, the bulk of who apply for asylum, increased around the turn of the century but was less than 7,000 a year at its peak. The unauthorized arrivals include both those coming by air without documentation and the 'boat people'.

As part of their controversial package of measures for asylum seekers the government introduced the Temporary Protection Visa (TPV). This was introduced in October 1999 and is granted to most of the asylum seekers who enter Australia unlawfully and who are assessed as meeting the requirements for refugee status. This is in contrast to those refugees who settle in Australia under the three traditional 'offshore' categories, and the substantial differences between the two groups in rights and access to services are documented.

The government maintains that this differentiation acts as a deterrent to undocumented immigrant arrivals and encourages refugees to stay in their country of first asylum, while critics argue that the creation of two classes of refugees is unfair and not within the spirit of the 1950 Convention. Nevertheless, the majority of asylum seekers on Temporary Protection Visas have been granted permanent entry visas following expiry of their TPV following agitation and pressure from advocates and political lobbying. The principal effect of globalization on movement to Australia has been not so much a change in the scale of immigration to Australia but in the nature of that movement.

Net immigration levels to the nation have varied between 25,321 in 1975-76 and 149,017 in 1969-70 but generally have been around 100,000. The biggest change in numbers has occurred in non-permanent in-movement, which shows that over the last two decades permanent arrivals increased by 58.5 percent while long-term immigration and short-term movement of visitors (as opposed to Australian residents) increased by 621.9 and 489.4 per cent respectively. These shifts in the balance between permanent and temporary immigration, together with a more general transformation in the global context of international migration, have greatly reduced the contemporary relevance of much existing research on Australian international migration. This presents a substantial challenge to researchers and policy makers alike.

AN INCREASING FOCUS ON SKILLS IN MIGRATION

One element of the new global context has been that contemporary 'theories of economic growth stress the importance of human capital to knowledge based economies' so countries increasingly are changing their goals 'from maximising stocks of gold and silver to maximising the brain power within their borders'. As a result one of the defining features of the new global migration as opposed to earlier eras of massive international population movement, such as that from Europe to North and South America and Oceania before World War I, has been the 'global quest for talent'.

Increased international mobility of highly skilled workers is an integral feature of contemporary globalization processes; the number of countries competing for the most innovative and skilled workers has increased, and labour markets for these types of workers have become increasingly internationalized and competitive.

In Australia, immigration policy has adapted quickly and forcefully to this dynamic global context. Australian immigration for settlement has been more highly controlled than in most other nations. Settlement occurs through one of the four main strands, skill, family, humanitarian and special eligibility; and annual targets and caps are set by government. A key element is the Points Assessment Test on which applicants can qualify for immigration through most 'skill', and some 'family', categories. Hence, there is a highly developed structure through which immigration for settlement to Australia is controlled.

Over recent times there has been greater government intervention to shape the content of the intake of immigrants so that it can better contribute to national development goals by increasing productivity through enhancing the national pool of skilled people. This has seen greater emphasis on skills in migrant selection, and in the development of business migration programs involved to attract entrepreneurs with substantial sums to invest in the destination country. Australia and Canada have micro-managed the qualifications of their migrant intake since the 1970s with the introduction of points assessment schemes. In Australia there has been a shift in selection toward skills-business migration.

In 1995-96, 24,100 skill visas were granted compared with 97,340 in 2005-06, while family migration fell from 57.4 per cent of the total immigration intake in 1995-96 to 28.8 per cent in 2005-06. However, the permanent settlement data give only a partial picture of the increased focus on skill in Australian immigration. As indicated in the previous section there has been a massive increase in temporary worker migration. The introduction of the 457 visa following a government inquiry in 1995 was a direct response to changing global labour markets and globalization processes.

The skill profile of the temporary migrants is even higher than that of permanent settlers. One study of 457-visa entrants compared their occupational profile with that of permanent migrants in the skill stream and found a greater concentration of 457s in the high skill categories. Hence, in response to globalization and the increased significance of the knowledge economy, there has been a massive change in the selection of immigrants wishing to come to Australia with a much greater focus placed on skill than ever before.

The increasing focus on skilled migrants not only in Australia and other OECD countries but also in fast-developing Asian economies in countries like Singapore has produced a significant ramping-up of international competition for skilled migrants. This has raised a number of issues in destination countries about the ability of the 'skilled' migrants recruited to meet their labour-market needs. It is clear that countries are finding it increasingly difficult to attract migrants with the combination of English language communication skills and expert skills and experience relevant to the local needs. Hence there is increasing concern with 'brain waste' as 'skilled' migrants struggle to find professional employment, not only in Australia but also in Canada and New Zealand.

EMIGRATION AND THE AUSTRALIAN DIASPORA

The effects of globalization in producing an increase in the scale and diversity of mobility between nations have been felt not only in movement into Australia but also with respect to emigration out of the country. This is evident, which is the companion but compares permanent, long-term and short-term movement out of Australia in 1982-83 and 2005-06. Here again the fastest growth has been in the long-term and short-term movement out of the country.

Of course these data partly reflect an increasing pattern of circularity in population movement between countries which is facilitated by relatively cheap and faster international travel, internationalization of business activity, globalization of labour markets and spread of information. The increasing circularity has other important implications such as to what extent it facilitates more people having multiple identities and commitments to more than a single nation-state. Australia in 2002 joined the increasing number of nations that allow dual nationality, but little is known about the extent to which globalization and mobility are reshaping patterns of national identity.

However, it will be noticed that whereas permanent immigration increased by 58.5 per cent over the period, permanent emigration increased by 103.2 per cent. There certainly can be no doubt that there has been an increase in the propensity for Australians to live and work on a long-term, or permanent, basis in other countries. There has been an increase in the ratio of permanent departures to permanent arrivals over recent years. While Australia has long been a significant country of emigration out-movement has increased with globalization.

The differentiation between permanent and long-term movement is on the basis of the stated intentions of persons leaving Australia, and intentions often are not borne out by reality. Osborne found that of people indicating that they had left Australia permanently in 1998-99 only 59 per cent by 2003 could be considered to have left Australia permanently. Of course a proportion of those who indicated that they were leaving on a 'long-term' basis will have eventually decided to stay away permanently as well. In considering this out-movement it is important to distinguish between that of the Australia-born and people who have come from other nations with respect to permanent emigration. It is apparent that while emigration of both groups has increased it is especially noticeable among the Australia-born.

In fact, 2001-02 was the first year that Australia-born permanent departures outnumbered former settlers leaving the nation. Each year since 1998-99 a new record number of Australia-born emigrants left the nation. In 2005-06 they numbered over 30,000 for the first time: two-and-a-half times the average for the 1990s (12,145) and almost four times the average of the 1980s (8,875). Long-term departures show similar patterns and have reached unprecedented levels in recent years.

Settler loss has been an important feature of the postwar Australian migration scene: more than a fifth of all postwar settlers subsequently emigrated from Australia, most of them returning to their home nation. There has been concern about this settler loss among policy makers but it has a number of components including a group of migrants who never intended to settle permanently in Australia, as well as people who are influenced by family changes, and those not able to adjust to life in Australia. In recent years it also includes many young people who have come to Australia as small children, grown up in Australia and travelled out of Australia as young adults.

Some, such as those from Greece and Italy, have returned to their country of birth, while others have been part of the exodus of young Australians to the UK and USA. The pattern of settler loss, while it varies between birthplace groups (e.g. it is high among New Zealanders but low among Vietnamese), has remained a consistent feature of postwar migration in Australia, and the fluctuations in its numbers are very much related to earlier levels of immigration. The impact of globalization here is that with the increase in the skill profile in immigration we can expect an increase in settler loss since skilled migrants have a greater chance of remigrating than family migrants.

The increased outflow of the Australia-born is selective of the young and well educated and tends to include two overlapping forms of movement, both of which have been strongly influenced by globalization. First, there is an increasing propensity for young Australians to engage in a type of 'rite of passage', temporary, but long-term, migration of a working-holiday type. While this phenomenon has a long history there has been a massive increase in its incidence as a result of globalization with the improved transport, higher level of education and knowledge of countries outside of Australia, higher proportions with family links in Europe and internationalization of labour markets.

There are also strong cumulative causation elements as the practice becomes embedded as customary behaviour among young Australians. The second main movement involves young Australians moving overseas as part of their career development. Whereas in earlier generations this type of movement was usually within Australian states or at most interstate, it is now often international. It has been encouraged by a number of developments such as the fact that many highly skilled regional and national labour markets have been usurped by labour markets which overlap international boundaries, the internationalization of capital, the exponential development of exchanges of all types through the development of communications, the reduction in real time and money costs of travel and the development of multinational corporations.

Increased levels of emigration have raised the spectre of brain drain in Australia, although Birrell et al. (2006) point out correctly that immigration of skilled persons substantially outweighs emigration. Moreover it has been argued that there are also positive developments which can occur in Australia because of emigration. First, most of the movement is not permanent in that many expatriate workers eventually return to Australia. Second, many emigrants are remitting substantial sums of foreign exchange to Australia-based families, investments and bank accounts.

Third, the extension of the skills and experience of the Australian emigrants can be harnessed to benefit Australia. Fourth, the links which are established between Australians and Australian companies and their overseas counterparts and markets assist in embedding Australia's economy internationally. Fifth, it may be creating opportunities for Australian companies to supply goods and services to other countries because the Australian expatriate workers will be most familiar with Australian-based suppliers.

Hugo, Rudd and Harris argued that Australia would benefit from developing a diaspora policy. The issue is not so much whether Australia is experiencing a 'brain drain' or a 'brain gain'; it needs to be recognized that as a small and peripheral (in the global economy) nation, Australia has a lot to gain from experiencing 'Brain Circulation' in which Australian skilled people go overseas and in which Australia receives skilled people from other countries. Hence Australia needs an international migration policy which embraces not only immigration but also emigration and especially circulation. This policy can be characterized as 'the four Rs': recruitment, retention, return, re-engagement.

Recruitment

Australia needs to build on its excellent and sustained record of recruiting highly skilled persons. There needs to be a public debate about the impact of this on less developed nations, and also associated policies considered which recompense the origin areas but also facilitate the immigrants having maximum developmental benefits on their home country.

Retention

Australia must ensure that there are opportunities for the small number among the 'brightest and the best' Australians to work productively and effectively in Australia so that they do not feel that it is absolutely essential for them to leave the country permanently to achieve their potential.

Return

We must realize that there is much to gain from young Australians leaving Australia and acquiring experience, knowledge and connections in foreign nations. However, if a substantial proportion can return, the country can gain a double dividend, not just retaining their talents but having those talents enhanced by the period away.

Re-engagement

It is apparent that many Australians resident overseas on a permanent or long-term basis still feel a strong sense of belonging to Australia and a deep concern for its well-being. There does appear to be a number of ways in which the expatriate community can be incorporated more into Australia. On a cultural level, it is important that expatriates who still consider themselves Australian are included more in the mainstream of Australian life. On an economic level, there are a myriad of ways in which the expertise, experience and contacts of the diaspora can be harnessed to benefit Australia in a rapidly globalizing economic, social and political context.

Accordingly, part of the new migration is undoubtedly the whole issue of emigration and diaspora. There are no simple blue-prints to follow to develop an effective policy in this area. There are many examples of diaspora-related programs, reverse brain-drain programs and expatriate intellectual networks, but a great deal of innovatory thinking will need to go into the development of such a policy for Australia if it is to be effective.

MIGRATION AND GLOBAL CITIES

One of the significant elements in globalization has been the emergence of 'world' or 'global' cities. These cities are the major links between nation-states and the outside world and contain the financial, cultural, societal, managerial, technological and producer activities which link nation-states to a globalizing world economy. One of the defining features of global cities is that a high and increasing proportion of their residents who are immigrants play important roles in both the higher-level and unregulated lower-level service jobs in those cities.

Hugo (forthcoming) has demonstrated that Sydney is a quintessential 'gateway' city linking Australia to global economy and culture, and that international migration plays a complex and significant role. Sydney is Australia's main international air and communications gateway, the primary location of transnational company command and control functions and associated producer services, the centre for many financial transactions and the location of more company headquarters than any other centre. International migration has been important in Sydney's growing global function.

The proportion of Sydney's population who were overseas-born increased from 23.8 per cent in 1991 to 33.4 per cent in 2001. Moreover, it is the pre-eminent destination of the growing temporary migration to Australia. Khoo, McDonald and Hugo show that 51 per cent of all 457 Temporary Business Migrants coming to Australia in 2001-03 went to Sydney. Hugo (forthcoming) also demonstrates that Sydney functions as an 'escalator region' whereby it attracts young immigrants from the rest of Australia who subsequently move to higher order global cities like London and New York.

CHANGING ENGAGEMENT WITH THE ASIA-PACIFIC ON MIGRATION ISSUES

As is the case in most important destination countries, Australian immigration policy is overwhelmingly formulated in terms of national interest, which in the past has involved little or no consideration of the impact of migration on origin nations. It has a long history of bilateral and multilateral engagement on immigration issues but until recently this has largely been with other OECD nations. Australia is a prominent player in SOPEMI, the OECD Continuum Reporting System on Migration, and in April 2003 Australia renewed its joint declaration with the European Union in a document entitled 'An Agenda for Co-operation'.

Until recently, engagement with the Asian region has been minimal despite the fact that Asian and Pacific countries have become important origins of migration to Australia and destinations for emigrants in the last quarter century. The situation is changing partly because of the increasing global discussion on the migration-development nexus, but also because it increasingly can be seen as being within Australia's national interest to change it. The 9/11 attacks caused a rethinking of security considerations in Australia as was the case elsewhere in the world.

This involved a re-evaluation of the nation's relationship with neighbouring countries and the realization that improving the security, stability and well-being of those nations is fundamental to Australia's future security. This has resulted in increased investment, capacity building and strategic interest in those countries by the Australian government. Part of this engagement has been increased Australian involvement in enhancing the capacity of migration structures and bureaucracy in some Asia-Pacific nations and in Australian engagement in a number of regional migration forums and activities. For example, Australia has been an important participation in a number of APEC activities to facilitate the travel within the region of executives, managers and specialists.

The increasing scale and significance of people-smuggling, trafficking and undocumented migration in the Asian region has seen a number of bilateral and multilateral initiatives of co-operation to combat such activity. Among the most inclusive and significant have been the meetings jointly convened by the Foreign Ministers of Indonesia and Australia in Bali on 26-28 February 2002 and 28-30 April 2003 as the Ministerial Conferences on People Smuggling, Trafficking in Persons and Related Transnational Crime.

This has come to be referred to as the 'Bali Process', which is intended to complement and strengthen bilateral and regional co-operation in this area. The initial meeting involved almost all countries of the region as well as a number of observer countries and organizations reflecting the increasing significance of this issue in the region as well as globally. Agreement was reached about the nature and importance of the problem, the principles for combating it, and the necessity of bilateral and multilateral co-operation to combat it.

Building on the Bali initiative, Australia greatly increased activity to use the institutional and technological expertise developed over a long period to improve the capacity of neighbouring countries to manage migration. While this is partly motivated by Australian security considerations, it reflects a new awareness that management of migration requires regional co-operation. Australian development assistance funds are being used for capacity building in immigration, border security, and customs in several nations in the region, especially Papua New Guinea, Fiji, Cambodia, Indonesia and Timor Leste. There has been a considerable expansion of the International Co-operation branch of the Department of Immigration and Citizenship which was established in 1999.

There has been knowledge transfer of information technology skills, document fraud detection, management and operational skills, information exchange and most importantly the development of a professional cadre of immigration officials who can operationalize effective migration management policies. While a significant motive is undoubtedly Australia's security concerns following 9/11, co-operation in capacity building in migration has certainly improved. What was largely an ad hoc process of co-operation and capacity building before the Bali Process has risen to a new level.

The Intergovernmental Asia-Pacific Consultations on Refugees, Displaced Persons and Migrants (APC) was set up at the end of 1996 following a conference in Canberra, and involved all Asian countries from Afghanistan east to the Pacific. It is largely a consultative forum rather than one which takes specific actions as is the case with the Bali Process. One plenary meeting and one or two additional subregional or expert conferences are organized each year.

The chair or co-ordinator of the APC rotates annually. While its achievements have been quite limited, it has served as an important forerunner of the Bali Process. It has set up channels of communication between Asian nations on migration issues, and the sophistication of its discussions has increased with each year. In 2006, for example, it convened in

Bangkok to discuss a regional response to the United Nations Secretary General's High Level Dialogue on Migration and Co-Development (United Nations 2006b).

In Australia the discourse remains limited on the role of migration in the development of origin countries of the Asia-Pacific. However, there is increasing evidence of the potential for migration to enhance development in the origin countries, and this suggests that a more 'development-sensitive' Australian immigration policy could contribute positively to the social and economic development of the Asia-Pacific nations from which migrants come to Australia. It may be possible to include in Australian immigration policy an element of development sensitivity which has positive developmental effects in both origin and destination. At present it would take a substantial conceptual leap for Australia to factor in the effects in origin countries as a major element shaping immigration-settlement policy.

Migration to Australia is clearly not the single way of remedying low development levels in origin nations, but it could contribute to some improvement of the situation of the poor in origin areas, and to the overall development process, but it will take policy intervention at both destination and origin to maximize such effects. At the very least there needs to be the development of a more substantial evidence base on which to consider policy formulation in this area. In the post-September 11 world Australian national interest will be served if neighbouring countries are stable and secure, and have populations whose well-being is improving; migration can help in achieving this outcome.

Achievements in this area will be incremental rather than massive and dramatic, as it is realized that 'win-win-win' scenarios can be formulated which enhance the well-being of migrants and their families, serve the labour market needs of Australia, and have a net positive development effect in the home country. Australia's immigration policies, especially as they relate to the Asia-Pacific, will be of crucial significance to the nation's economic, social, demographic and political future. They will impinge upon many aspects of Australians' lives as well as those of many people in the Asia-Pacific.

In the last few years, there has been a transformation of the scale, characteristics and significance of international population movements. This demands a continuous reassessment of Australia's immigration policy and program as well as a full assessment of the global situation influencing population movements to and from Australia. Australia can no longer confine its consideration of immigration to what is happening in Australia.

The globalization of capital, the transformation of international travel and communications systems, the instant worldwide distribution of information, the increasing levels of education, the internationalization of many labour markets and the creation of political and environmental refugees, are among the processes and trends which are producing an exponential increase in all forms of international population movements and opening up such movement to a much broader spectrum of the world's population. As Richmond has eloquently shown, no nation can isolate itself from the global system of which population movement is an important part.

These changes have important implications not only for people wishing to come to Australia, but also for Australian residents wishing to move elsewhere. The new widespread consciousness of international migration as an option for people to improve their life chances in the Asia-Pacific has great implications for Australia located on the edge of the region. Economic, social, environmental and political change in the region is likely to produce more pressure for immigration to Australia.

From an Australian perspective it is crucial that any future developments of Australian immigration policy and variations in the immigration program should be undertaken with full appreciation of the rapidly changing international migration situation, especially with the Asian region. This is imperative for the maintenance of good relationships with other Asian nations, to be fair and equitable to all potential immigrants and to safeguard the well-being of resident Australians.

All of the world's nations are facing challenges associated with the new global regime of international migration in what has been termed the 'Age of Migration'. However, few are as well positioned to meet those challenges as Australia. The long experience as a 'country of immigration', especially during the post-World War II era, has given Australia an almost unique capacity not only to cope with new migration pressures but also to develop policy and program approaches which maximize the benefit of those developments. Australia has developed a culture of migration in which there is broad acceptance in the community of the benefits that immigration can deliver, contrasting sharply with community attitudes in many nations.

Moreover, Australian politicians have developed a more sophisticated understanding of the issues surrounding migration and settlement than in most other nations, so that there is considerable capacity for sound and effective policy. Finally, it is often overlooked that Australia is one of very few nations in that it has for more than half a century had a federal government department devoted to immigration and settlement. This has meant that a skilled and committed cadre of immigration bureaucrats has developed over a number of generations.

This substantial body of people with professionalism, knowledge and experience gives Australia a huge advantage in confronting the challenges created by the New Migration. The need for 'Management of Migration' has become the mantra emerging from international forums, conferences and meetings concerned with international migration. However, an essential element in any migration management is the availability of human resources, institutions and infrastructure to develop and operationalize effective management strategies, and Australia is extremely well-positioned in that respect.

All immigration policy formulation in Australia should be undertaken in full recognition of the fact that the world immigration situation of the twenty-first century is new. It is part of a set of powerful international processes which are creating new political, economic, financial, cultural and information links between countries. These forces of globalization are crucial to an understanding of changing global immigration trends. To view immigration as an autonomous process in isolation from other international flows and links could lead to the development of irrelevant and ineffective policies. Sassen, in discussing the situation in the US, has put this argument very strongly:

> The Achilles' heel of US immigration policy has been its insistence on viewing immigration as an autonomous process unrelated to other international processes. It should be clear by now that powerful international forces are at work behind the outflow of emigrants from the developing world and the influx of immigrants into the United States.

While this may be a somewhat extreme statement, it does correctly draw attention to the fact that policies relating to international migration must take account of it being an integral part of a complex system of flows and links between countries. Australia's policies relating to immigration cannot be formulated in isolation from other policies and relationships with those countries.

9

Restructuring and Labour in Rural Communities

The forces of contemporary capitalism are radically altering the structure of business enterprise, the organization of labour, the quality of life on and off the job and the role of the state in shaping these in Canadian society. The study reported on here attempts to expand upon our knowledge of this transformation through empirical research, in particular research that is situated in a rural community context. This context is terra incognita as far as Canadian social science is concerned. We situate our study within the broad debate around the implications for labour, and ultimately the wider society, of economic restructuring in Canada.

We then examine three case studies of corporate restructuring in rural communities of Southern Ontario. The survey we conducted of the former plant labour forces points to some common and disturbing outcomes of the restructuring process. We interpret these in light of the theoretical debate around the directions of contemporary Canadian capitalism.

THE DEINDUSTRIALIZATION VS. RENEWAL DEBATE

That contemporary capitalism has undergone a substantial, indeed profound, change since the 1960s is a point around which there is some agreement on the right and left, at least in the

Canadian context. However, this concordance of views ends when it comes to evaluating the consequences of this process and the policy responses necessary to survive and prosper in this new economic environment. This is where the real debate lies. The following passage encompasses both the unanimity and the fundamental disagreement existing over this issue.

> We have a society in which firms have been merged and acquired, downsized, deindustrialized, multinationalized, automated, streamlined, and restructured. In the process, the rich have gotten richer, the poor poorer, and the life for the middle class more and more precarious.

The first part of this statement would likely not attract much of an argument from Canadian neoconservatives. It is the last sentence, summarizing the writers' views of the outcome of this economic process, that is hotly contested. Few studies dealing with the restructuring of contemporary capitalism successfully link macro-economic developments to a careful empirical analysis of the impact of these developments at the level of the job structure and the quality of work. The landmark studies by Barry Bluestone and Bennett Harrison in the United States were among the earliest and most comprehensive attempts to do this.

At the macro-economic level, Bluestone and Harrison have carefully documented for the U.S. the powerful wave of capital migration by American industrial firms to low-cost countries abroad, stimulated by the much-discussed crisis of profitability that developed around the late 1960s. With this new phase in the globalization of American corporations, firms were now replacing domestic manufacturing with manufacturing abroad. The greater reliance on foreign assembly, the "outsourcing" (subcontracting) of components to foreign manufacturers, the introduction of co-production arrangements with foreign firms and the licensing of technology to foreign competitors were all resulting in the "hollowing out" of American industry, they argued.

The "de-industrialization" thesis of Bluestone and Harrison and others sparked a vigorous and trenchant debate in the U.S. by the early 1980s. It echoed the potent reverberations of massive plant shutdowns and corporate relocations that affected one state after another in the old industrial heartlands of the northeast and north central U.S. Ironically, despite the relative calm in the Canadian manufacturing sector at the time, Canadian scholars in the political economy tradition had already anticipated their American counterparts with the de-industrialization issue.

The trenchant critiques of Canada's "dependent" development that emerged in critical social science circles in Canada-work that was crystallized at the political level in the interventions of the Ontario Waffle faction of the NDP-posed the threat of Canada's possible de-industrialization by the early 1970s. This Canadian literature explored the significance of the apparent dominance of the resource or "staples" fraction of the Canadian capitalist class, together with the manifest weakness of the manufacturing sector in Canada. The high degree of American control over the Canadian manufacturing sector through branch-plant operations was seen to be linked to serious structural weaknesses, such as the very low level of R&D activity carried out in Canada, and our relatively high dependence on imported capital goods.

Moreover, foreign ownership was seen to be at the core of the de-industrialization threat. As James Laxer warned at the time, the Nixon administration's strategies to oppose the growing competition from the Japanese and European economies were "designed to encourage multinational corporations to shift their production from branch plants to the United States".

However, a serious branch-plant exodus was not to materialize in Canada until some 15 years later with the signing of the Free Trade Agreement (FTA), in early 1989. To the extent that Canadian manufacturing was threatened by a de-industrialization process in this earlier period, it was linked more to imports from low-wage industry regions of the Third World, which had considerable impact on such Canadian-owned industries as clothing and textiles.

There would seem to be a growing consensus that a number of changes in Canadian society in the 1980s when taken together constitute a major qualitative shift in the the way the economy is structured. This shift to "neo-capitalism," or "global ,capitalism", entails a change in the logic of accumulation from the Fordist model to some kind of post-Fordist regime of accumulation that remains yet to be fully defined. At the macro level this new model of accumulation is centred on transnational financial institutions and the formation of continental economic spaces in North America, Europe and Asia. At the more micro level of capitalist enterprise, this model entails a host of changes that have rather dramatically reshaped the structure of employment and the quality of worklife in our economy.

Canadians could not expect to remain unscathed by the pressures emanating from international capital to restructure its operations worldwide, particularly given the overwhelming presence of multinational branch plants in our economy. Indeed, even in the U.S., branch-plant operations of multinational firms were found to be more likely to be affected by economic restructuring than by local independent firms. However, the FTA represents one particular strategy for accommodating to the shifting global economic environment. Now, several years after the agreement was signed, we are still analysing and debating the consequences of it all.

One way to interpret the FTA is that it constitutes a vehicle for organizing the corporate response in Canada to global economic pressures in one specific way. This way corresponded by and large to the interests of the most powerful sections of the Canadian capitalist class, particularly in the resource and financial sectors, and to the interests of the foreign owners of much of our manufacturing sector.

The FTA shaped the restructuring process in Canada along two important dimensions. These have been summarized by Jackson as follows:

It has totally removed any concern on the part of business that relocation to the U.S. would be followed by any "discrimination" on the part of Canadian governments. The core of the FTA is the promise of "national treatment" for U.S.-based enterprises and the systematic removal of Canadian public policies favouring Canadian-based companies.

Moreover the FTA has prevented the Canadian government from implementing policies that might otherwise have been pursued to address the almost unprecedented scale and severity of the crises. More important than removing tariff end non-tariff barriers to trade, then, the FTA and the more recent North American Free Trade Agreement (NAFTA) have been about changing the "rules of the game" by which business and government interact to construct the economy.

There is strong evidence that the combination of the FTA and monetary policies that kept the Canadian dollar at artificially high levels produced massive plant shutdowns in the industrial heartlands of Canada. Published data compiled by the Canadian Labour Congress indicate the magnitude of the job destruction that took place before the onset of the sharp downturn of the business cycle that set in by 1990. The more than 400 plant closures that occurred between late 1988 and June 1990 affected small, medium and large manufacturing firms alike.

Moreover, data compiled by the Canadian Centre for Policy Alternatives demonstrates that more than 100 of the plant shutdowns occurring in Ontario until June 1992 involved relocation of production outside Canada, largely to the United States and to some extent Mexico. This fact underscores the argument that many of the shutdowns taken together constitute more or less permanent structural changes to the economy, and not simply temporary closures that will re-open with an upswing in the business cycle.

THE HUMAN DIMENSIONS OF RESTRUCTURING

What, then, was the impact of this type of economic change on incomes, job structure and beyond? With respect to these human dimensions of the restructuring process, we may again turn to Bluestone and Harrison to consider their thesis on what has happened in the American economy. Basically, in an effort to adapt to a variety of new competitive pressures and restore former levels of profitability, U.S. firms since the late 1970s have elaborated a series of strategies that are, to a large extent, designed to increase labour "flexibility"- a euphemism for cutting their wage bill.

These strategies include: a) unremitting pressure for concessions from unionized and non-unionized workers in order to reduce their wages and overall compensation packages; b) the introduction of a two-tiered wage structure into the workplace whereby newly hired workers are paid much less than previously hired workers doing what is basically the same job, and this lower wage rate continues for a much longer period than had previously been the case; c) the promotion of part-time contingent work schedules, which include the introduction of a growing cadre of part-time or temporary workers within the firm itself, and/or the growth of subcontracting, where workers are supplied by another, typically non-union, lower-wage employer; and d) promoting the strategy of "union avoidance" whereby firms increasingly "outsource" production to non-unionized firms at home or abroad, while downsizing or shutting down entirely unionized plants.

Bluestone and Harrison point to the fact that while one in three American workers was represented by an independent union in the years after World War II, only one in six was projected to be so represented by 1990. In summarizing the thrust of these processes, the authors write that:

> Altogether, almost 4 out of 5 workers displaced from manufacturing jobs found themselves skidding into unemployment, skidding completely out of the labour force, or skidding down the wage scale and for these workers to hold on to a middle class lifestyle required that there be two or more workers in the family.

The conservative critique of these arguments has focussed on the emerging service economy and the high-technology electronics industry. Proponents of the "de-industrialization" thesis have been criticized for ignoring the dynamic dimension of capitalism in these new sectors, which have stimulated the growth of an impressive number of jobs in the 1980s. Job growth there is proof of the dynamic nature of "open" market economies. And while some critics do not deny the painful aspects of the transition to an information-based society, they argue it will be a short-term one and a necessary evil if we are to have the dynamism that is responsible for long-term increases in living standards. As one critic has put it:

> Many of the country's jobs were destroyed because of the jobs that were created-that many jobs are lost simply because workers prefer other and better employment. . . . The interdependence of job creation and job destruction is so complete that we might just as well use the rate of job destruction as a sign of economic vitality rather than as a sign of economic distress.

However, critics of the emerging "service economy" point to disturbing evidence of what has been somewhat inaccurately dubbed the "hourglass" economy because of its shrinking middle tier of managerial and blue-collar unionized workers. As Drache has argued in the Canadian context:

> While there are better paying jobs in services in a few areas, the service economy is first and foremost a low-wage economy. This is the main reason why job growth has changed the shape of the wage pyramid right across the face of the entire economy.

Interestingly, studies in the United States have argued that this is true even in metropolitan areas where leading-edge high technology and financial services firms are prominent. Here, the emergence of a technical and financial elite has also brought forth a host of low-wage jobs to service the new economy, jobs disproportionately populated by women, visible minorities and new immigrants.

Empirical evidence to support these contentions is particularly rich for the United States. Evidence is less abundant for Canada, but a few important studies suggest the emerging pattern. As in other developed economies, the shift in the job structure toward service-economy employment has accelerated and is now quite advanced. While the "goods producing" sector, primary industries (agriculture, fishing, forestry and mining) and manufacturing accounted for about 40% of employment in 1967, this had declined to 29% by 1988. The decline in the primary sector has been particularly dramatic in Canada (from 10.6% to 6%).

By the latter date service-sector employment accounted for just over 70% of jobs in Canada and almost 90% of job growth in Canada since 1967. What, then, are the essential characteristics of this new economy that is rapidly replacing the one based on resource industries and manufacturing? There is evidence that service sector growth has contributed to the phenomenon of "occupational skidding" noted above. The growth of "nonstandard" work forms-those that do not conform to full-time, full-year work, has increased quite dramatically. Part-time work had grown from 4% of total employment to 15% by the 1980s, and it contributed to an average of 30% of overall employment growth in Canada between 1976 and 1988.

Other forms of "nonstandard" employment, including short-term jobs, self-employment and temporary help agency work, have also increased substantially in the 1980s. These types of employment are known to be overwhelmingly non-unionized, and less likely to be covered by fringe benefits. Wages are likely to be lower than those of full-time, full-year jobs as well. Sectoral analysis of job trends indicates that these types of jobs are particularly concentrated in what has been termed the "traditional" services (over 40% of jobs there being "nonstandard"), but also prevalent in the more "dynamic" service industries as well.

Of course, it is precisely in these areas that most of the job growth in Canada is taking place, and where many ax-employees of the restructured manufacturing sector must seek work. It is noteworthy, however, and in keeping with the American experience, that various types of "nonstandard" employment have also seen growth in primary resource and secondary manufacturing industries, where by 1986 they amounted to more than 20% of employment. We shall return to this matter below. What, then, of the longer-term economic impact of this structural change? Has it led to the growth of an "hourglass" economy with a decline in the middle tier of employment and the consequent polarization of incomes, as has been persuasively argued in the U.S.?

One major research report based on Statistics Canada data for the period 1967-1986 found that there has in fact been a definite decline in the middle stratum of income earners, and of this "declining middle" nearly three-fifths were redistributed into the lower group. This had produced, even by 1986, a measurable increase in income inequality in Canada as compared with 1967. Further studies have since corroborated this growing inequality. The study by Yalnizyan et al. indicates this trend has even accelerated in the last few years. The authors also present data that indicate dramatic shifts in market income among Canadian families in the period 1973-1991.

By 1991 the richest Canadian families with children had increased their share of market income by about 14%, while the income share of the poorest 10% of families had plummetted 47% since 1973. They note that only government transfer payments to these families have prevented "a free fall into destitution". This relative growth in jobs at the bottom of the earnings distribution is argued by some to be mainly the result of declining relative wages among young people, a decline that is manifest in all economic sectors including manufacturing and resource industries.

It has also been argued that there is strong evidence in Canada that a growing polarization of hours worked, especially among male workers, accounted for much of the growing earnings inequality in the 1980s. This was likely due to a shift for some from full-time to part-time work, but especially full-time workers having to work longer hours. Overall, while it may still be too early to say with certainty that these changes are more than a cyclical phenomenon (and therefore may soon be reversed), at least one well-known study has argued that the "pervasiveness of the polarization does suggest that the changes that are taking place in the workplace and within industries are fundamental and systemic".

If the nature of employment shows definite signs of change, how then have the characteristics of unemployment changed? While there is not complete unanimity on this issue, there is strong evidence in Canada of a rather substantial and disturbing increase in the proportion of unemployed individuals experiencing long-term unemployment. Indeed, in 1989, even after seven years of economic "recovery," the incidence of long-term unemployment was 100% higher than the level prevailing in 1980. Moreover, there is evidence of the development of sharp interregional differences in the duration of unemployment in the most recent recession.

The duration of unemployment for permanently laid-off workers in Ontario has increased by 100% in the early 1990s, as compared to the 25% increase for the rest of Canada. Older workers in recent years have fared considerably worse than was previously the case with respect to duration of unemployment. In fact, the gap between the incidence of re-employment of younger workers and those over 45 has substantially widened since the late 1970s.

Long-term unemployment imposes considerable social and private costs. For society, its presence in significant numbers leads to the marginalization of a segment of the labour force, and therefore to higher costs for unemployment insurance and other social programs. For the individual it erodes work skills, limits the prospects for further employment, and ultimately undermines morale.

Finally, it must be pointed out that almost all of the studies on restructuring and job changes have either focussed on data at the national level or, in a few cases, data for metropolitan areas. Relatively little has been written about rural/urban differences. Fitchen's study of upstate New York is an exception. Her study shows that some rural communities, at least, are even more dependent upon manufacturing activity than major metropolitan areas such as New York City.

The decline in manufacturing activities there poses a special problem for rural communities, because service sector growth that could ameliorate this process has not been strong. Rural communities have also been further stressed by the longer-term crisis in the farm sector, a crisis that dates from the high interest rates and collapse in land prices that occurred with the recession beginning in 1981. However, the loss offactories in rural communities has had a more pervasive and deeper impact, according to Fitchen, than has the decline in farms.

In other respects, Fitchen's findings in rural New York state reflect much of what restructuring has meant outside rural areas: evidence of definite "occupational skidding" to lower-paying, often part-time work with limited fringe benefits. Older workers, particularly men and the less-educated, were particularly disadvantaged, and it was common for workers to experience a decline in the quality of life on the job, typically as a result of less favourable working conditions and/or the necessity to commute farther to the new jobs.

The present study helps to fill a void that exists with respect to research on the rural dimension of corporate restructuring in the Canadian context. In what follows we discuss some findings from a study of rural Southern Ontario and conclude,by relating these findings to the issues raised above.

This research is part of a larger study of communities in a rural Ontario county and the effects of corporate restructuring. Our methodological approach is intended to complement macro-economic and social data by providing a close look at the texture of peoples' lives under restructuring. By focussing on a rural county relatively far (in Southern Ontario terms) from major transportation routes, we can demonstrate diversity within the province and raise concerns about overlooked rural areas. We take the region under study to be fairly typical of rural communities that are relatively diversified economically.

In contrast with many communities in the Canadian hinterland that are heavily dependent upon either single-industry resources (such as forestry-, hardrock mining- or fishing-based communities) or on monocrop agriculture alone, many Southern Ontario rural communities have drawn on a range of economic activities, including a diversified agricultural base, manufacturing in both monopoly and competitive sectors, and in some cases resource extraction. We employed ethnographic data collection techniques, including the use of questionnaires and both structured and unstructured interviews with key informants and 68 plant workers. Interviews took the form of lengthy structured conversations which covered our research questions, but also allowed unanticipated issues to emerge.

North Wellington County is a rural region comprising 11 municipalities north of Fergus with a total population of 25,835. Although the local economy was rooted in agriculture, with older manufacturing facilities created to process locally produced foodstuffs, economic development over the past couple of decades has favoured new industrial parks and provided economic incentives for diverse industries to relocate. Since the late 1980s plant closures, layoffs, relocation of businesses and farm failures have led to increased unemployment. The welfare caseload increased some 500% for the rural county as a whole between 1987 and 1991, indicating economic hardship across the county.

The present study examines the impact of the closure of Canada Packers plants in Elora, Harriston and Mount Forest, and of a Westinghouse plant in Mount Forest. The Canada Packers food processing plant had existed in Harriston for most of the century. The plant was unionized early, and made a variety of mainly dairy products. In 1984 ice cream production was discontinued to avoid new capital investment. In 1990 Canada Packers was acquired by the British food processing giant Hillsdown Holdings PLC, which set out to radically restructure Canada Packers.

The strategy concentrated on high profit areas such as value-added food products, and joint-venture operations with American agribusiness to take advantage of the continental market opened up by the FTA. During the two-year restructuring period Hillsdown sold off entire divisions and closed down twenty plants, including those in Harriston and Mount Forest in January of 1991. The Westinghouse plant opened in a custom-built facility in Mount Forest in 1981, moving some operations from Hamilton. The move may have been, as some workers saw it, to "get away from the union,'" but a number of employees relocated from Hamilton, and the workers at the new plant were soon certified with the United Electrical Workers.

The plant produced electrical products for government, public utilities and industry. During the late 1980s senior management decided to use the company's consumer credit division to make a foray into speculative real estate and other high-risk investments. In the words of a leading U.S. business magazine, "Westinghouse Credit Corp., known in the company simply as Credit Corp., shoveled loans out the door with the speed and abandon of a go-go S&L. It poured money into high-risk, high-return ventures like hotels, shopping centres, junk bonds and leveraged buyouts. Now it's paying the price".

The collapse of the North American real estate markets with the onset of the recession in 1990 proved very costly for Westinghouse. A little more than a year after CEO Paul Lego had boosted his annual compensation package from $1.4 million to $1.7 million, the company was forced to write off $2.7 billion in assets and begin a masse restructuring to cover bad loans that would force the sale of whole corporate divisions and layoffs of several thousand employees.

In 1989 the Canadian subsidiary began decentralizing, and some product lines were moved to South Carolina. In 1993 Westinghouse announced that it had sold 38 of its production facilities to Eaton Yale Co., including eight in Canada, and the employees at Mount Forest were told that their plant was one of three in Canada to be closed. The new company had bought the capital equipment of the plant only, and not the building itself. The equipment was removed and shipped south of the border to enhance the company's operations in the southern United States.

THE HUMAN DIMENSIONS OF CORPORATE RESTRUCTURING IN RURAL COMMUNITIES

We now turn to examine the impact of these plant closures on the workers themselves. When the Canada Packers plants in Elora and Harriston closed in 1991, 130 and 101 workers respectively were laid off. Westinghouse in Mount Forest, which at its peak in 1989 had employed 250 workers, began laying off employees in October 1991 and finally closed in July 1994. Our sample comprises data from 68 in-depth, face-to-face employee interviews.

Since the time between layoff and our interview varied considerably, some people had had relatively more time in which to look for work, and in some cases to find it, than others. At the time of interview, however, 24 (35%, comprising nine men and 15 women) were entirely without work, of whom seven (five men and two women, all over 60) were receiving various pensions and considered themselves effectively retired. Age is a significant factor among those still unemployed at the time of interview. Of the 17 unemployed and looking for work, 10 (58%) were over 50, while only 25 of the 68 in our overall sample (37%) were in that age bracket.

The remaining 44 (65%, comprising 17 men and 27 women) had managed to find some kind of work by the time we interviewed them. The periods these people had spent in unemployment varied widely, partly because of the staggered layoffs from Westinghouse, yet 27 of those who were working when interviewed (61%) had spent at least a year unemployed. A striking feature of this number is the gender breakdown-24 women and three men. Some workers had managed to find work within a few weeks of layoff, and one or two had found new jobs pre-empting actual layoff, yet those jobs usually led to a huge drop in annual income and an erosion of reasonably good work conditions.

Overall, if we compare the average hourly wage before layoff to that received after layoff, the percentage change is perhaps less dramatic than one might expect, although, women fared less well than men. Five of the 17 men had managed to find work at a higher hourly wage than that of their former jobs. In a number of ways, average hourly wage figures may obscure more than they reveal. For example, if an individual's former wage level was for 1991, a similar current wage level does not take into account the kinds of wage increases that the union might have been able to negotiate during the intervening three years.

As well, and perhaps more significant given the low rates of inflation of the early 1990s, the average hourly wage differential conceals the fact that a large proportion of workers were forced to shift from working full-time hours of at least 40 hours per week, often with overtime, to working at part-time jobs. Indeed, the Westinghouse workers whose hourly wage on an individual basis had dropped the most, often by as much as half or more, were the most likely to be continuing in full-time employment. Those whose hourly wage was still within a dollar or two of their pre-layoff rate were more likely to be in part-time jobs. This finding is analysed further below.

If we look more closely at changes in income level, it becomes quite clear that the direct economic impact of these plant closures upon workers and their families was very hard indeed. The change in annual income from the last year workers were employed by Canada Packers or Westinghouse to their projected income for the year in which they were interviewed is quite dramatic, especially when the workers are disaggregated by age and gender. Of the 34 people with jobs who provided this information, 19 were women and 15 were men.

Of the 19 women, only one had experienced a raise in income, while 16 had experienced a drop in income of at least $11,000. Among the 15 men, five were making more than in their previous jobs. For one, this was because he now had to work six days per week instead of five, and for two others the additional costs of a long commute ate up most of their pay raises. Of the remaining 10, eight had lost a minimum of $6,000 per year; the other two were coping with the loss of more than $16,000 per year. An interesting feature is the number of couples employed in the same plant. We interviewed both members of nine such couples and there were an additional five where only one spouse was interviewed.

The literature on single-industry towns usually deals with steady male employment in the primary resource sector, where employment for women in the same establishment is relatively rare. Where both men and women are employed in the same company in what is effectively a single-industry town, the plant closure hits doubly hard. While the existence of two incomes in the family is usually seen as providing insurance against job loss, in this case it has simply increased the family's vulnerability. As in single-industry towns, the heavy dependence on one employer in the community may have repercussions for the whole family. One couple was hit twice when both the husband and the parents of children cared for by the wife were laid off.

A significant reason for the dramatic drop in annual income is that more and more of the jobs that are available are part-time, temporary-contract or home-based jobs, rather than full-time, permanent jobs, supporting the observation that the contingent workforce is growing. In such jobs, workers can be easily let go if the work drops off; thus even minimal short-term job security is denied. In a couple of cases Westinghouse used its own laid-off workers on a contingent basis. One worker was rehired on a short-term contract to clean up before the plant was vacated; another worker laid off in Mount Forest accepted short-term work at other locations owned by the same company. She had worked spells of a few weeks at Georgetown, Burlington, Georgetown (again), Oakville, and Georgetown (yet again).

Of the 44 who were working when interviewed, 16 (36%, comprising 2 men and 14 women) were in part-time work. The average hourly rate for part-time work compared to full-time work is shown. While the average wage of men dropped significantly when they accepted part-time work, for women, it was full-time replacement work that represented the largest hourly wage decline, and the difference between full-time and part-time was much less significant than for men. For some, working part-time meant holding a number of jobs at one time to try to make up for the shortfall in income. Five of the 16 in part-time work were juggling two or more part-time jobs to try to make ends meet.

It is worth noting again that older workers fared differently from their younger co-workers. Eight of the 25 workers over 50 were employed at the time of interview; of these, six were in part-time jobs, and another was employed on a six-week contract. Most workers moved from a unionized job environment to one where unions are absent, or where as casual employees they were not eligible to enter the bargaining unit. There were a number of stories of hiring promises not fulfilled, lengthy struggles to effect agreed-upon pay raises, and so on.

Although a few argued that working in a non-union environment was preferable, even these recognized that their severance package and assistance received after layoff was primarily the result of the union's work. We would argue that although the reality of being in a non-union workplace may not have hit workers whose experience there was as yet relatively short, the consequences of this will become noticeable as they attempt individually to negotiate pay raises, deal with grievance situations and avoid apparently arbitrary firing or layoff without cause.

A major financial blow to workers was the loss of job-related benefits. The unions at both companies had negotiated decent benefit packages for their members, which included things like extended health care, increased vacation with seniority, and dental and optical benefits. As workers moved to nonunion employers, they lost a large part of these packages. If their new work was part-time or casual they would not accrue vacation or sick-leave time, nor would they be eligible for the other significant benefits they were used to. Workers themselves raised the issue of loss of benefits, or pointed out that where benefits were still available, they tended to be less comprehensive.

At Westinghouse the union had successfully negotiated an extension of benefits after layoff from three to six months, but since-as we have observed-many people remained unemployed for far longer, this would clearly have been insufficient. More generally, the social benefits of seniority, such as progressive vacation entitlement, recall provisions and priority for promotion and transfer, were entirely lost as workers moved into non-union employment situations. At Canada Packers the collective agreement stipulated that employees with 20 years' service received five weeks of paid vacation, and those with 25 years, six weeks. Given the high levels of seniority within the plant-in 1991, 19 employees had 25 years' service-this represents a significant loss.

A major factor in many workers' lives, and a change related to their work, was the requirement to commute to new jobs. For those used to walking to work, this was a major adjustment:

I remember one day a bunch of us were sitting around the coffee table and one of us said, "Well we're going to have to make up our minds, if we're going to work, we're gonna have to drive to it." I could count on my hands how many times I drove. Sometimes I would drive to work, waLk home, and wonder why the car wasn't there.

Many of those who had found relatively well paying jobs had been forced to look quite far outside their communities. As noted above, one woman was travelling daily from Mount Forest to Burlington, Oakville and Georgetown; others commuted into Guelph, while other work destinations included Erin, Kitchener and Cambridge. The distance from Mount Forest to these places of employment was between 60 and 120 km, one way.

There were mixed feelings about this, no doubt because of the felt conflict between needing to work and the negative aspects of commuting. Some workers dismissed the problems, both financial and social, though one, whose previous job had been straight day shifts 15 minutes from his home, admitted that driving 60 km following a night shift was both unpleasant and potentially dangerous. Another worker who had lived a five-minute walk from the factory and was now commuting 80 km each day pointed out that the $2 per hour increase over his former job rate was eliminated by having to put a car on the road, insure it and keep it running. Another worker described it this way:

Sure, I could take this job [in Guelph] at $15 an hour, but with the driving that's an extra 20 hours a week, and you're only making $10 an hour. And if it costs you $6 a day in gas, that's another $30. So now you're down to $9 an hour and that doesn't include repairs on the car, tires; that's just the gas and the time that you're spending.

Clearly, in addition to the financial burden of commuting, there are social and environmental implications. Commuters frequently lost two to three hours per day in travel time-time they would formerly have spent with their families or in community activities they could no longer perform. Another issue is that where one partner takes the car to work, the other is often left at home without transportation, since the overall loss of income has either forced the selling of a second vehicle or prevented the purchase of one. This is a much more significant factor in rural areas without public transportation than it would be in urban settings.

Although a few workers attempted car pooling, long-distance commuting adds to the atmospheric impact of excessive private car use. While a few workers who had held skilled jobs were able to find similarly skilled jobs elsewhere, a majority were forced to accept semi-skilled or unskilled work. Those who had held semi-skilled jobs were likely to be forced to revert to unskilled jobs, such as retail sales, bar and restaurant work, house cleaning, babysitting and unskilled factory work.

Thus there is considerable evidence among our sample of "occupational skidding." These workers, who formerly held well-paid, full-time, skilled or semi-skilled, unionized jobs with good benefits, have seen their reasonable working conditions eroded. Overall, there was a clearly discernible decline in the quality of working conditions. When we asked how their new job compared to their old one, the common response was simply that it did not. Workers were often quite effusive about how much they had liked their old jobs.

The women laid off from Westinghouse frequently talked about the challenge presented by their old jobs and how they enjoyed the skills they had required. They missed the stimulation those jobs had provided, as well as the camaraderie of the work group. Now in unskilled jobs, often in the small workplaces of the service sector, they lamented the loss of both of those elements. It is not surprising that the greater wage decrease experienced by women is related to the nature of the jobs they were able to find after layoff.

Men were more likely than women to find equally skilled work, and for this the price was frequently a long commute into cities 50 km to 80 km away. For many women, entering more distant labour markets was simply not a viable option, because of children or other family responsibilities. They were then limited to seeking work in the micro labour market close to home, where the possibilities for work of any kind were scarce, and for more skilled and better-paid work, practically non-existent. The three communities where women were employed before layoff show different patterns in terms of the type of job they found after layoff.

For Harriston and Elora 11 of the 14 women found part-time work, at least half combining two or more part-time jobs. Mount Forest, however, shows a different pattern. Here, nine of the 12 women found full-time jobs. Seven of these had in fact taken work at a local sporting goods factory, K Brand, which was hiring at the time the Westinghouse layoffs were taking place. This company offered the women full-time jobs within minutes of their former workplace, a definite advantage for single-car families and for those hoping or needing to stay fairly close to home.

The trade-off for this valued proximity was, however, a dramatic loss of income. The pre-layoff average hourly wage for women at Westinghouse was $12.98. Those who moved to K Brand averaged $7.27 (one woman was making $9.50 an hour, the remainder averaged $6.90). Men were unwilling to settle for factory work at this rate of pay and, as well, perceived the kind of work being done to be inappropriate for them, as men. One woman described her husband's reaction (and her own) when she handed him an application for work at K Brand:

He said, "I'm not working at K Brand." He wouldn't make enough money there. Even the men thought I was stupid quitting early to go to a minimum-paying job, because I could have stayed there and made $14 until the end of May. But how many of them are going to have a job when they finish there? They are so stupid. That's what really made me mad.

As fieldwork was continuing in August of 1994 we learned that, because of the Major League Baseball players' strike, K Brand was laying off workers. During the following months layoffs and rehirings continued due to exogenous factors unrelated to the company's own performance. While typical of firms operating in the competitive sector, this is quite far removed from the security of operation enjoyed by a company like Westinghouse before it ran into problems caused by its own mismanagement.

THE COMMUNITY DIMENSION

The broader impact of these changes upon the small communities where most of these workers lived, shopped and socialized is not easily summarized, either in quantitative or qualitative terms. While in-depth conclusions are beyond the scope of this chapter, a few tentative remarks should be made. To begin with, the immediate economic impact must have been considerable. For the community of Mount Forest, with a population of 4,095 in 1991, we have conservatively estimated that the gross pay of employees in the Westinghouse plant at the peak of its operations would have amounted to at least $150,000 per week. The loss of this money being pumped into the village economy, together with the company tax revenues lost by the municipality, which were approximately $220,000 annually by 1989, must have been a serious blow to the community. Former plant workers had noticed changes in the community:

Merchants talk and say sales are right down. The community attitude is even different. It's very depressing for the whole community. Everyone's depressed because their friends and family are out of work.

It's really bad for the whole community, not just for those people who were laid off. Another noted:

It's hurt everybody in Mount Forest. At one point there [were] close to 300 people in the plant which meant houses, which meant tax dollars, which meant grocery stores dollars, which meant appliances, which meant cars-you name it, they bought it. There were people from Owen Sound, Listowel, Guelph, Atwood, all over. I think you could probably ask anybody on Main Street and they would say it's hurtful. Because those people aren't spending their dollars in Mount Forest anymore.

One woman reported that when Westinghouse closed, the local bank that handled the direct deposit of their pay cheques had laid people off while individuals and families felt and accommodated for the impact of income loss on their particular lifestyle in a variety of ways, personal choices around these issues had consequences for the vitality of the local economy. People reported changing their shopping habits, seeking out "specials" more diligently, and visiting several markets to take advantage of good prices. One woman described her own changed practices:

You look for cheaper stuff, bargains, and sales. You go to different stores for sales. Now that I have a job, I still do it out of habit. And you think twice about buying something. You don't want to go into debt. I tried to keep it in my own town because you waste gas by going out of town.

Given the usual gender division of labour, this would normally mean an intensification of women's work in this area. Those who had made regular trips to the shopping malls of Guelph and Kitchener now made them less frequently or had stopped going altogether. The general reduction in spending, however, meant that staying close to home did not necessarily translate into benefits for the local economy. Store closings continued, and buying shoes, for example, now required an out-of-town trip. This went against a sentiment among some that "we make the money in the town, we should leave it in the town."

Christmas shopping was cut back, and one woman was saddened at nor being able to spoil her grandchildren. Often it was the anticipation of Christmas that brought home the impact that unemployment was having, when "you didn't have the extra money to buy things, some of what you wanted to buy for the kids."

Eating in local restaurants and entertaining were also severely curtailed. One family told of annual holidays in the Caribbean replaced by cottaging and camping, and eventually by skipping holidays altogether to save money, and because in new, insecure jobs vacation time was no longer automatically available. People worried that during these times even dropping in to visit friends and family could be viewed as "mooching," and in any case represented a drain on overstretched resources. Thus one man said he visited less often to avoid such embarrassment.

Nagging worries about money and, in some cases, frank financial distress, placed a heavy strain on family relationships, as did the necessity to work longer hours or spend time commuting. As a result, there were a number of short-term or permanent family breakups. Less direct forms of impact were felt by the community and noticed by those active at the community level. A man who now worked as a bartender at the Legion reported people were spending less there.

The annual operating deficits of community-based resources like the arena and the curling club had risen. One couple had given up their weekly outing to a local bar in order to save money, and they recognized the broader effect of such actions: "When Westinghouse was good Westinghouse basically supported that bar. It is on the main street and it's still there, but it is nothing like it used to be." Community service clubs also felt the financial crunch as people cut back their social activities. Company-sponsored social events were also missed in communities with few alternative social attractions. Events like dances had been free to employees and their spouses, so, as one woman put it: "It was a night out-all you really had to worry about was a babysitter."

Other social costs of the plant closures included a double impact on local students. One woman observed: "It would have been a lot of kids that never could have gone to university or college if not for the Packers." Partly this was because of the secure, reasonably high income earned there by their parents-often both mother and father. But there was also the loss of summer jobs for local students. In Harriston Canada Packers had provided summer jobs for 50 or 60 students, many of which were lost when the ice cream division closed, but which have now completely disappeared.

This puts additional financial pressure on families, and as well students find themselves spending the summer untrained and idle. The plant closures also eliminated decent long-term job opportunities for young people: "Our son's been looking for a better job for a lot of years. He works in a store in Listowel, but it's not a good paying job, and he doesn't get a lot of hours. It's very difficult for the younger people." Obviously, the reduction in such local employment opportunities forces younger people to seek work out of the community altogether.

Neoconservatives have been successful in putting forth the argument that a restructuring of our manufacturing sector, unfettered by government regulations and controls, is vital if Canadian business is to compete in a global marketplace. The hegemony of this worldview today is confirmed by the lack of public debate around the merits of such restructuring, and public policies that might play an important role in shaping the way in which restructuring occurs. Private-sector firms essentially have carte blanche when it comes to designing and implementing a restructuring strategy, and beyond minimal legislation regarding severence pay, the public purse is left to deal with the social consequences.

Public acquiescence to restructuring in its present form is likely due in part to the absence of a credible alternative agenda. This situation is no doubt related to the crisis of the chief political alternative in Canada in recent times-the New Democratic Party. But this acquiescence is arguably also due to a general absence of information about the realities of restructuring for many, perhaps most, of those involved. Our study provides a glimpse into the world of rural Canada, and it shows that this world has not escaped the turmoil that has convulsed the Canadian urban manufacturing economy.

Overall, our study supports the view that corporate restructuring has entailed deterioration in the lives of working people. For most of our respondents, restructuring has meant a substantial drop in household income even when reemployment occurred and paradoxically sometimes even when reemployment meant a job at a higher wage rate. The prevalence of part-time work in the new economy taking shape is largely responsible here.

Evidence of "occupational skidding" was the norm, not the exception, for our respondents. Work at a substantially lower wage in a non-union shop, sometimes part-time contingent work, was the lot for most of those lucky enough to find new employment. We also found considerable evidence that the quality of work had deteriorated for most upon reemployment, whether this meant worse job conditions as compared to their previous work, and/or extra stresses entailed in securing the new job, as with the addition of a commuting burden to their lives.

In the rural communities we have studied, there is little evidence of the "good jobs" that some writers argue are associated with the new "information economy." While the older manufacturing economy was dispersed, to some degree, into rural Canada, it may well be that the benefits of the new service sector economy, to the extent that they exist, are even more geographically restricted than was the case with manufacturing.

Our study also tended to confirm what the few macro-level empirical studies of changing job structures in Canada have argued. A disturbing proportion of the samples have faced long-term unemployment, with older workers being particularly disadvantaged. What may be more unique to the rural milieu is the particularly harsh impact of restructuring on women plant workers. The very limited employment opportunities for women in rural communities together with the extra domestic burden may have restricted their ability to secure good replacement jobs farther afield. These are important determinants in the lives of women after restructuring.

10

Women's Work in Traditional Production in Northern Chile

Recent changes in the global political economy have had dramatic effects on the lives of women as they are incorporated into globalization processes, such as the expansion of agribusiness, in often marginal and unstable ways. However, it is vital to consider how these globalization processes are mediated by women in ways that reflect local geo-historical contexts. This chapter explores the expansion of the fruit export sector; land tenure, community organization and female employment in agriculture in northern Chile. Agro-export production has marginalized but not destroyed the small-scale farming sector and large-scale export farms co-exist with small-scale domestically-orientated farms.

Female labour has been very important in the success of fresh fruit exports and many rural women negotiate both waged work in the fruit export economy and unwaged work on family farms. The paper explores the women's perceptions of agricultural work and how these relate to their identities as unpaid workers on the family farm a nd as waged workers in the agro-export sector. The paper thus attempts to explore the multiplicity of ways that women experience rapid changes in the agrarian sector and how these changes relate to the maintenance of more 'traditional' practices and identities.

This chapter explores women's employment in the fruit export sector of northern Chile and how this is related to the particular community contexts of the women, and the outcomes that this has for their identification with waged work and family farm work. The situation in the Guatulame valley in Chile's Fourth Region is explored as it represents a site where there has been significant growth in the production of table grapes for export. There has been an increased feminization and seasonality of agricultural production associated with the agro-export economy in the Guatulame and while these patterns may be visible across the majority of fruit exporting regions of Chile, a heterogeneous rural population experiences the expansion of non-traditional exports in different ways.

Therefore, this chapter examines the specificities of land tenure and community organization in the Guatulame to set the context for the changes that have taken place in both traditional and agro-export production syste ms. In this region, many women have become involved as temporary waged workers (known as temporeras), working in the fields and packing plants of the grape economy.

Many women in the Guatulame valley also maintain work on the family farm, producing for the domestic market in what can be termed 'traditional' agricultural production. The women, therefore, negotiate their participation in a variety of agricultural sectors at different times of the year and in different ways. The paper attempts to explore the multiplicity of ways that women experience rapid changes in the agrarian sector and how this relates to the maintenance of more 'traditional' practices and identities.

Recent changes in the global political economy have had far-reaching and dramatic impacts on the lives of women in many parts of the world who have become integrated into the world's production and consumption processes. 'Women have been affected by globalization in the most diverse aspects of their lives and in the furthest reaches of the world'. The generation of a global fruit market in which a variety of products are sourced year-round from different countries as the seasons rotate represents one such process. In many developing countries the nature of agriculture is changing as governments promote agro-export production as part of an overall strategy of economic restructuring.

The export of fresh fruits is frequently central to these changing agricultural production systems, and changing consumption patterns (led by the Northern elites) mean that this type of produce is consumed throughout the year, irrespective of season and location. The global environment, therefore, i ncreasingly shapes local patterns of agricultural production and employment. A common feature of this globalized production of fresh fruits (and other nontraditional agricultural exports) has been the employment of large numbers of women.

This is the case in Chile, where the expansion of fresh fruit production has led to the integration of thousands of women into the rural wage labour force, working to export fresh fruits such as kiwi fruit, apples and table grapes to the Northern markets. However, the spread of globalization processes within agriculture is not uniform and unproblematic and it is important that we explore the heterogeneity and complexity of agrarian life under processes of re-structuring and agro-export production and attempt to disaggregate the experiences of women under globalization processes.

The increase in the level of female employment, much of it temporary and unstable, is one of the most striking changes brought about by the expansion of agro-export production in Chile. The female seasonal workers or temporeras are employed for a few months each year, particularly during December to March (the main fruit harvest season). Employment in the fruit sector is highly gendered, with women's work concentrated in the packing plants, where their perceived and often imaginary 'female' characteristics such as manual dexterity have made them the desired labour for handling the delicate fruit.

They do also work in the fields where there is a much less marked gendered labour market. There are no precise figures for the numbers of women employed, but estimates put the figure at about 150 000 or approximately half of the total temporary agricultural labour force. Overall, studies have shown that a minority, approximately, 35 per cent, of Chilean temporeras are single and that the average age of temporary workers is 30. The age and marital status of temporeras, therefore, contrasts with other studies into women who have become involved in export sectors, who tend to be young and single.

This study, therefore, helps to focus our attention on the ways that older, married and rural women have become incorporated into paid employment and the impact that this has on their lives. The impacts of employment in the export sector on gender roles and relations are debatable but there is a growing literature on gender and non-traditional agricultural exports that explores the patterns of female involvement in waged work and the outcomes that this brings.

Certain globalization processes such as structural adjustment, economic liberalization and export promotion and their impacts on women have been well documented and in many cases there is some similarity with the findings of studies on diverse employment sectors and in a variety of countries and the studies into women's participation in non-traditional agricultural exports. These studies have highlighted the fact that although women's employment is often highly unstable and relatively poorly paid, whether it is the export factories of South East Asia or the Colombian cut-flower sector, it does bring with it the potential for their empowerment and the re-working of household relations. In some instances women may actually be able to earn more than men in a given production process because they are concentrated in the most highly 'skilled' jobs such as packing delicate fresh fruit for export.

There appears to be a shift in earning patterns and limited empowerment for some women who value the opportunity to take control of their own wages and escape the domestic routine. In addition waged employment frequently gives women access to organizations that challenge traditional gender roles and campaign for women's rights. For example, Stephen found that women who participated in the Seasonal Workers Union in Chile have 'challenged men's notions about the "natural" character of their own gender roles...In addition their political activism has led them to challenge the traditional gendered division of labour'.

So waged employment does bring some benefits for women in terms of earning potential, increased decision-making within the household and participation in organizations beyond the domestic realm. However, what many of these studies also show is that even when women are earning a significant proportion of the household income, old patterns of male dominance and women's central role in caring for children and housework remain slow to change.

While some evident similarities emerge from these studies, the outcomes of women's involvement in these re-structuring processes are certainly not clear cut, they are highly contingent on a variety of factors including the:

- Type of production processes;
- Working and pay conditions;
- Woman's family and household situation;
- Position in the life cycle; and
- Alternative employment opportunities.

Moreover, in rural areas experiencing agro-export expansion, they are also dependent on the agrarian structures of the region and women's position within them. Agro-export expansion rarely takes place in a pristine environment; rather it is overlaid on existing social, political and economic conditions that can shape the nature of women's incorporation into the export economy. For example, in Chile, rural women frequently work on the family farm for part of the year and in the fruit economy during peak periods of labour demand such as the harvest. They thus maintain not only their roles within the household but also their roles in two contrasting agricultural sectors.

The diverse impacts of globalization, therefore, need to be understood through detailed research grounded in the specificities of particular places that is mindful of the way that a complex set of relationships, in which 'diverse sites (household, workplace, state, community resources) interact in spatially specific ways'. In the case under consideration, community organization and land tenure systems have helped shape women's involvement in both 'traditional' agricultural production and the modern agro-export sector. There has been an incomplete transformation of the agricultural sector and women negotiate both waged and unwaged agricultural work in ways that reflect their household/family circumstances and the interaction between the two agricultural systems.

FRUIT-EXPORT PRODUCTION AND AGRARIAN TRANSFORMATION

Chile has promoted non-traditional exports as part of a general outward-looking economic strategy to the extent that between the mid- and late-1980s nontraditional exports grew at a rate of 222 per cent. It is an excellent example of a country that has successfully integrated itself into non-traditional agricultural exports, exports that are regarded as contributing to the Chilean economic 'miracle'. Non-traditional exports refer to three distinct phenomena; they may be:

1. Products not produced in a country before;
2. Products traditionally produced for the domestic market and now being exported; and
3. Products exported to a new market.

The expansion of agribusiness in areas of Chile supplying the world market with these types of exports has led to a radical transformation of the rural sector. Agricultural production systems have become increasingly capitalized, active land markets have developed and there has been a dramatic alteration in agricultural employment structures. It is generally the large-scale commercial farmers who have enjoyed the benefits of the export growth and it has been argued that Chile's impressive agro-export growth has re-concentrated land ownership, thus reducing peasant access to land and stable employment. As Chile has become further integrated into the world market, peasant farmers have found it increasingly difficult to remain competitive.

There is thus an increasingly large economic disparity between capitalist and peasant farming and even under the recent attempts by the state to support peasant agriculture, a process known in Chile as Reconversion, the peasant economy remains precarious. However, these changes are locally specific. The expansion of export production does not necessarily herald the destruction or marginalization of more 'traditional' forms of agricultural production. In some cases the local systems of land tenure and community political and social organization have allowed the small-scale farmers to negotiate the form of their relationship with the export sector and to survive alongside it (albeit in an increasingly marginal position).

There is a vital link between locally-specific land tenure systems and the shape and form of export agriculture and female involvement in this export economy. In the case under consideration, there has been an incomplete transformation of agricultural production systems. While export production has expanded dramatically and some local small-scale farmers have been marginalized, the pattern is complex. Small-scale farmers in some cases remain an important part of the productive landscape, producing crops for the domestic market alongside the large highly-capitalized firms producing for export.

This is certainly true of the Guatulame valley located in the Fourth Region in Chile's semi-arid Norte Chico. This part of Chile had traditionally been characterized as a relatively poor and underdeveloped region, where a mixture of petty commodity farmers and minifundistas, alongside some larger-scale farmers produced crops destined for the national market. From the early 1980s the Guatulame valley has been the site of dramatic expansion of table grapes for export.

In the basin of Chanaral Alto (in the Guatulame valley), there were no table grapes planted in 1980; in 1994, however, there were 1800 hectares under export table grapes. The majority of the grapes are grown on large-scale estates (known as parronales) owned by commercial farmers who have received financial support from international marketing companies and now demand large numbers of seasonal employees, especially during the Summer harvest season. In addition to the large-scale export oriented farms in the

Guatulame valley, there are locally-specific agricultural communities, which unusually for Chile include elements of communal land-holdings.

These communities, with their complex systems of land holding have played a crucial role in the development of the grape economy as sources of land (and labour) for grape production. They are also the sites where, to a certain extent, the traditional system of agricultural production has been maintained with the attendant social and political organizations of the communities. Each community is composed of a fixed number of members or comuneros who hold 'rights' or derechos to use the communal land and form the community committee.

In the Fourth Region in 1993 there were 166 communities with 12731 community members undertaking some form of agricultural production. With a total population of 76386 and a total landholding of 946 932 hectares, they constitute d 58 per cent of the rural population of the Fourth Region and occupied 25 per cent of the land. Within the communities, land ownership is based on three types of exploitation, one of which is individual while two are communal. The community grants the use of the communal lands to a comunero for a certain number of years, then on death or migration, another comunero may receive the right to use the land. It has been argued that since the early 1980s the communities have been strongly challenged by both external and internal forces and that the development of a market for community land is one of the main challenges.

In some communities land tenure has been legally regularized and it is now possible to sell land rights to individuals (but not companies) who are not members of the community. In these communities an active land market has developed, and land has been sold to large-scale export producers. Other communities have not regularized land tenure and are not legally able to dispose of communal rights to non-members. The alienation of community land to non-members is per haps the most important factor in the weakening of the communities' traditional economic, political and social organization.

In the Guatulame the weak development of a land market

has been significant for many aspects of community life including the gender aspects of employment in the export and domestic agricultural sectors. The difference in the legal status of individual and collective ownership within the various communities has produced dramatically different patterns of agricultural production. These patterns have become more obvious with the expansion of the table grape economy in the region.

Although the community legislation of recent years has sought to define and limit the exchange of land within the communities, especially its removal from communal use and transfer to the private sector, a land market has always been present and since the early 1980s has become much more influential. As land has been sold to export producers many local residents of the communities have lost access to their land and have had to look for alternative income sources.

For example in the village of Chanaral Alto, which lies at the heart of the community of Chacarillas, the regularization of the land tenure system and the subsequent shift to private ownership has transformed the local land market. Traditionally the economy of the village was based on small-scale farmers (with plots of less than five hectares) producing tomatoes, beans, peppers, garlic and melons for urban centres in Chile. However, the community has experienced the effects of the dynamic land market in the valley, as a significant number of community members have sold their land to large-scale producers.

By 1990, 126 of the 216 community 'rights' had changed hands, with the majority of them going to the commercial farmers who were not previously community members. These commercial farmers have installed vineyards, transforming the village into an important centre for table grape production. At the same time, the small-scale producers who had sold their land generally remained in the community to work either permanently or seasonally in the vineyards and associated packing plants.

In contrast, in the communities without regularized land ownership such an active land market has not developed, and commercial grape farming has not substantially taken-off. For example, in Tome Alto in the community of El Tome, there are no large-scale grape farms and the landscape is dominated instead by small plots of land under the plastic protection used for the tomato crops. As land tenure is not regularized, thereby preventing comuneros from selling to a third party, vineyards have failed to encroach on the settlement and the list of community rights showed very few of them changing hands (in 1994 no rights had been sold to large-scale producers).

However, the small-scale production of crops such as tomatoes does not necessarily provide the farmers with a reliable income. So although the majority of the population is directly involved in cultivating crops for the domestic market, they also work temporarily in the grape economy during the harvest season (December-January). For the women of the communi ties these changes in land tenure and the expansion of the export economy more generally have impacted on their ability to retain access to land and provide them with employment opportunities that extend their roles as unpaid family labour.

TRADITIONAL RESPONSIBILITIES AND NEW OPPORTUNITIES

Historically women's involvement in productive work in Chile has been severely under-estimated. This is especially true in rural areas where women's inputs as agricultural workers have been virtually ignored. In many ways, women were 'invisible' in the pre-agrarian reform estates in Chile as their work was seen as supplementary to the predominantly male head of household. As women's contribution to the labour of the estate was so under-recognized, it made it all but impossible for women to gain access to land in their own right, a discrimination that existed into the period of agrarian reform.

Rural women or campesinas had and in many cases still have a myriad of responsibilities including the raising of animals, care of the family garden (huerto) and work on the family farm. Yet women's activities have been virtually ignored by the census. For example in the Comuna of Canela in the Fourth Region, 76 per cent of women were categorized as being economical ly inactive. A fact that lends support to the argument that the women in the agricultural communities have a tradition of work that has been under-estimated and under-valued in official statistics. Under the neo-liberal model women have had to intensify their work in both 'peasant' and capitalist production, yet the state has been slow to recognize that women are workers who make important contributions to the rural economy.

Women now, however, find that they form a highly-visible part of the labour force in the fruit export economy, although again the state has been slow to implement polices, such as the provision of child-care, that are specifically designed to support the temporary labour force. The changes that have occurred with women's involvement in export production in the Norte Chico have been mediated through the pre-existing social and economic systems of the agricultural communities. There is little doubt amongst Chilean writers that the agricultural communities have been, and to a large extent still are, run on patriarchal lines.

Within the actual decision-making bodies of the agricultural communities of the Fourth Region, women are under-represented and, therefore, have diminished powers to influence the organization of the communities. In the community of Chacarillas, women held 38 per cent of the land rights in 1995. It should also be noted that some of these rights to community land were in the name of women from families involved in export agriculture, women who were not, therefore, directly involved in agricultural work or connected to the community. Women are excluded from decisions about the use of and access to communal land and the power structures within the communities.

For women in areas of agro-export expansion any new employment opportunities are set within the context of traditional systems of production and social organization, in this case the agricultural communities. The paper now explores the way that the women of the Guatulame have negotiated both their more 'traditional' responsibilities within the agricultural communities and their new roles in fruit export production. The following sections draw on semi-structured in-depth interviews with women who have all been involved with work in the agro-export sector. The objective here is to:

1. Draw out the complexities of women's experiences in traditional and export agriculture;
2. See how women combine and negotiate work in both sectors; and
3. See how the transformations in traditional agriculture have shaped their experiences.

Women are employed in the grape economy throughout the year but their employment is especially concentrated during the grape harvest when they work in both the fields and packing plants. The majority of the women from both villages work for some time in the grape economy, although the women from Tome Alto are more likely to work for shorter periods than the women from Chanaral Alto. For both 1992 and 1993, none of the women in Tome Alto, who participated in the study, had worked for longer than six months and in both years the majority of the women worked for just two months during the harvest. In contrast, in Chanaral Alto, although the majority of women worked for five months or less, some women did work for longer than six months.

A similar pattern is discernible with respect to the actual tasks undertaken by the women. In general the women are concentrated in the tasks associated with the packing plants, the selecting, cleaning and packing of the grapes. In Tome Alto fewer women work outside the packing plants, although some may be involved in work in the fields such as pruning. For the women from Chanaral Alto, there is a greater variety of tasks with at least 50 per cent of the sample in both years working in both the fields and packing plants.

Many women from Chanaral Alto work for longer periods and in a greater variety of tasks in the grape economy than do the women from Tome Alto. Overall then, women are concentrated in certain tasks that reflect the gendered nature of the agro-export labour market and this concentration is evident for the women from both villages. However, there is a difference in the length of time that women from the different communities actually work and the extent of their involvement in the agro-export economy.

PERCEPTIONS OF AGRICULTURAL WORK

How do women from the Guatulame perceive their work in both the agro-export and family-farm sectors? From the interviews it emerged that there are clear differences in attitudes towards work on the family farms and in the grape economy. Although the women who work on domestic agriculture tend to be very negative about the work itself, they regard it as fundamental to the maintenance of their households. In contrast there was a much wider range of attitudes expressed towards work in the grape economy. In many ways it represents an enjoyable indeed even liberating experience, but at the same time brings with it many problems such as long hours, repetitive work and exposure to chemicals.

For many of the women from Tome Alto who work in both the grape-packing plants and on their own family tomato plots, they prefer the working conditions experienced in the regimented but shaded packing plants to working with their own tomato crops. The main objection to the tomatoes is the relentless nature of the work, with constant care of the plants essential for several months each year. The women who work on the family farms describe the hard, back-breaking work carried out whether it is raining in winter or baking hot during the summer.

The language that the women used to talk about their work on the tomatoes revealed a great deal about some of its negative aspects. Throughout the interviews, many women used words such as 'hard', 'sacrificial' and 'risky' to describe their work on the family farm. They used these words to describe both the actual work that needs to be done to care for their crops, such as planting and weeding and also to talk about the life of the small-scale farmer struggling to surviv e in an economic climate favouring export-producers. These points are reflected in the following quotes from women in Tome Alto:

> The hardest months working on the tomatoes are June and July. You have to look after the plant before the fruit

comes in August. It's very cold and you have to wear an overcoat and if it rains you have to get up two or three times in the night to make sure there are no little floods. When the work is really hard you want to throw in the towel.

Rachel, Tome Alto

In addition to the poor working conditions, are the problems of profitability and risk within tomato cultivation and sale? The majority of the interviewees in Tome Alto reflected on the risks inherent in relying on tomato production as their sole source of income. For example:

Well on the tomatoes it's very individual, if you want to work hard you work hard, but it's very risky. You invest lots but you don't know if you're going to recoup the investment. You put in money and work and not only one person from the family but all the family and if the tomatoes are going well then everything, the whole village goes well because everyone relies on tomatoes.

Ana, Tome Alto

Life is very sacrificial, very hard. The life of the farmers is very hard and sometimes it's not for profit. For example this year it was very difficult for us. We lost absolutely everything. Now we are just waiting and hoping we get work on the grapes. In the packing we will earn a little bit of money.

Maria, Tome Alto

Although small-scale production remains central to the women from Tome Alto, they are very aware of the hard work that is required and the risks involved in making a living from it. For them, the working conditions in the grape-packing plants were preferable and their work there had allowed them to make decisions about how to spend their wages. One woman had bought a washing machine with her money from the grapes and several described the way it helped them support their children's education:

Yes the money from the grapes is useful. I used to worry about going out to work so as to get things for the children for school. Every year I did it. Now it's two years since they (two sons) started working and they buy their own things. But I have one who is very little and I still have to provide for him. And little things for him, sometimes a bicycle. Anyway the older children buy their own things from the grapes and I have to buy for the little one. But the work on the grapes is OK. I work every year.

Celia, Tome Alto

However, many women from both Tome Alto and Chanaral Alto expressed ambiguous ideas concerning the working conditions in the packing plants. On the one hand many explained how they preferred working in the shaded packing plants, where conditions were considered by one woman as 'beautiful' and food was provided, but on the other they expressed concern over the long working hours and the difficult nature of some of the work. This ambiguity is captured in this quote from Clara:

I had a friend, a supervisor and she told me 'I'll give you a job which you'll find easy, it's clean'. 'You will pack because cleaning is very difficult for one thing and it's also dirty because you dirty your hands, this liquid gets onto the scissors and stains your hands, so it's very difficult. So packing is better because the grapes come to you clean and already chosen so you will pack and wrap them'. So I went to the packing plant and it was very good. Yes, I've no real complaints.

Clara, Chanaral Alto

There are many comments that directly reflect the problems inherent in such work. Work in the packing plants is much regulated; the women cleaning and packing the grapes stand in line and in many packing plants are not allowed to talk to each other except during breaks. The grapes that have been picked need to be processed and shipped the same day, which means that work in the packing plants continues until the day's harvest is on its way to the port. Working hours can, therefore, be very long with workers staying until the early hours of the morning and then returning to work just a few hours later. Much of the work in the packing plant is paid at piece rate to encourage the workers to be more productive.

While this may allow a skilled packer to earn more money than workers being paid per day, it promotes a competitive working environment that can be extremely tiring for the workers. Some of the work in the fields is also paid per piece e.g. pruning the grape plants, and as one woman wo rking in a vineyard near Chanaral Alto remarked 'you work per plant, so you work harder because otherwise it's just like working per day'.

A fundamental problem with work in the packing plants is that it represents the only significant source of waged employment in the valley. The extreme dependency of women on work in fruit is not simply because they prefer it to other work; it is because there is a scarcity of other work. In addition, work in the fields and packing plants offers almost no opportunity for career progression, the temporary workers may be skilled but they are constrained by the specific demands of the agro-export economy and the lack of alternative employment.

Marta described some of the limitations inherent in this work as she talked about her experiences of being a temporera and also migrating in search of alternative employment. She is single and lives with her parents in Chanaral Alto and has worked in several different packing plants in the Fourth Region. In the past she has travelled north to look for work but has returned to the village as she now has a young son. For Marta the work in the packing plants is her primary so urce of income, which has led her to question both the working conditions and the lack of other local employment opportunities:

I like my job more or less but lately I do not like it because I realise that the work in the grapes is the only possibility to be able to earn a little bit more. And you're on your feet all day long. Yes on your feet all day working because if you sit down you slow yourself down. And you can find that suddenly you're very, very tired but you have to put your tiredness aside because if you stop well it's less boxes and less boxes means less money ...I went to Iquique to look for work, there's nothing here but I had to come back for my son.

Marta, Chanaral Alto

Some of the most commonly cited problems experienced by temporeras are those associated with the pesticides used on the export crops and the gases used to treat the fresh fruit in the packing plants before shipping. Many temporeras are exposed to these chemicals over extended periods of time, either in the fields or the packing plants, and their lack of a coherent worker organization coupled with the relatively lax controls over chemical use means that their struggle for safer working conditions continues. The interviews revealed many health concerns about work in the packing plants, not only related to the chemicals but also the problems of standing for hours at a time and the strain from repetitive cleaning and packing the grapes:

Well they spray the grapes with gas in the packing plant. They have some rooms to do that, so they take all the boxes from the vineyard and they put them in these rooms. And before processing them they put them in these rooms and spray to get rid of insects. So often they give them five minutes of air, no more before they give them to each person. They don't give the grapes long enough to air. I think that if they gave them half an hour to be aired that would be better. It's dangerous. The gas is dangerous for us. But there aren't any more profitable jobs for us and at least all the machines are the same.

Celia, Tome Alto

This quote reflects many of the contradictions experienced by women working in the grape economy. Celia describes the tangible problem of exposure to potentially dangerous chemicals but also adds that there is a dearth of alternative employment opportunities. Work in the grape economy in some respects has better working conditions than traditional agriculture and provides women with their own wages but at the same time this is qualified by the fact that there are many shortcomings in such employment and that it is effectively the only waged work open to large numbers of women.

CAMPESINA/TEMPORERA: WORK AND IDENTITY

Women's insertion into the modern agro-export sector as temporary workers interacts with their more 'traditional' roles as set in the context of Chilean rural society more generally and the agricultural communities in particular. A previous study by Valdes found that the majority of temporeras viewed their work in a favourable light and that it improved their self-esteem but that they viewed it as very much secondary to their roles within the domestic sphere. Valdes concluded that the temporeras did not have a clear 'work identity', based on their temporary employment, although the 'category' of temporera was beginning to develop a greater coherence in terms of bargaining for better working conditions.

In the Guatulame, many women negotiate both waged and unwaged work in the export and domestic agricultural sectors, working in the different sectors on different tasks and at different times throughout the year. They, therefore, move between different employment sectors that bring with them contrasting ideas about suitable gender roles and relations. How do women from the agricultural communities think about their interaction with the notions of what it is to be a campesina and what it is to be a temporera and do they take on these identities in ways that reflect their changing agricultural activities? What emerged from the interviews is that women think about their different types of agricultural work (and in some cases their associated identities) in a kaleidoscopic fashion.

Their attitudes relate to their particular family and community contexts and also change throughout the year as different types of work take priority. For many of the women from communities such as Tome Alto, where land tenure laws have limited the expansion of the export economy, work on the family farms remains fundamental in helping to shape their identities as campesinas. For example the majority of women in Tome Alto work first and foremost as unpaid family labour for nine months of the year and work as temporeras for a limited period during the grape harvest.

This is reflected in their discussion of the relative importance of their different agricultural work. Even in a community experiencing rapid agrarian change, the family farm remains of fundamental importance in providing an income and regulating social change. We work most of the year on the tomatoes, from March to December. The whole family works together. Most of the things for the house we buy from the tomatoes.

Luisa, Tome Alto

Yes, well with the tomatoes when things are good it's OK. We buy things for example we bought a small van from the tomatoes... And the things from the house we buy from the tomatoes because the work from the vineyards is no big deal.

Lucilla, Tome Alto

Many women in Tome Alto perceive their work on the tomatoes as central to their lives and their identities as campesinas. They were keen to take advantage of the wage-earning opportunities offered by the grape farms but did not see the agro-export sector as a viable alternative to small-scale production. This could be seen as a retreat to the local that Hall suggests takes place under the increasing impacts of globalization, in this case the spread of agro-export production across the landscape.

As the community land remains in tact, along with traditional systems of community political and social organization, people are able to take advantage of the seasonal work in the grapes but rely primarily on small-scale production in the context of traditional community structures. The people of Tome Alto are in effect keeping the impacts of this agro-export production, such as in-migration, a land market and deeper identification as temporary waged workers at bay. This of course is a locally-specific example and in Chanaral Alto, this 'retreat to the local' remains less of an option because of the sale of community land and the attendant weakening of community relations.

In Chanaral Alto many women referred to the changes that had taken place with the expansion of the grape economy and the impacts these changes had had on small-scale producers. Only a minority of the interviewees in this village dedicate themselves to small-scale cultivation as their primary economic activity. Instead they work in a variety of occupations including domestic service, local government offices and also for extended periods as temporeras. For example, Alicia is from Chanaral Alto and is married with five grown-up children. She and her husband sold their land when the tomatoes were no longer profitable and invested their money in a small shop. Every year she goes to work on the grape harvest to earn some extra money, but more importantly to escape the domestic routine.

Although Alicia takes advantage of the opportunity for seasonal employment offered by the grape economy, she expressed concern at the changes it had wrought in the village. Her comments concerning the impacts of the grape economy a nd her apparent nostalgia for the time before when people 'had their own land' are representative of many interviewees' views:

Men arrived and offered us a good price for the land. Times had changed and so people were fed up. They said 'everything is so expensive' and they sold up everything, their little plots of land. So now there's nowhere to plant tomatoes. Because before people had their work season and then after that you could rest. The house always had food and you had money in your pocket. But now no, the money is weekly only. Of course the houses seem more ordered or nicer because now the women are working they are using that to their advantage. It's their money but in terms of business, things were better before in the time of the tomatoes.

Alicia, Chanaral Alto

There is both an understanding that in some ways it is better for women to have access to their own wages but that life in the village was more autonomous before the expansion of the export economy. Another interviewee from the village reiterated this latter idea:

If it weren't for the grapes the people would work on the tomatoes, as they did in the past. Nearly everyone worked on the tomatoes..... I think it is better for people to have their own land and the means to work it. It's better for people to work like that and not have to work for someone else.

Sara, Chanaral Alto

For many in this community, the loss of community land and the penetration of capitalist agro-export production have fundamentally altered labour systems in the village. The process of agro-export expansion and its concomitant impact on land tenure and wage-earning potential has had contradictory impacts. It provides some women with their own income but has also marginalized small-scale farmers and made the population reliant on wage labour that is unstable and rarely permanent. While few women explicitly described themselves as 'temporeras', they had become more fully integrated into the export economy than the women in Tome Alto.

In effect the relative robustness of community structures has played a role in shaping women's involvement as temporary workers in the grape economy and their identities as temporeras and/or campesinas. In Tome Alto the majority of the women combine work in the 'traditional' and export agricultural sectors, negotiating both waged and unwaged work. While work in the grape economy does bring some material benefits, it is seen as a supplement to work on the family land. In contrast, in communities where land has been sold to large-scale grape producers, the agricultural transformations have been felt more immediately and women (and men) have become more 'deeply' involved in the export economy as waged workers. In Chanaral Alto a significant minority of women work for at least six months of any one year in the fields and packing plants of the grape economy extending their roles as temporeras.

As Chile continues to promote the expansion of nontraditional agricultural exports, the exporting areas will continue to experience changes in land tenure and labour organization. In this particular instance some of the 'traditional' agricultural producers have been able to maintain their small-scale production for the domestic market. This does not mean though that they are not involved in the export economy, it is just that they are able to work in the grape economy at certain times of the year to earn extra income. The expansion of the grape economy in the Guatulame has led to the development of a complex set of interactions between various sectors of the rural economy.

The pattern is by no means a simple one and there is a need to develop a nuanced understanding of the impacts of export expansion on a heterogeneous rural population if responsible and reactive polices for the support of small-scale producers and temporeras are to be developed. The fact that small-scale agriculture remains viable in some ar eas of the Guatulame valley is not the direct result of government policies. It is instead the result of a combination of factors including the non-regularization of land tenure in the communities and the production calendars of the domestic and export crops.

It is important to remain mindful of the varied shape and impact of globalization processes, for example the spread of agribusiness. In this case, rural women negotiate their involvement as waged workers in agribusiness in a variety of ways that reflect their access to land and their perceptions of different types of work, as waged workers and as workers on the family farm as well as with respect to other wage-earning opportunities. Overall though, there has been an incomplete transformation of the agricultural sector - the small-scale farmers have not necessarily been marginalized or removed from the landscape.

This reflects the uneven and partial integration of modern agribusiness into this region of Chile, providing an example of the way production for the domestic market is interwoven with export activities. The variations in land tenure and the seasonality of output facilitate the multiple roles of women. While temporary employment on the grape farms has come to be an important source of income, it may be in addition to the income from their own properties. Thus the temporera labour force remains fragmented, but in possession of long-term strategies for income generation where small-scale farming continues to be of fundamental importance.

Bibliography

Anker, R. and C. Hein, 'Why Third World Urban Employers Usually Prefer Men', *International Labour Review*, Vol. 124, No. I, Geneva, 1985.

Beech, C., *Women and Women into Information Technology*, a report by the British Computer Society, 1990.

Byrne, E., *Women in Science and Technology: The Institutional Ecology Approach*, Interim Research Report, Department of Education, University of Queensland, 1988.

Chew. S.B. and R. Chew, 'Information Technology as a Strategy Human Resource Development', in E.C.Y. Kuo, C.M. Loh and K.S. Raman, *Information Technology in Singapore Society: Trends, Policies and Applications*, Singapore University Press, 1990.

Davidson, M.J. and C.L. Cooper (eds), *Women and Information Technology*, Psychology and Productivity at Work Series, London, John Wiley and Sons, 1987.

Deakin, R., *Women and Computing: The Golden Opportunity*, London, Macmillan Press, 1984.

Eriksson, I.V., B.A. Kitchenham and K.G. Tijdens (eds), *Women, Work and Computerization: Understanding and Overcoming Bias in Work and Education*, Amsterdam, North Holland, 1991.

Faruqui, A.M., M.H.A. Hassan and G. Sandri (eds), *The Role of Women in the Development of Science and Technology in the Third World*, proceedings of the conference organized by CIDA and the Third World Academy of Sciences, Trieste, Italy, October, 1988.

Harrison, P. (1983), *The Third World Tomorrow*, NY, Pilgrim Press and Harmondsworth, Penguin

Irvine, J., 'Women into Information Technology', *Information Technology and Public Policy*, Vol. 8, No. 3, Summer, 1990.

Kluzer, S., *Computer Diffusion in Black Africa: A Preliminary Assessment*, unpublished paper, SPRU, University of Sussex, Brighton, UK, 1988.

Lim, G.K., 'Women's Participation in the Computer Industry in Singapore', in Ken Tijdens *et al.* (eds), *Women, Work and Computing: Forming New Alliances*, Amsterdam, North Holland, 1989.

Lovegrove, G. and B. Segal (eds), *Women into Computing: Selected Papers*, 1988-1990, London, Springer, 1991.

Mitter, S., 'Computer Aided Manufacturing and Women's Employment: a Global Critique of Post Fordism', in I.V. Eriksson, B.A. Kitchenham and K.G. Tijdens (eds). *Women, Work and Computerisation: Understanding and Overcoming Bias in Work and Education*, Amsterdam, North Holland, 1991.

Mumford, E., *Where are Tomorrow's Top Women Executives ?*, Manchester Business School Review, Vol. 4, No. 3, 1980.

Ng, C. (ed.), *Technology and Gender: Women's Work in Asia*, Women's Studies Unit, UPM and Malaysian Social Science Association, 1987.

Ng, C. and J. Othman, 'Information Technology, Gender and Employment in Malaysia', in S.C. Bhatnagar and M. Odedra (eds) *Social Implications of Computers in Developing Countries*, New Delhi, Tata-McGraw Hill, 1992.

Odedra, M., *Information Technology Transfer to Developing Countries: Case Studies from Kenya, Zambia and Zimbabwe*, unpublished Ph.D. thesis, London School of Economics, 1990a.

Odedra, M., 'Poor Management leads to Gross Under-utilization', *Computer in Africa*, Vol. 4, No. 5, July, 1990b.

Parikh, I., *Women in Management: an Annotated Bibliography with Emphasis on Commonwealth Sources*, London, Commonwealth Secretariat, 1987.

Stamp, P., *Technology, Gender and Power in Africa*, Ottawa, international Development Research Centre, 1989.

Subramaniam, P.R., *The Future for Women in Information Technology*, M. Sc. dissertation, London School of Economics, 1991.

Tijdens, K., M. Jennings, I. Wagner and M. Weggelaar (eds), *Women Work and Computing: Forming New Alliances*, Amsterdam, North Holland, 1989.

Virgo, P., 'The Case for Women into Information Technology Campaign', *Information Technology and Public Policy*, Vol. 6, No. 3, Summer, 1988.

World Bank, *Sub-Saharan Africa: From Crisis to Sustainable Growth*, Washington DC, World Bank, 1989.

Wright, B.D. (ed.), *Women, Work and Technology: Transformations*, Chicago, University of Michigan Press, 1987.

Index

I

L

M

N

O

P

R

S

T